Foreword by Jack Hayford

God's Final Answer

A Series of Studies on the Book of Hebrews

By

Harold E. Helms

What does God say when your faith is challenged so severely that you're about ready to give up? In former days He spoke in various ways, but in these last days He has given us
His Final Answer!

To
Winona

My wife of 57 years-
My closest friend, my dearest companion,
Who has validated the poet's words:
"Grow old along with me; the best is yet to be."

Foreword

❧

There are at least three criteria by which a book distinguishes itself to my mind: content, use and character of the author.

Content? Who wants to read, much less recommend, a book without substance—either spiritual, intellectual or both?

Use? Who should bother with a book if it is only verbiage without a practical focus or purpose? Shouldn't my reading contribute something "functional"—even if the only function is that it stirs the juices of our thinking or passion?

Author's character? For my part, I am interested in the source as well the substance or usability of a book and its content. Ultimately, I am imbibing of more than ideas, because a book transmits something of the "spirit," of the "life-stuff" of the writer. I don't want to drink from a toxic well.

So, having described a standard I think worth measuring a book by, let me offer a few words in commending this book to you, reader—let me elaborate my delight regarding all three measuring sticks. I do so in reverse order to my above listed criteria.

First, I am thankful for those who open this book, because whether you ever meet the author or not, you are drawing from a fountainhead of fidelity and fruitfulness—as a man, as a minister and as a messenger.

I have known Harold Helms for nearly all my 45+ years in serving the Church—the flock of God. He is a man of proven devotion to his family, his friends, and to the congregations he has served. His *steadfastness* to the elements that constitute a life of trustworthiness in leadership has been manifest for over a half-century of pastoral, pulpit and professional labors. Harold, as my grandkids say, is "the real deal!" His character alone warrants listening to what he has to say.

Second, there are multiple points of practical value to this book, but to select one, let me note its *soundness and health*. Today, sloppy thinking about God and His Son is far more rampant than many realize. Our "mega-mindset," which supposes that a crowd on the church grounds guarantees worth in the content of what's being offered there, brings Gershwin's lyric to mind: "It ain't necessarily so!" Pop approaches to Christian living may set feet to taping, but not necessarily to walking the path of discipleship.

"Make disciples" is as much Jesus command as "preach the gospel." The Church is about more than "saving souls," it's about growing people; and it takes solid truth to *grow* solid lives. That's why I'm so happy for the strength and solidity for life and living that abound on these pages. You'll grow as you read—and at the same time, be reminded: there is *nothing more practical* to life, strengthening to relationships, nourishing to families or effective in producing success in your life-vocation than *truth-made-livable* through Holy Spirit ignited communication. And, dear reader, I congratulate you: you have a handful of the same, right here on this book's pages.

Finally, I am especially pleased with the content. A lifetime of observing the fruit of Bible exposition breeds an appreciation for seeing it well done. My friend and esteemed associate, Harold Helms, has always been known as a masterful speaker—beloved and welcome across the spectrum of widely varied church environments and enjoyed by listeners of every age or ethnic group. However, here he demonstrates his skill as a *master expositor*—unfolding the Word of God, phrase by phrase through one of the most enriching portions of the Bible.

The Book of Hebrews is God's consummate statement regarding His Son. Harold Helms refers to it as *"God's Final Word"*—a fit and focused theme for people like us—people upon whom *final times* have come.

Jack W. Hayford
Pastor, The Church On The Way
Chancellor, The King's Seminary
Van Nuys, California
March, 2004

Endorsements

(Continued from back cover)

One of the greatest gifts Dr. Helms gives to the readers of this stimulating book is what is most needed in today's culture—practical theology. As you read God's Final Answer *you will be inspired, informed, and invigorated by a fresh look at the challenging book of Hebrews.*

JAMES RANGER
Pastor, New Life Center, Bakersfield, CA

In his book on Hebrews Harold Helms reminds us that the only way to "tune out" the confusion about Life and Purpose is to "tune in" to the Person of Jesus Christ, God's Final Answer.

GLENN BURRIS
General Field Supervisor, Int'l Church
of the Foursquare Gospel

The balance between a good study book and good preaching material has been found in this refreshing and needed revelation from the Book of Hebrews. Some have difficulty in putting into practi-

*cal application the jewels located in Hebrews, but **Dr**. **Helms** has **blended** these truths into a seamless exposition of foundational and yet challenging study. I not only urge you to read it, but to also **share** its truth with others.*

DAN STEWARD
President, LIFE Pacific College, Los Angeles, CA

Preface

After a severe earthquake shook the Los Angeles area the words "things which cannot be shaken" kept coming to my mind, but I could not immediately remember where these words were found, although I knew that they were in the New Testament. I soon found them in Hebrews 12.

The Sunday morning after the earthquake as we gathered for worship under Angelus Temple's massive dome I sensed that the congregation, as well as the pastor, needed a sense of serenity. It was amazing to actually see the Word of God bring healing and peace as it was spoken, a process pastors often observe especially during times of crisis.

Two things happened that morning: first, I sensed that the Word was bringing healing and quietness to our nervous spirits. Second, I realized that I had been unexpectedly captivated by a book which I had not adequately appreciated and from which I had preached little in over 40 years of pulpit ministry. I knew that Sunday morning that I was "hooked on Hebrews."

It took well over a year, with time allotted to special occasions, to finish the 43 weekly studies in this remarkable letter. Together, congregation and pastor found that Hebrews offers warning, encouragement, inspiration, practical teaching, as well as insight into the Person and work of Jesus not found elsewhere.

After using this material in Angelus Temple and on its radio station, KFSG, I have also been privileged to use it in teaching the

Book of Hebrews in Angelus Bible Institute in Los Angeles and in **New Life** Center's School of Ministry in Bakersfield, California.

These studies have been printed primarily to provide encouragement, inspiration, and practical help to believers today who, like the first century Hebrew Christians, may be facing opposition in their Christian walk.

In Appreciation

I must express my thanks to computer genius and friend, Richard McCutcheon, and to efficient and conscientious secretary, Charlene Steiner, who both provided invaluable assistance helping to prepare this material for publication. Scholar and friend, Don Pickerill, who taught the Book of Hebrews in Life Pacific College for many years, was willing to read the original manuscript and offered invaluable suggestions. And, as she has done for 57 years, my wife, Winona, offered her assistance by providing an atmosphere conducive to study and writing.

Finally, I want to especially thank God for the privilege of serving as Senior Pastor of Angelus Temple, where these 43 messages were preached. During the 18 years Winona and I served there we saw this church open its arms and facilities to at least 42 nationalities. What a joy to serve a church where the Gospel was preached in eight different languages each week and where thousands of people each month were provided with food and clothing.

Table of Contents

God, who at various times and in various ways spoke in time past to the fathers by the prophets, has in these last days spoken to us by His Son, whom He has appointed heir of all things, through whom also He made the worlds; who being the brightness of His glory and the express image of His person, and upholding all things by the word of His power, when He had by Himself purged our sins, sat down at the right hand of the Majesty on high, having become so much better than the angels, as He has by inheritance obtained a more excellent name than they.

Hebrews 1:1-4

CHAPTER 1

God's Supreme Revelation
(Study No. 1 in the Book of Hebrews)

S ome consider the Book of Hebrews to be "the most important and useful of all the apostolic writings." Although we are not sure of its authorship, some translations boldly claim it to be "The Epistle of Paul the Apostle to the Hebrews," while others believe that it may have been written by Luke, Apollos, or Clement.

We do know that the book was written to a certain group of Hebrews who had accepted Jesus as Messiah but were considering going back to their former religion. The writer warns them that abandoning their faith was not the solution to the problems they faced.

The recipients of this letter had allowed persecution and pressures to rob them of their peace and confidence. They were beginning to ask serious questions about the relevancy of their faith. If their new Christian faith was genuine, why were they subjected to so much harassment? Where was the peace, the contentment, the joy?

As their commitment wavered they began to question their faith and were dangerously close to apostasy. They were at a crossroad in their spiritual journey. The situation was so desperate that the writer urged them to take certain prescribed actions. We will consider five of his exhortations but pay particular attention to the first two.

First, the writer says that they should **pay close attention to the Word of God.** He warns, "Therefore we must give the more earnest heed to the things that we have heard, lest we drift away"

(2:1). Furthermore he writes, "See that you do not refuse Him Who speaks. For if they did not escape who refused Him Who spoke on earth, much more shall we not escape if we turn away from Him Who speaks from heaven" (12:25).

Second, they were to **fix their thoughts on Jesus Christ**. "Therefore, holy brethren, partakers of the heavenly calling, consider the Apostle and High Priest of our confession, Christ Jesus..." (3:1).They would be wise, he says, to continue "looking unto Jesus, the Author and Finisher of our faith, Who for the joy that was set before Him endured the cross, despising the shame, and has sat down at the right hand of the throne of God" (12:2).

Third, they were to **spend more time with other Christians, particularly in encouraging one another**. They were to "exhort one another daily" (3:13) and to "consider one another in order to stir up love and good works, not forsaking the assembling of ourselves together, as is the manner of some, but exhorting one another, and so much the more as you see the Day approaching" (10: 24,25). "Let brotherly love continue" (13:1) was another strong word regarding their mutual relationship.

Fourth, they were admonished to **hold firmly to the faith they had professed in the Lord Jesus**. "Seeing that we have a great High Priest Who has passed through the heavens, Jesus the Son of God, let us hold fast our confession" (4:14). "Do not cast away your confidence, which has great reward" (10:35). Regarding their present suffering he wrote, "If you endure chastening, God deals with you as sons; for what son is there whom a father does not chasten?" (12:7). He further warns, "Do not be carried about with various and strange doctrines. For it is good that the heart be established by grace..." (13:9).

The author's fifth admonition had to do with **approaching the throne of grace boldly in prayer**. "Let us therefore come boldly to the throne of grace that we may obtain mercy and find grace to help in the time of need" (4:16). He pleads, "Let us draw near with a true heart in full assurance of faith, having our hearts sprinkled from an evil conscience and our bodies washed with pure water" (10:22). And he mingles prayer with praise as he writes, "Therefore by Him let us continually offer the sacrifice of praise to God, that is, the fruit of our lips, giving thanks to His Name" (13:15).

Of these five admonitions our purpose is to consider the two which have to do with **the Word of God** and **the Son of God**. First, the **Word of God**. Notice how this letter begins: **"God"**! What a way to start a letter! What authority! Of the 27 New Testament books 19 begin with the author's name (Paul, James, Peter, John, Jude). Here is the only book in the Bible which begins with the very Name of God. Here is the God Who speaks, Who reveals Himself, first, through the prophets of old, but ultimately through His Son, *God's Final Answer.*

The God Who has chosen to reveal Himself cannot be discovered sufficiently by man's personal searching. We could never have known God were it not for His self-revelation. If the barrier of our sin was ever to be penetrated God had to take the initiative...and He did! Through the 39 books of the Old Testament we see God going to great length to show Himself to His people. In all the ways by which He revealed Himself, ways which are recorded during the 1500 years when the Old Testament was being written, He was preparing for His supreme revelation in His Son, Jesus Christ. God has chosen various ways to reveal Himself—visions, dreams, angels, mental impressions, and circumstances, all with various degrees of clarity; but now in these last days He has spoken to us through His Son—*God's Final Answer!*

The Old Testament seems in some instances to be complex, especially as we contrast it with the simplicity of the New Testament. God used the Old Testament prophets in a most marvelous way. Verse one reminds us that God spoke to His people through these men and women. He used these anointed personalities, though most were not appreciated and many were martyred. They have been called "the most distinguished group of men who ever lived" and yet, when God spoke through them it was in a piece-meal manner, by one prophet after another, one truth now and another later. It all seemed so slow. Some complained of the prophet's message, "precept must be upon precept, precept upon precept, line upon line, line upon line, here a little, there a little" (Isa. 28:10). But verse two claims that in Jesus Christ the final revelation of God came clearly into focus! He was *God's Final Answer!*

The fact that Jesus Christ was, and is, God's supreme revelation does not suggest that earlier Old Testament revelations are unreli-

able. No matter what God says, or how He says it, His revelations **are** reliable!

Second, consider **the Son of God.** "In these last days God has spoken to us by His Son" (v. 2). "The last days" simply means that these days will not be followed by any further revelations of God's grace. The songwriter asks, "What more can He say than to you He has said?" The answer is *nothing*! **This** is the time to embrace the Lord Jesus. There will be no better opportunity.

The Spirit Who exalts the Lord Jesus, here inspires the writer to pen one of the most beautiful chapters in all the Holy Scripture concerning Christ. See how he describes Him: **He is God's Son** (v. 2). God has many sons and, if they are sons, they are also heirs. But this Son is **Heir of all things** (v. 2)! Everything that exists belongs to Him. How incredible that we are joint-heirs with Him (Rom.8:17)!

He is also the Creator of all that is created (v.2). John says, "All things were made through Him, and without Him nothing was made that was made" (Jn. 1:3). Paul agrees that, "By Him all things were created that are in heaven and that are on the earth, visible and invisible, whether thrones or dominions or principalities or powers. All things were created through Him and for Him. And He is before all things, and in Him all things consist (hold together)" (Col. 1:16, 17).

Furthermore, **He is the Brightness of God's Glory** (v.3). Isaiah predicted, "The glory of the Lord shall be revealed, and all flesh shall see it together; for the mouth of the Lord has spoken" (Isa. 40:5). John tells of the day when Isaiah's prophecy was fulfilled, "And the Word became flesh and dwelt among us, and we beheld His glory, the glory as of the only begotten Son of the Father, full of grace and truth" (Jn. 1:14). Speaking of the miracle at Cana of Galilee John wrote, "This beginning of signs Jesus did in Cana of Galilee, and *manifested His glory;* and His disciples believed in Him" (Jn. 2:11).

When the writer says that Jesus is the "Radiance of God's Glory" he does **not** mean that Jesus reflects God's glory as the moon reflects the light of the sun. "Radiance" suggests light coming from a luminous body. The **inherent** splendor and the **exhibited** splendor are essentially the same. If one compares the sun to God, then the sunshine is Jesus! "The Lord is my **Light** and my salvation"

(Ps. 27:1). "The people who sat in darkness have seen a great **light**" (Matt. 4:16).

An ancient legend tells of a cave that heard the voice of the sun calling it to come out into the light. The cave could not understand for it had never known anything other than absolute darkness. When the sun continued to call for the cave to come out it finally emerged from its place in the ground and came to the surface for the first time. The brilliance of the sunlight amazed the cave and it wanted to reciprocate. So it invited the sun to come down and visit. When the sun entered the cave there was no darkness at all for the sunlight spilled into every single corner.[1] When Jesus Christ came into this world He dispelled all obscurity about the character and compassion of God. He came not only to drive darkness from our lives but to fill us with His purifying light.

Christ is also the Express Image of God's Person (v. 3). When we read in scripture that man was created in the "image" of God (I Cor. 11:7) another word is employed rather than the one used here of our Lord Jesus. This word means that He is visibly exactly what God is in essence. This word for "image" is not used of man. The word used of man "suggests" God, as our shadow "suggests" us. Only Jesus Christ could truthfully say, "He that has seen Me has seen the Father" (Jn.14:9).

We are further informed that our Lord Jesus **upholds all things by the word of His power** (v. 3). There are two words in the Greek New Testament for the term "word"—"logos" and "rhema." The term "rhema" may indicate "a spoken command." The latter is the word used here. "He holds all things up, or bears all things up, by His spoken command." He commands the sea, "Come to this spot and no further"; He orders the sun, "Shine"...and it does! He is still in absolute control. Without such perfect and exact control we would have no science as we know it today. God is never haphazard!

A miracle which far exceeds His control of nature is expressed by the words, **He by Himself purged our sins**" (v. 3). To be purged means that we have been cleansed thoroughly. Cleansing was not provided simply for these Hebrews, but for the whole world! He did not do this with the blood of goats and bulls, but with His own precious blood. His own life had to be offered for no man could take His life. **He** would lay it down **He** would take it up again (Jn. 10:38)!

After our dear Lord completed the greatest work He could ever do He then **sat down at the right hand of the Majesty on high** (v. 3). The Great King seats the Highest Honored One on His right hand. Now the blessed Savior is seated. His work is finished. He can add nothing to it! What blasphemy to imagine that anyone might add one jot or tittle to the work of Calvary! It is finished! The Aaronic priests were always standing because their work was never completed. They constantly repeated their sacrifices, but our Lord paid the price once and for all! "So then, after the Lord had spoken to them, He was received up into heaven, and sat down at the right hand of God" (Mk. 16:19).

Verse four tells us that **Christ was so much better than the angels, as He has by inheritance obtained a more excellent name than they** (v. 4). The Hebrews, to whom this book is addressed, had a great regard for angels. Recall that Paul had to warn the Colossians about worshiping angels (Col. 2:18). The writer says that in consequence of Christ becoming a man, entering into this world, suffering, and dying for our sins, He had earned the Name which had been given to Him by divine order. His Name is Jesus! Call Him "Jesus," the angel said, "for He will save His people from their sins" (Matt 1:21).

None of us can ever be what God intended us to be without Jesus. A farmer in western Kansas found a young eaglet whose wing had been badly hurt. When he saw that the bird could not fly he took it back to the farm, cared for its wound and put it in the chicken pen. The eagle walked about on the ground and was soon mimicking the chickens scratching for worms in the ground. In a few weeks the wing was as good as new but the eagle made no attempt to leave the chicken pen. He continued to eat with the chickens and dig for worms. His beautiful feathers became dirty and his sharp beak became dull and discolored as he lived the life-style of a chicken. One day a young man visiting the farmer noticed the eagle and was horrified to see this once magnificent and beautiful creature scratching around in the dirt. When the farmer told his guest what had happened the man said, "It was good of you to help the eagle but surely now that his wing is healed you will free him to fly again. He certainly wasn't made for this." The farmer protested, "But he wants to stay here. Nevertheless, I will agree to take him out to the area where I found him." They drove to the edge of the hills where the young man held the eagle out on his arm and cried, "Go, boy, go!" but the eagle refused to leave. Just then a mighty shriek was heard from a huge mother eagle who was circling overhead. The shrill sound came again. Then ever so gently the eagle tested his wing, and with a mighty push, left the man's arm. At first he circled slowly just above their heads, then with a new sense of freedom, he climbed into the sky to join the older bird. The two men stood and silently watched the beauty of the soaring birds until at last the young man said, "That's what he was meant to do. That's what he was meant to do!"[2]

A person who has discovered God in the Person of His Son, Jesus, can never be content living by barnyard standards. Not only do we find in Christ a Deity worthy of our worship, we also discover the meaning of real life, life with a capital L!

For to which of the angels did He ever say: "You are My Son, Today I have begotten You?" And again: "I will be to Him a Father, and He shall be to Me a Son"? But when He again brings the firstborn into the world, He says: "Let all the angels of God worship Him." And of the angels He says: "Who makes His angels spirits and His ministers a flame of fire." But to the Son He says, "Your throne, O God, is forever and ever; a scepter of righteousness is the scepter of Your kingdom. You have loved righteousness and hated lawlessness; Therefore God, Your God, has anointed You with the oil of gladness more than Your companions." And: "You, LORD, in the beginning laid the foundation of the earth, and the heavens are the work of Your hands. They will perish, but You remain; and they will grow old like a garment; like a cloak You will fold them up, and they will be changed. But You are the same, and Your years will not fail." But to which of the angels has He ever said: "Sit at My right hand, till I make Your enemies Your footstool"? Are they not all ministering spirits sent forth to minister for those who will inherit salvation?

Hebrews 1:5-14

CHAPTER 2

Higher Than Angels

(Study No. 2 in the Book of Hebrews)

Christmas is a magnificent season, especially for those who are aware of its significance. Some, unfortunately, are confused about the reason for the season. One cartoon shows a little girl, with her baby brother on her lap, explaining the meaning of Christmas. She says, "Jesus was born just in time for Christmas up at the North Pole surrounded by eight tiny reindeer and the Virgin Mary...then Santa Claus showed up with lots of toys and stuff and some swaddling clothes...the three wise men and elves all sang carols while the Little Drummer Boy and Scrooge helped Joseph trim the tree... in the meantime, Frosty the snowman saw the star..." [1] Confusion about Christmas is not limited to children!

Christmas is more than mistletoe, fir trees, gifts, and cards. One lady who had waited until the last minute to send her cards rushed into the store and bought 50 cards without reading the message inside. She hurriedly addressed 49 of them and mailed them to her friends. After things quieted down she read the leftover card and to her horror found that the message on the cards was, "This card is just to say, a little gift is on the way."[2]

The text tells us that Jesus was God's "begotten" Son. The sending of this Son into the world is what Christmas is all about. Angels, who are an integral part of the Christmas story, are in these verses **compared with Jesus Christ.** What we **think** about Jesus and angels may be interesting, but here we have absolute **facts** about both Christ and angels, for we have what **God** says about them. The writer, in these few verses, quotes from the Old Testament at least eleven times. New Testament writers obviously had great confidence in the inspiration of the Old Testament.

First, consider **the information that we are given here about angels**. We are told that angels **are spirits** (v. 7). They are not confined to a body, but they may assume a body, when necessary, for the service of their Lord. Some think of spirits as eerie or frightening. Biblical accounts tell us that angels do often frighten those to whom they appear. Awareness of our sinfulness would promote fear during an angel visit. As long as we are in this present sinful state we might well believe that if an angel appears he may not have come with good news!

A little girl was afraid to go to bed in the dark by herself. After three or four trips to her parent's bedroom, her father tried to reassure her. "Look, honey," he said, "You are not really alone in your bedroom. God is watching over you. Since God is everywhere He is in your bedroom too." She was not very reassured by this, and as she started back to her room she stopped at the door and said in a loud whisper, "God, if You are in there, please don't say anything. You'll scare me to death."[3] When we talk about spirits we do not always comfort people!

Angels are ministering spirits (v. 7). Whether cherubim, seraphim, or archangels like Michael or Gabriel, they are still ministering spirits. Very early in man's history they were placed as guards at the east of the Garden of Eden (Gen. 3:24). Lot and his family were delivered from Sodom by angels (Gen. 19:1, 15, 16). Jacob, returning to meet Esau, saw a host of angels (Gen.32:1, 2). An angel prepared food and water for Elijah when he was disheartened and fragmented by his confrontation with Jezebel (1 Ki. 19:5-7). Daniel, in the lion's den, was protected by an angel (Dan. 6:22). The Christmas story is replete with angelic visitations. Zacharias learned that he and Elizabeth were to have a child through the visit of an angel (Lk. 1:11-13). Mary, mother of our Lord, received the wonderful news about the birth of her Son from Gabriel. Joseph, in a dream, received angelic assurance concerning his espoused wife (Matt. 1:19-21). Shepherds were filled with awe when they, of all people, were visited by a host of these heavenly beings (Lk. 2:9-14). An angel instructed Joseph and Mary to take the young Child to Egypt to escape the wrath of Herod (Matt. 2:13). Angels ministered to the Lord Jesus after His temptation in the wilderness and during His Gethsemane agony (Matt. 4:11 and Lk. 22:43). At His arrest in Gethsemane Jesus said that He could ask for 12 legions (72,000) of angels and His Father would send them (Matt. 26:53). Angels came to witness concerning the resurrection (Matt. 28:2-7; Mk. 16:5-7; Lk. 24:4-7; Jn. 20:11-13). At the Ascension two angels reminded the disciples that Jesus would return (Acts 1:10, 11). Paul tells us that an archangel will shout at the return of Jesus (1 Thess. 4:16), and Matthew says that the holy angels will come with Him (25:31). Luke writes that the apostles were delivered from prison by an angel (Acts 5:18-20). Philip and Cornelius were given instructions by angels (Acts 8:26; 10:3-6). Peter was delivered from prison by an angel (Acts 12:7-10). Paul was reassured by an angel that he and those on board a ship would be saved from the storm (Acts 27:23, 24).

Some time ago San Francisco celebrated a major anniversary of its Golden Gate Bridge. When the bridge was first being built there were no safety devices to protect the workers and 23 men fell to their deaths. Later a huge safety net was installed at the cost of $100,000.00. At least 10 men fell into the net but none were injured. An impressive side benefit was that work on the bridge progressed 15 to 25 percent faster because the workers were no longer afraid.[4] How often in scripture do we hear the angels of God say to those whom they are visiting, "Fear not!"?

All about us this very moment the heavenly hosts are encamped. The word "host" is a military term which suggests protection. One lady said that she "felt like a six piece pie that is being served to ten people." When times of frustration come it is proper to rest in the Lord. He has instructed His angels to care for us and we can trust in God's provision!

And, by the way, *He* gives the angels orders, not us! Two little boys turned their tree house into a space station. Their lively imaginations had them fighting Star Wars all over again. Suddenly the mother of one of them stood beneath the tree and shouted, "Johnny Jones, you come home right now." One of the little fellows said sheepishly to the other, "Uh, oh! I believe I hear earth calling."[5] You and I do not exercise that kind of authority over the angels, but when our Lord speaks they very well may say, "I hear heaven calling."

There is scriptural basis for the belief that angels are absolutely committed to do the bidding of the Lord whether sent on a mission of mercy or judgment. They evidently serve us out of perfect obedience to their Lord, not because they have a great love for us. On the other hand, our Lord reaches out to us out of love. In 1980, the day before Christmas, little Richard Ballenger's mother in Anderson, S.C., was busy wrapping packages and asked Richard if he would shine her shoes. Soon, with the proud smile that only a seven-year-old can muster, he presented the shoes for her inspection. His mother was so pleased that she gave him a quarter. On Christmas morning as she put her shoes on to go to church, she noticed a lump in one shoe. She took it off and found a quarter wrapped in a paper. Written on the paper in Richard's scrawling handwriting were the words, "I done it for love."[6] When we think of all God has done for us in the Person of His Son, Jesus, we should all remember of our Lord that "He done it all for love."

Angels are ministering spirits to those who will inherit eternal life (v. 14). Imagine the joys that await us! We *will* inherit eternal life. We have it now but the half has never been told! We have already experienced justification, sanctification, the infilling of the Holy Spirit, the healing of our infirmities, and we anticipate our glorification. Our future is as secure as His promises!

Second, note **the facts which God gives about His Son.** He says of Christ, **"You are My Son, today I have begotten You"** (v. 5; Ps. 2:7). So the Lord Jesus is called "begotten" (v. 5), and "first begotten" (v. 6). Theologians refer to this truth as the "eternal generation" of the Son. A dangerous heresy grew up around this doctrine in the third century. A man named Arius taught that God had created Christ before the world was made and had endowed Christ with creative powers. Therefore, Christ was not really God, but only similar to God. Concerning John 1:1 — "In the beginning was the Word, and the Word was with God, and the Word was God" — Arius would say, "Amen," to "The Word was *with* God." But he would have difficulty accepting the statement, "The Word *was* God." The argument was over whether Christ was "of *one* substance" with the Father or whether He was "of *like* substance" with the Father. This debate almost tore the Christian world apart. Christianity itself rested on the outcome of this argument. Athanasius, the man who stood against Arius, claimed that God did not merely *send* a Messenger when Jesus Christ came to earth, but that the Christ Who came **was God manifested in flesh**. He contended that to know Christ was to know God, Who is essentially revealed in Christ.

Ralph Waldo Emerson, who broke with his church over this doctrine, stated that he could not celebrate Communion because it offered more reverence to Christ than he could show. You can see how dangerous such a doctrine is. Hebrews ascribes not only **pre-existence** to Christ, but **eternity** as well. We believe that He is not only **divine**, but **Deity**! We read in Scripture that Christ became a **man**, but we never read of Him **becoming** God. He has always been, and will forever, be God. A fellow was far away from home in a small town and the only money he had was a thousand dollar bill. He was famished for food but could buy nothing, because no one would take his thousand dollar bill. It was only after he found a way to break that bill that he could finally have his needs cared for.[7] That story illustrates why Jesus came as He did. If He had arrived in all His inherent Splendor fellowship with Him would have been impossible. But he came as a Man and revealed God to us in ways that we could comprehend. He was not only the **Revealer** of God, He was **God Revealed**! He was not simply **similar** to God, or **like** God; **He was, and still is, God**!

The words in verse five are taken from Psalm 2:7, and are also quoted by Paul in Acts 13:33 in his sermon at Antioch, as well as in his epistle to the Romans (1:4). In both instances Paul associates this verse from the Psalms with the resurrection of Christ from the dead. We must not misunderstand Paul to say that Christ **became** the Son of God by being raised from the dead, but that Christ was **declared to be** the Son by the resurrection, i.e., the resurrection gave conclusive evidence of His Lordship.

Consider **the Father-Son relationship.** "I will be to Him a Father, and He shall be to Me a Son" (v. 5). There is no suggestion of **superiority** or **inferiority** in that statement. Christ is eternally, and equally, God. He did not **become** the Son when He was given, but was, instead, the Son Who **was** given.

The Father, Son, and Spirit were involved in our redemption. Some have suggested that the Father was ready to judge the human race but that the Son interceded; however, John 3:16 tells us that God so loved that **He sent** His Son. There has never been a division in the Godhead.

We do not wonder that **Christ is worshiped by angels** (v. 6). No angel could ever claim such eminence as Christ in being the **first-born** and the **only-begotten Son of the Father.** Upon His entrance into the world a multitude of the heavenly hosts praised God and said, "Glory to God in the highest heaven, and on earth peace among men with whom He is well-pleased, men of good will, of His favor" (Lk. 2:14, Amp.).

What comfort to know that **His throne is to be forever** (v. 8)! We nearly despair over the weakness of human governments. C.S. Lewis, in one of his science-fiction books, illustrates the frailty of human governments. A scientist from earth lands on another planet and makes friends with the inhabitants there. The earthling tells them the history of his planet. As he gives the story, he notices with embarrassment that he is telling of war after war. One of the creatures to whom he is recounting the story concludes that the constant fighting on earth must be because earthlings have no God. Another creature offers a more logical explanation. Earthlings behave like that, he concludes, because each of them wants to be a little god. As usual, Lewis hit the nail right on the head. [8] If we are not centered in God, self will always be on the throne.

Isaiah tells of a day when "the government will be upon **His** shoulder..." and "of the increase of **His** government...there will be no end" (Isa. 9:6, 7). The angel announced to Mary, "**He** will be great, and will be called the Son of the Highest; and the Lord God will give **Him** the throne of His father David" (Lk.1:32).

We need have no fear of His governance for we read that **His scepter is one of righteousness and that He loves righteousness and hates lawlessness** (vv. 8, 9). Loving righteousness and hating lawlessness are inseparable. We can not love God and at the same time love sinful behavior. One little six-year-old girl said to her mother, "The number one problem in the United States is pollution. I read that in my Weekly Reader. Everybody knows that the number one problem in the United States is pollution—everybody but our preacher. He thinks that it is sin. I feel that is just because he is a preacher."[9]

Many of us think that we can embrace Christ and sinful behavior at the same time. Some flaunt their immorality. Many advertise their sins on bumper stickers. Hollywood gossip columnists are provided with more fodder than they can use, not only from the movie industry but from the church world as well. We not only need to avoid sin, we desperately need to **hate** it! When someone wrote, "No heart is pure that is not passionate," he meant that unless we hate iniquity we simply do not love God. Augustine said, "Love God and do as you please." We may not fully accept this statement since our love for God is imperfect; but we understand that his premise must have been, "If we really do love God we will find it pleasing to please Him."

Because the Lord Jesus rules in righteousness and hates lawlessness **He is anointed with the oil of gladness** (v. 9). Righteousness and anointing go hand in hand. The anointing speaks of the Holy Spirit. Jesus said, "The Spirit of the Lord is upon Me, because He has anointed Me to preach the gospel..." (Lk. 4:18). Samuel anointed Saul and then David. Moses made a special oil to anoint Aaron and his sons. Whenever there is an anointing there is an accompanying freedom that promotes gladness. The "yoke" is broken by the anointing (Isa. 10:27).

God has not given us a spirit of fear, but of "power, love, and of self-control" (2 Tim. 1:7, TCNT). Satan tries to bind people with chains of fear and doubt. The anointed man can "do all things through Christ Who strengthens" him (Phil. 4:13). When Aaron was anointed the oil ran down his head, his beard, across his garments, and to his feet, suggesting the mighty baptism of the Holy Spirit! This anointing comes in sanctifying power. Everything that Moses touched with the anointing oil became holy, separated unto the Lord's service. So the anointing sets people free to serve. When David was anointed king, the Spirit of God came upon him "from that day forward" (1 Sam. 16:13). Leaders in the Church especially need God's anointing.

The anointing of God also sets us free to give. Many are held in bondage to mammon. Needs that demand sacrificial giving cry out to us; and the Holy Spirit wills to free us to give cheerfully. God links giving with cheerfulness: "But this I say: He who sows sparingly will also reap sparingly, and he who sows bountifully will also reap bountifully. So let each one give as he purposes in his heart, not grudgingly or of necessity; for God loves a cheerful giver" (2 Cor. 9:6, 7).

I believe that God gives a special anointing to saints who are getting ready to leave this world through death. Paul said, "For we know that if our earthly house of this tent is destroyed we have a building from God, a house not made with hands, eternal in the heavens" (2 Cor. 5:1). Again he wrote, "O death where is your sting? O grave, where is your victory? But, thanks be to God Who gives us the victory through our Lord Jesus Christ" (1 Cor. 15:55).

We are also reminded that Jesus Christ **laid the foundation of the earth** and that **the heavens are the work of His hands** (v. 10). Evidently, the angels watched in awe as Christ created the universe! Job 38:7 says that "all the sons of God shouted for joy" on that occasion. But all things that He made of this present heaven and earth will pass away. They will **perish, grow old, be folded up, and changed** (vv. 11, 12). All that can be accumulated by man will be destroyed. Nevertheless, Peter says that we "look for new heaven and a new earth, in which righteousness dwells" (2 Pet. 3:13).

While all of this is being accomplished **Jesus Christ remains the same** (v. 12). Since He is forever the same there is never a reason for His people to despair. A PEANUTS cartoon shows Linus dragging his blanket and saying to Charlie Brown, "Charlie Brown, you look kind of depressed." Charlie Brown replied, "I worry about school a lot." He paused. "I worry about my worrying about school. Even my anxieties have anxieties."[10] Some of us who identify with Charlie need to remind ourselves that Jesus is still the same. If all these truths about our Lord are reliable, and they are, then why not commit all our todays and tomorrows to Him?

Since a day will come when all His enemies will become His footstool why not determine now to be on the victory side? The decision is clear. In that final day we will either be seated at His side, or we will be under His feet. The choice is ours; we **do** have a vote in the matter.

Therefore we must give the more earnest heed to the things we have heard, lest we drift away. For if the word spoken through angels proved steadfast, and every transgression and disobedience received a just reward, how shall we escape if we neglect so great salvation, which at the first began to be spoken by the Lord, and was confirmed to us by those who heard Him, God also bearing witness both with signs and wonders, with various miracles, and gifts of the Holy Spirit, according to His own will?

Hebrews 2:1-4

CHAPTER 3

The Danger of Neglect
(Study No. 3 in the Book of Hebrews)

⚜

There is probably no other book in Holy Scripture which exalts the blessed Lord Jesus more fully than Hebrews. Perhaps the writer does this because he was deeply distressed that some of the Christian Jews were considering turning back to their former lifestyles and religion. He offers compelling arguments why they should not forsake the superior realities they had found in Jesus Christ for the shadows and rituals of their former religion.

The Bible proves itself to be as up to date as our morning newspapers for we face this same problem with increasing frequency today. Some believers today have not only looked back, but have actually gone back. They have, by their lifestyles and sometimes by their confession, denied the very Lord Who rescued them from sin's dominion.

I am not suggesting that Christians today in a wholesale manner are deliberately deciding to forsake their Lord. The matter is not so clear-cut or traitorous. It is, instead, a more gradual thing...more a "drift" than a "rift." The light in many lives which once burned brightly has diminished so gradually that the decreasing of its brilliance is hardly noticed until at last the feeble light flickers out.

Not only is there a drifting today, there is also a pernicious, devilish deception abroad. Satan tells believers that they need not be vigilant, that they can, without risk, be "at ease in Zion."

In our nation unprecedented blessing and prosperity have encouraged many of our brethren to embrace a doctrine of affluence and proclaim it as a vital part of their faith. When such humanistic teachings begin to crumble the tendency may be to abandon the Christian faith altogether. Whether we have money has little to do with our Christian faith and it should have no bearing on our faithfulness to the Lord Jesus.

These early Hebrews were daily enduring such persecution and pressure that they were beginning to doubt the reality of their faith in Christ. If the Christian faith were relevant why were their lives not free from conflict? Why commit to Christ if life was simpler, easier, and less complicated in the traditional Hebrew religion?

Responding to their dilemma the writer gives a warning in our text. First, **this passage admonishes us to pay close attention to those things which we have heard.** Second, **we are told why it is imperative to give earnest heed to those things which have been told us.**

Concerning **that which we have heard**, the writer calls it "**so great a salvation.**" A salvation which is "so" great suggests a God Who "so" loved the world!

If you can measure the "**so** loved the world" statement, perhaps you can also measure a salvation which is **so** great!

Although this scripture is often used to present the message of salvation to unbelievers, this entire letter was written to believers who had been walking with the Lord for some time. The word "salvation" suggests more than deliverance from sickness or weakness, or from suffering due to hereditary or environmental problems. "Salvation" deals with the fact that all people everywhere are **lost** forever lost, without Christ. We have not accepted Jesus as some high Ideal which we must emulate; He is our only Way to God!

Salvation is also a process. There must be a perpetual appropriation of the cleansing which our Lord provides. It is foolish to believe that we do not need to constantly pray the Lord's Prayer which calls for the forgiveness of sin. If we think that we need no such prayer then we need to see ourselves in the light of God's holiness! John wrote, "If we walk in the light as He is in the light, we have fellowship with one another, and the blood of Jesus Christ, His

Son cleanses us from all sin" (1 Jn. 1:7). So cleansing occurs while we are walking in the light!

Paul wrote concerning this salvation, "Work out your own salvation with fear and trembling; for it is God Who works in you both to will and to do for His good pleasure" (Phil. 2:12,13). These words indicate interdependence in working. None of us would be saved if we depended on our "working," but it is also true that we "work out what God has worked in." There is a personal responsibility.

This great salvation was **"first...spoken by the Lord"** (v. 3). We are told of "the word spoken through angels" (v. 2), the law of Moses, but the word spoken by our Lord is none other than the message of grace, a message confirmed by those apostles who actually heard the Lord speak. Not only did they hear Him, they also saw Him work signs, wonders, and miracles. He imparted various Spirit-inspired gifts to others enabling them to continue His work.

One of the qualifying words given here regarding signs, wonders, miracles, and gifts is **"according to His own will."** We must remember these words in a day when some seek to exercise the gifts of the Spirit for their own purposes rather than for the edification of the Church. These convincing evidences of the truth of the gospel are given "according to His will."

Why were these Hebrew Christians not to be casual about this warning? The reason is that the word, whether given by angels or by the Lord Himself, was **steadfast**...it was sure to stand! There was simply no way that sin, either by neglect or by commission, would escape punishment.

The writer did not expect these Hebrews to refrain from sin merely because of the fear of punishment. A person is not under conviction for sin if he stops sinning only because he is fearful of punishment. When a person is fully awake to the awful fact of sin he sees its terrible contaminating influence. That is its agony. Fear of punishment cannot be a prolonged motivation for living the Christian life. "Perfect love casts out fear" (1 Jn. 4:18), but it is also true that perfect love **generates** fear. Until we are in a right relationship with God we are afraid that God will punish us; but when we are in right relationship with our Lord we are fearful lest we should hurt **Him,** lest we should bring sorrow to His heart.

In this passage we do not read of overt sin. We read about neglect. If we neglect our salvation (and we must **have** it in order to neglect it) the result is still the same, for neglect leads to a sinful lifestyle. The verse does not talk about denying our salvation, simply neglecting it. Admitting that Christ is Savior is not the same as actively serving Him.

Some who at one time were careful in their worship habits, who judged it important to gather with those of like precious faith to worship the Lord Jesus, are today content to give the lovely Lord a moment of their time in the same manner that they would toss a bone to a dog. When it is convenient they will gather for worship; but if it is costly, in terms of time or money, they neglect to do so.

St. Mark's Church in Mayfair, England, was declared "redundant," unnecessary, because no one worshiped there. The Bishop said that it would probably be sold for commercial use and be turned into a restaurant. Howls of protest came from the well-heeled residents, and they appealed to the Bishop to stop the sale. His reply was incisive: "Had they been in the habit of attending the church in question," he said, "the issue would never have arisen." [1] We never neglect that which we really love.

How may we neglect our Lord? We can choose our profession without consulting Him. We can move to another location without asking Him about it. We can run our lives as we very well please without His counsel, i.e., until a crisis arises. We may neglect our spiritual life until faced with an emergency. That's what the word **neglect** means. When we treat our very salvation as a trivial thing we are neglecting it...and we cannot escape the inevitable consequences of such neglect.

Neglect can kill a marriage. Ron Lavin offers this description of neglect between a husband and wife: "Their wedding picture mocked them from the table, these two whose minds no longer touched each other. They lived with such a heavy barricade between them that neither battering ram of words nor artilleries of touch could break it down. Somewhere between the oldest child's tooth and the youngest daughter's graduation they had lost each other.

"Throughout the years, each slowly unraveled that tangled ball of string called self, and as they tugged at stubborn knots, each hid his searching from the other. Sometimes she cried at night and begged the whispering darkness to tell her who she was. He lay beside her, unaware of her winter, for she warmed herself in self-pity.

"She took a course in modern art, trying to find herself in colors splashed on a canvas, and complained to other women about men who were insensitive. He climbed into a tomb called an office, wrapped his mind in a shroud of paper figures and buried himself in customers.

"Slowly the wall between them rose, cemented by a mortar of indifference. One day, reaching out to touch each other, they found a barrier they could not penetrate, and recoiling from the coldness of the stone, each retreated from the stranger on the other side. For when love dies, it is not in a moment of angry battle. It lies, panting and exhausted, expiring at the bottom of a carefully built wall it could not penetrate."[2]

Neglect can kill a relationship. Likewise, when we neglect our salvation and choose other things, we become imprisoned by the things we have chosen. It is dangerous to neglect our salvation during those times when the sea is calm, but to do so when the storm is raging is absolute madness. We are certainly not in a calm period today. There is danger today for the Body of Christ collectively and for believers individually. We dare not neglect our salvation one moment. These Hebrews lived in a similar time. Notice the perils the writer points out:

1. The danger of drifting onto the rocks (2:1).
2. The danger of divine retribution for disobedience (2:2).
3. The danger of failing to reach the promised goal (4:1).
4. The danger of the terrible sin of apostasy and its penalty (6:4-6).
5. The danger of falling away (6:6).
6. The danger of forsaking the edifying assembling of themselves together (10:25).
7. The danger of neglecting the needs of others (13:1-3).

It is easy to rely on our own spiritual attainments and make them the foundations of our confidence. How easy then to fall! Someone has said that "Christian men should never lose the look of forgiven men." O how we need God's continual cleansing! Those who say that they have no sin and therefore do not need to ask for forgiveness have little concept of the holiness of God. We must never allow the assurance of our future salvation to make us careless about our walk today.

For He has not put the world to come, of which we speak, in subjection to angels. But one testified in a certain place, saying: "What is man that You are mindful of him, or the son of man that You take care of him? You have made him a little lower than the angels; You have crowned him with glory and honor, and set him over the works of Your hands. You have put all things in subjection under his feet." For in that He put all in subjection under him, He left nothing that is not put under him. But now we do not yet see all things put under him. But we see Jesus, who was made a little lower than the angels, for the suffering of death crowned with glory and honor, that He, by the grace of God, might taste death for everyone.

Hebrews 2:5-9

CHAPTER 4

The Neglected Gift

(Study No. 4 in the Book of Hebrews)

The recipients of this letter knew what it was to be exposed to prolonged persecution and have their property confiscated (10:34). Other Jews considered them traitors and, because they had no visible gods, the Romans viewed them as dangerous atheists. Constant struggle against social, political, and commercial bigotry was beginning to take its toll on them. When we are drained by the fight and drift into indifference and indolence, we are in peril of apostasy. Some of the gravest dangers to the Christian life are losing interest in the things of God, becoming inattentive to the Word of God, and being careless about our relationship with God. The devil likes nothing better than for a person to neglect the Word of God and neglect fellowship with God and His people. We see, then, the necessity for the warnings given by this concerned author.

Our previous text pointed out **the great peril, the great penalty, and the great provision. The great peril** is pointed out in verse one, "Therefore we must give the more earnest heed to the things we have heard, lest we drift away." "Therefore" suggests the writer is drawing a conclusion from all he has written in chapter one, where he says that God had spoken, and had spoken in many ways. Finally, in the supreme revelation, He had clearly spoken through His dear Son. No matter how God speaks we should obediently respond, but since He has at last spoken through His Son, we should especially hear and retain the message. Both **attention** and **retention** are stressed. And in this instance the Medium and the Message are one! How could they then fail to hear Him? The plea of the writer, a warning, is not only to those in that day, but to us today as well.

The danger is that of **drifting**. The image is that of a ship drifting on by a safe harbor to its sure destruction. This is no intentional drift away from the loving care of the Lord, nor a deliberate decision to abandon their faith. Other priorities were gradually crowding out those things that had originally seemed so pivotal. The writer sees the great peril of these dear souls drifting toward their own personal Niagara. Perhaps the Spirit is alerting you to this danger.

He then cautions them about **the great penalty**. They were not to see themselves as a lost coin that could not help but lay where it had fallen, or a lost sheep that ignorantly nibbled itself out of the shepherd's presence and could not find its way back again. Personal responsibility is emphasized. He does not allude to any conscious rebellion against the Lord, but a growing lukewarmness in the hearts of these people, a lukewarmness that could ultimately issue in alienation from God.

This is why he writes of both **"transgression and disobedience"** (v.2). "Transgression" suggests an act of offense against the will of God, while "disobedience" has to do with neglecting the will of God. Sins of omission may often be as destructive as sins of commission.

The writer reminds his readers that the law of Moses had been spoken by angels and every infraction of that law brought its own just punishment. How, then, could **they** hope to escape if they disregarded words, not spoken by angels, but by God's own Son? They could not deny the logic of this argument—**the greater the light the greater the responsibility.** Though God does not strike out in a fit of rage when His law is transgressed, His own holy nature demands that sin be dealt with. Grace and judgment are forever intertwined. If we do not obey God we always suffer for it. We do have a vote in our destiny.

Following the writer's warning concerning the great peril and the great penalty, he mentions **the great provision**, calling it "so great a salvation" (v. 3). It is great **because it was first spoken**

by the Lord (v. 3). This message of salvation came from the lips of the Lord Jesus. Earlier the Word of God came through angels, but salvation's proclamation came through Christ. John the Baptist proclaimed the way to salvation, but he did not preach the final word. Jesus, Who first proclaimed it, commissioned others to preach it to the end of the age.

An old hymn asks, "What more could He say than to you He hath said?" No further recourse remains after the Son of God has spoken! He is God's Supreme Revelation, God's Final Word. In Christ God said all He could say and gave all He could give. How might one grade God when it comes to giving? How much did He give of what He could have given? The answer, of course, is that He gave **ALL** in giving the very life of His own dear Son!

Second, the provision **was attested to by eye-witnesses who had heard Christ** (v. 3). John writes, "That which was from the beginning, which we have heard, which we have seen with our eyes, which we have looked upon, and our hands have handled, concerning the Word of Life—the Life was manifested, and we have seen, and bear witness, and declare to you that Eternal Life which was with the Father and was manifested to us—that which we have seen and heard we declare unto you, that you also may have fellowship with us; and truly our fellowship is with the Father and with His Son Jesus Christ"(1 Jn. 1:1-3).

Jesus Christ came as a specific, identifiable, Human Being. He came, as it were, with name, rank, and serial number. In essence, He said, "If you want to know what God is like, look at Me. If you have seen Me, you have seen the Father."

None of these things were done in a corner. The Christmas story is about common people hearing the message that God had invaded His own planet in the form of a little Baby. Wesley described this Baby as "God contracted to a span," the distance between a man's thumb and the little finger. For the first time it could be said that the mother looked like the Baby! He came to this planet with pre-written history. This pre-existent One made the very ground His mother walked on. He created the water she drank and the air she breathed. There is nothing mythical about the Person of Jesus Christ, nor about His wondrous works or words.

Someone told me that they enjoyed Christ-centered preaching. I agree! Sometimes I run the risk of sounding a bit like the Sunday School teacher I read about. A mother asked her son how he liked Sunday School. He replied, "Oh, all right." "Was it just all right? How was your teacher?" He responded, "Well, I don't know but she must have been Jesus' grandmother because He was all she talked about." [1] It is good for preachers and teachers to sound a bit like "Jesus' grandmother," for He alone meets the needs of their hearers.

Third, the provision is also great **because God the Father, Himself, authenticated it by signs, wonders, miracles, and by the gifts of the Spirit** (v. 4). Though we often use these words (signs, wonders, and miracles) synonymously, they are distinct. God gave Noah the **rainbow** as a **sign**. A sign may often be explained. We know what causes a rainbow. A **wonder** differs from a sign in that it is something we cannot explain. Light is a wonder. We know that light travels both in straight lines and in waves; but light remains a wonder. A sign and a wonder together, as seen in the burning bush, constitute a **miracle**. These phenomena were a **sign** to Moses, but a **wonder** also. A sign may not always be a wonder and a wonder may not always be a sign. **But when a sign is a wonder and a wonder is a sign, the result is a miracle.**

Our Lord's miracles issued from His compassion. Yet, who can deny that the works He did proved that He was indeed the Son of God? John gave an account of the miracles of Christ so his readers might believe that Jesus was the Christ, the Son of God, and that believing they might have life in His Name (Jn. 20:31).

In our age we have witnessed possibly the greatest outpouring of the Spirit with accompanying spiritual gifts than in any other time. The fastest growing segment of Christianity today is the Charismatic/ Pentecostal group. From a humble beginning in Los Angeles in 1906 this movement has spread around the world touching all denominations. Wherever He has found open hearts the Holy Spirit has played "leapfrog" with our denominational barriers and has filled hungry believers all over this planet. The gifts of the Spirit signify that this salvation, this provision, is great indeed! It is greater than our own biases, greater than denominational labels, greater than social barriers, and greater than racial prejudices. "Greater is He that is within you, than he that is in the world" (1 Jn.4:4).

Fourth, this provision is also great **because it comes through the death and resurrection of Jesus Christ** (vv. 5-9). This is one of the most exciting passages in Scripture, for it tells us that all that man lost in the fall will ultimately be restored by virtue of the sacrificial death and victorious resurrection of the Lord Jesus.

The world to come, the restored earth, will not be under the administration of angels, but under the administration of God's redeemed people (v. 5). In Adam our position of authority was forfeited; in Christ it is not only restored, but enhanced!

Psalm 8:4-6 teaches that man was made a little lower than the angels. When the writer says "one testified in a certain place" (v. 6), he is not suggesting that he does not know where this place is found in the Old Testament. This expression, a common way to quote high authorities, implies reverence and humility, rather than ignorance. The term "son of man" (v. 6) refers, not only to Jesus Christ, but to man himself, for that is the thrust of these verses from Psalm 8. We are made a little lower than angels and are presently inferior to the angels in strength, wisdom, and beauty. This, however, is temporary, for the redeemed will **judge** angels.

What the human race forfeited by Adam's transgression is absolutely staggering. God gave Adam dominion over **all things**. When this was forfeited by man's failure the whole creation suffered. All the works of God's hands were meant to be under man's authority, even the moon and the stars (Ps. 8).This dominion, lost by Adam's failure, will be restored in the future! God created things for our enjoyment, our pleasure, our convenience, as well as for His own glory. We have a God Who is forever looking out for our welfare.

Injustice, sorrow, fear, sickness, and death filled the earth as a result of man's sin. God had "put all in subjection under him (man), He left nothing that is not put under him. But **now** we do not see all things put under him" (v. 8). This is obvious. Since man is incapable of even ruling over himself there is no possible way that he, by his own goodness or cleverness, can regain what he lost. Nor does he have the qualities necessary to satisfy the demands of God's holiness.

We do not see our ultimate position restored now, "But we see Jesus...!"

(v. 9) What an amazing picture! If you see Him you need see no other! When you see Jesus, you see Life! For the first time the author uses our Lord's human name...**Jesus! O how sweet the Name!**

Our hope is in that Name, not in religion! C.S. Lewis tells a little fantasy about a liberal bishop of the Church of England who died and went to meet the Lord. The bishop was a skeptic, who, in spite of his ecclesiastical position, always had more questions than answers about faith. He had no great sense of commitment toward Christ or the Church. Religion for him was merely a matter of intellectual speculation. In Lewis' story the bishop is given one last chance to visit heaven to decide whether he would like to stay. But heaven was not appealing to the good bishop. I suppose it threatened him to bow down to another, even God. Before he left he engaged one of the inhabitants of heaven in a speculative discussion about religion. "Oh, we don't know anything about religion here," answered his new heavenly acquaintance. "We only know Christ."[2] How wonderful to be obsessed with Him!

Verse nine embraces the great gospel of Christ– His incarnation, His suffering of death for every human being, and His exaltation at the throne of God. Knowing that Christ had ascended, the disciples no longer wondered who was in charge. They knew that Christ now sat at the right hand of God, and they were connected to Him by the Spirit.

"He was made a little lower than the angels, for the suffering of death crowned with glory and honor, that He, by the grace of God, might taste death for everyone" (v. 9). (Note the unfortunate punctuation in the KJV.) The Christmas story testifies that Jesus "was made a little lower than the angels." The incarnation exposed Him to all the trials we face. No one can truthfully say of Jesus, "He just doesn't know how I feel." We can say that of angels, but not of our Lord. When we are told that He "tasted death," the term means more than our understanding of the word "taste." It implies that He "experienced death to the very limit;" and this He did for every one of us.

Some stumble over the fact that Jesus paid the price of their redemption leaving no payment for them to make. It seems too easy. When Betty Crocker first marketed her cake mixes they required only that water be added to them. The cake mixes were a colossal market failure. The company officials could not understand. After all, the mix only required water to achieve a creamy batter and a fine cake. They commissioned their research department to find the answer and discovered that the public felt uneasy about a mix that only required water. It was too easy! Consumers felt that they had to **do something**; so the company changed the formula and required that an egg be added. Immediately the mix was a great success! [3] Betty Crocker might make such an adjustment, but when it comes to the finished work of Calvary it is exactly that—**finished!** Nothing can be added! *Jesus is God's Final Answer!*

At Christmas we are reminded of Jesus' lowly birth in Bethlehem, His positioning Himself below the angels, becoming a Man, a Servant. But this was not the end of the story. Because He came and suffered death He is now crowned with glory and honor. He is a Baby no longer! He now reigns at the Father's right hand, and someday soon the kingdoms of this world will become the kingdoms of our Lord and of His Christ!

For it was fitting for Him, for Whom are all things and by Whom are all things, in bringing many sons to glory, to make the captain of their salvation perfect through sufferings. For both He who sanctifies and those who are being sanctified are all of one, for which reason He is not ashamed to call them brethren, saying, "I will declare Your name to My brethren; in the midst of the assembly I will sing praise to You." And again: "I will put My trust in Him." And again: "Here am I and the children whom God has given Me." Inasmuch then as the children have partaken of flesh and blood, He Himself likewise shared in the same, that through death He might destroy him who had the power of death, that is, the devil, and release those who through fear of death were all their lifetime subject to bondage. For indeed He does not give aid to angels, but He does give aid to the seed of Abraham. Therefore, in all things He had to be made like His brethren, that He might be a merciful and faithful High Priest in things pertaining to God, to make propitiation for the sins of the people. For in that He Himself has suffered, being tempted, He is able to aid those who are tempted.

Hebrews 2:10-18

CHAPTER 5

Bringing Sons to Glory
(Study No. 5 in the Book of Hebrews)

The central theme of all Scripture is found in this beautiful and compelling passage. Whatever else one may think about, speak about, or sing about, there is no other thought nearer to the heart of God than "**bringing many sons to glory**"(v. 10), a reference to our Lord's redemptive work.

Our purpose is to consider the **priority** of our Lord's work, His **procedure** in His work, and His **pleasure** from His work in bringing sons to glory. The author shows the **priority** of our salvation by simply mentioning the fact that all creation came into being through Christ and that everything was created for His glory. It is as if he is recording this great truth, "for Whom are all things and by Whom are all things" (v. 10), almost incidentally.

Jesus Christ, he says, is the "Final Goal" as well as the "First Cause" of the universe. All those things which we see and know about, as well as things invisible and unknowable, were created for the glory of God. Until we consider creation from that perspective we never fully appreciate it. We sing from Revelation 4:11, "...and for Thy pleasure they were created, Thou art worthy O Lord." How true! God, by His spoken word, brought this universe into being. The Genesis creation account reads with almost monotonous regularity, "And God said...and God said." By divine fiat all that is was made.

…However, when God executed the plan for our salvation He did not speak it into being. He personally became involved in the plan by becoming one of us. God became a Man! We read in the Old Testament of the six days of creation and the seventh day of rest. The New Testament account of our salvation is not measured in days; our Lord spent 33 years among us, identifying with us in every possible way, revealing Himself especially to the poor. He breathed this world's polluted air, walked and talked with sinners, the love of God spilling out of Him everywhere He went. By this He demonstrated His amazing love for us.

Sam Levenson once said, "I pay my psychiatrist sixty dollars an hour and all he does is ask me the same question my father used to ask me all the time: 'Who do you think you are anyway?'"[1] Our Lord tells us who we are! We are the "apple of His eye!" He laid down His very life for us.

Rather than distancing Himself from human suffering, He identified with our distress. When the author says that Jesus was "made perfect" through sufferings (v. 10) he means that Jesus "qualified" to redeem us by becoming one of us. He did not stand back and look at the awful river of death; He plunged into it and experienced its terrible pollution. All our sin was **on** Him, but none, thank God, was **in** Him.

His identification with us was not accomplished by His taking one small step downward. Can you imagine yourself becoming a worm? It is even more remarkable that Christ became a Man. God so loved that He sent His Son. The priority of this mission exceeded any other work Christ could do. The importance of His redemptive work is emphasized in that the writer simply mentions Christ's creative and sustaining work and then emphases the grandest theme— our great redemption, the bringing of many sons into Glory.

How was this redemption accomplished? Consider the **procedure** in His work. His first step was identification with us; "...He Who sanctifies and those who are being sanctified are one" (v. 11). Since we are not perfect, we are not one in character, but in family. We are awed by the thought that Jesus Christ stooped to become our Brother! What an altogether incredible thing for Him, without reluctance, to do!

Were you or I trying to accomplish our salvation we would surely have designed some elaborate system of works and rewards. We would have made sure that only those who "deserved" heaven would have gotten in! And we might have excluded those who differ with us doctrinally. Whitefield and Wesley were the best of friends, but they had a falling out over Whitefield's strict adherence to Calvinist doctrine. Whitefield was asked, "Do you expect that you will see John Wesley in heaven?" "No," answered Whitefield. "That's what I thought you would say," his questioner replied. "But you don't know what I mean," said Whitefield. "Wesley will be so far up there near the great Throne, I will never see him."[2] God help us never to think that because our doctrine may be purer than someone else's that we are therefore purer than they! Jesus, knowing that none of us would ever deserve anything other than hell itself, came to planet earth to redeem us, not because we hold a flawless creed, but by His grace, a grace which is forever greater than our sin.

This grace of God is so magnanimous that we are offered acceptance without hesitation. Can you imagine such love, acceptance, and forgiveness that Jesus Christ Himself is not ashamed to call us brothers (v. 11)? Some people are concerned about choosing the "right" friends, and are fearful that they will not be accepted by others. Paul's statement, "I am not ashamed of the gospel of Christ," meant he was proud of it. The fact that Jesus is not ashamed to call us brothers means that He is *proud* to be related to us! How wonderful that God calls us *sons* and Jesus calls us *brothers*! How could any of us, in view of His acceptance, ever fail to accept others?

A story is told about John Hinckley, Jr., the young man who shot President Reagan. Prior to that event the family received a telephone call from young Hinckley in New York. The boy was incoherent, broke and hungry. He begged for a ticket home. Receiving the ticket he flew to Denver and was met at the airport by his father.

At Hinckley's trial his father described his son at that meeting. He could hardly walk from the plane. They went to a waiting room and talked. John Hinckley, Sr. said, "I told him how disappointed I was in him. How he had let us down. How he had not followed the plan we had agreed on. How he left us with no choice but to not take him back again." Mr. Hinckley gave his son a couple hundred dollars and suggested that he stay at the YMCA. At this point in the trial, John Hinckley, Sr. had trouble speaking, but he reported these final words to his son, "Okay, you're on your own. Do whatever you want." Mr. Hinckley concluded, "In looking back on that I'm sure that was the greatest mistake in my life. I am the cause of John's tragedy. We forced him out at a time in his life when he just couldn't cope. I wish to God I could trade places with him right now." As he spoke Mr. Hinckley began weeping quietly into his handkerchief. [3]

We cannot say that the Hinckley son merited acceptance, but things might have been different, his father thought, if he had responded to John, Jr. differently. What mercy is it that you and I have been received by a holy God Who had every possible reason to reject us!

Jesus' forgiveness and acceptance of us demanded, not only His identification with us, but identification so intimate that it led to His own death (v. 14). Mankind had never experienced such unconditional love, a love based on *our* need, not His. The lyrics of a song has a young man repetitiously crying, "I need you, baby; I need you, baby." That young fellow is simply saying, "I want to use you, baby." Much of what we think of as love today is just the opposite... it is selfishness. Jesus Christ did not leave the purity of heaven and come into a filthy world to meet His own need. "He looked beyond my fault and saw *my* need."

To accomplish His death Jesus went into the devil's domain and, on the enemy's own turf, defeated him! Through death He destroyed him who had the power of death, that is, the devil (v. 14). "Destroy" means "to bring to naught, to render powerless, to put a stop to, to break the power, to neutralize, to dethrone, to paralyze, to crush, to render impotent," and (I really like this one.) "to reduce to a zero!"

It naturally follows that **fear of death is conquered** (v. 15). This is one of the great and present victories that we enjoy as a result of the death and resurrection of Christ. When facing death, peace is one of the most treasured possessions of the saint of God. No longer do we fear the cold hand of death, for "to be absent from the body is to be present with the Lord" (2 Co. 5:8).

So much effort is spent today cosmotizing death. Graveyards are referred to as "parks" or "lawns" and we are often forbidden from erecting monuments which would remind us that people are actually buried there. The bodies of our loved-ones are placed in "slumber rooms," and the word "death" is carefully avoided. Even insurance salesmen avoid that terrible word by saying to their prospective customers, "You really need this policy for what would your spouse do *if something should happen to you?*" I once interrupted a man to ask, "What do you mean by 'if something should happen to me'?" It was interesting to see him groping for words, which he hoped might be inoffensive, to tell me that he was talking about my death. When we speak of death we needn't bother with a conditional "if!" Honesty demands that we say, "When," for "it is appointed for men to die once, but after this the judgment" (Heb. 9:27). The movie actor, Woody Allen, said concerning death, "I am not afraid of dying. I just don't want to be there when it happens."

One of the strongest proofs of the veracity of the Christian faith is that Christ gives His followers the ability to cope with death and dying. I am not suggesting that death, your own or that of a loved-one, will be met without tears and pain. But we do not "sorrow as others who have no hope" (1 Thess. 4:13). Christ has removed the fear of death!

A Dr. John Mitchell relates a story about a friend who was dying. When Dr. Mitchell came near his bedside, the man reached out and grasped his hand. "Oh, John," he whispered, "I'm so sick." Then his head dropped back and they thought he was gone. But after a moment he opened his eyes again. "John, is that you?" he asked. Dr. Mitchell replied, "Yes, it is." The dying man said, "My, my, I'm so disappointed. I was expecting to see the Lord and all I saw was you."[4] Our greatest expectation is to see Christ!

How is it possible that Jesus Christ could be both "merciful *and* faithful"; merciful to mankind, yet faithful to the holiness of God which demands sin's punishment? Since the wages of sin is death it is logical that the human race must experience sin's awful penalty. Jesus was *merciful* in offering us forgiveness, yet *faithful* in that He Himself took sin's just penalty. Billy Graham tells of having been caught for speeding. The judge found him guilty, but then proceeded to pay the fine. What an illustration of our Lord's mercy *and* justice.

Another great benefit of our redemption is that **Jesus Christ is a very present help in the time of trouble.** Because He was personally tempted when He was here on this earth in the days of His flesh, He is now able to "aid (succor, KJV) those who are tempted." The word "succor" literally means that He will "run to the aid" of those being tempted and tried. Williams translates this portion, "He is able to give immediate help to any that are tempted."

We have seen the priority of His work and the procedure in His work, but does our Lord get **pleasure** from His work? Verse 12 is a quotation from Psalm 22, a Messianic psalm. After saying that Jesus is not ashamed to call us brothers the writer says that the Lord Jesus will "declare Your (God's) Name to My brethren." To "declare God's Name" means to speak of God's character. Nobody ever did this as Jesus Christ. He came to let us know for a certainty what God was really like.

Not only does He speak about the character of God, He also sings about it. He **speaks** about God's character to the "brothers" (He called His disciples "brothers.") and He **sings** praises to God in the assembly (the Church). We have pleasure in talking and singing about that which is nearest and dearest to our hearts. Our Lord gets pleasure in declaring the Father's Name in word and deed. His delight was to do the will of God.

No work is more precious to the Lord than bringing God and man together. Thus we see the **priority** of this work. The **procedure** of the work is His identification with us, and the **pleasure** from His work is apparent in the way He sings about His Father to His followers.

The newspapers carried a human interest story about a little boy who was riding a bus across town. He was huddled close to an exquisitely dressed lady and was swinging his leg out into the aisle when he accidentally rubbed his shoe against the woman who sat across from him. Angrily she protested, "Pardon me, but would you make your little boy remove his dirty feet from this seat?" The well-dressed lady took a hard look at the youngster as if she had not been aware of him before and giving him a shove she said, "He's not my boy. I never saw him before."

Embarrassed, the little boy moved aside and sunk down into the seat as if to shrink from view. It was obvious that he was fighting back the tears. "I'm sorry," he said to the lady whose dress he had soiled. "I didn't mean to." The lady felt badly at the way she had responded. "That's all right," she said. "Are you going somewhere alone?" He lowered his head and answered, "Yes, I always travel alone. My mommy and daddy are both dead so I live with my Aunt Maggie. But when she gets tired of me, she sends me to Aunt Elizabeth." The lady asked sympathetically, "Are you on your way to Aunt Elizabeth's now?" The child answered, "Yes, but Aunt Elizabeth is hardly ever home. I hope she is home today though. It sure is cold." "You sure are young to be riding the bus alone," the lady said. "It's O.K.," said the boy, "I never get lost, but sometimes I get awful lonesome. So when I see someone I'd like to belong to I sit real close to them and pretend that they are family. That's what I was doing when I got your dress dirty. I forgot about my feet." The lady moved over and put her arms around a little boy who just wanted badly to belong to someone. [5]

The amazing truth of this passage is that you and I belong to Someone. We are in His family. He calls us "brothers" and "sisters" and God calls us "sons" and "daughters." In "bringing many sons to glory" Christ is, in reality, bringing us back to Himself.

Therefore, holy brethren, partakers of the heavenly calling, consider the Apostle and High Priest of our confession, Christ Jesus, who was faithful to Him who appointed Him, as Moses was also faithful in all His house. For this One has been counted worthy of more glory than Moses, inasmuch as He who built the house has more honor than the house. For every house is built by someone, but He who built all things is God. And Moses indeed was faithful in all his house as servant, for a testimony of those things which would be spoken afterward, but Christ as a Son over His own house, whose house we are if we hold fast the confidence and the rejoicing of the hope firm to the end. Therefore, as the Holy Spirit says: "Today, if you will hear His voice, do not harden your hearts as in the rebellion, In the day of trial in the wilderness, where your fathers tested Me, tried Me, and saw My works forty years. Therefore I was angry with that generation, and said, 'They always go astray in their heart, and they have not known My ways.' So I swore in My wrath, 'They shall not enter My rest.'"

Hebrews 3:1-11

CHAPTER 6

The Danger of Delay
(Study No. 6 in the Book of Hebrews)

Those Hebrews who first read this letter had embraced the Christian faith and had consequently experienced persecutions and ostracism by friends and family members. Life had become one problem after another. Focused now on their problems, rather than upon their Lord, they were tempted to abandon their faith. A man in New York was arraigned before a courtroom on some minor charge. The bailiff announced, "The State of New York versus John Jones," to which the defendant, John Jones, threw up his arms in despair and cried, "I give up! I can't beat them odds."[1] When believers are ready to give up, they do not understand the situation any better that John Jones did.

These Hebrews were now considering going back. The faith that they had accepted as fulfillment of all the types and shadows of the Old Testament now seemed to produce more problems than blessing. During a Monday night football game between the Chicago Bears and the New York Giants one of the announcers observed that Walter Payton, the Bears' running back, had accumulated over nine miles in career rushing yardage. The other announcer remarked, "Yeah, and that's with somebody knocking him down every 4.6 yards!" Walter Payton, an incredibly successful running back, proves that everyone—even the very best—gets knocked down. He also teaches us that the key to success is to get up and run again just as hard. [2]

None of us look for trouble, but we must not be surprised when it comes. Br'er Fox said to Br'er Rabbit in *Uncle Remus* tales, "You can't run away from trouble. There ain't no place that far."[3]

A sequence on a TV program, *All in the Family*, had Archie Bunker arguing with his son-in-law, "the Meathead," a professed agnostic. The son-in-law asks, "Archie, if there is a God why is there so much suffering in the world?" There is a long, awkward silence. Finally Archie yells, "Edith, would you get in here and help me. I'm having to defend God all by myself."[4] God doesn't need our defense, but our creed may need defense if it does not allow for struggle.

In the midst of their troubles these Hebrews Christians were addressed as "holy brothers," partakers of a "heavenly calling" (v. 1). They are reminded that they should consider Jesus Christ, "the Apostle and High Priest of their confession." The writer confirms that the ministry of angels was historically significant and that the work of Moses and Joshua was important; but he declares that all these ministries were fulfilled in the work and Person of the Lord Jesus. They probably agreed with his observations. Yes, his reasoning concerning Christ being the fulfillment of the law and the priesthood was rational. Yes, all he wrote could be confirmed by scripture, as well as by their own experience. **But their problem was not an intellectual problem.** It seems invariably true that when we begin to draw back in unbelief our unbelief expresses itself in disobedience...and disobedience issues in death, spiritual death. So their problem was spiritual, not intellectual.

The Holy Spirit does not **argue** with us. He states the case in clear, rational ways and then makes His plea. So the Spirit-inspired writer says that angels, Moses, the Priesthood, are all fulfilled in the Lord Jesus. Since that is true, he writes, "**Therefore** as the Holy Spirit says: 'Today, if you will hear His voice, do not harden your hearts as in the rebellion, in the day of trial in the wilderness'" (vv. 7, 8).

Their own history was all too familiar to them. It was "your fathers," he said, that had so tested God that He swore in His wrath, "They shall not enter My rest" (vv. 9-11). They, indeed, had not.

That entire generation perished in the wilderness. Every Israeli father rehearsed this familiar story with his family.

Though the writer penned these words, it is "the Holy Spirit" Who speaks and the words which He chooses are from Psalm 95:7-11. "As the Holy Spirit says: 'today, if you will hear His voice, do not harden your hearts!'"(vv. 7, 8) Notice three truths from this text. First, there are some **sound assumptions,** second, some **sure warnings** and third, a **suggested gospel.**

First, consider the **sound assumptions.** The first assumption is that **once we hear we become responsible to His voice.** Once we have heard the voice of God we must respond, or else bear the responsibility for what happens as a result of our failure to respond. Light always creates responsibility. When God speaks to our hearts we must never be casual about it.

This raises an interesting question. **How can we know when God speaks to our hearts?** Let me suggest a few ways. Ask yourself the question, **"What is the nature of the thought I am presently entertaining?"** When the thought comes to my heart that I should forgive someone of a wrong that I suffered from them, perhaps years ago, where do you think that thought originated? When a deep conviction comes that I should pray for that one who has abused me, what, I ask you, is the source of that message? When I am mysteriously prompted to give beyond my normal means to the work of the Lord what gave birth to this idea?

I may hear a hundred sermons on forgiveness, or prayer, or giving and never once feel that the preacher is talking to me. I may secretly wish that someone else had heard **that** sermon for after all, **they** really needed it! So it is not the preacher who is ultimately responsible for our hearing the voice of God.

The very moment you and I hear in our hearts a call to forgiveness, to prayer, to giving, we are hearing the voice of the Lord. When we sense a call to exalt the lovely Lord Jesus we have heard the voice of God. When we are firmly rebuked for our wrongdoing we are hearing the voice of God. When we begin to see the corruption rather than the attraction of sin we are hearing the voice of God. Make no mistake about it; we do not have it within our own capacity to give birth to such sanctifying thoughts.

Let me suggest still another way. **A sense of responsibility always accompanies the voice of God.** Whenever the Lord speaks to our hearts we are personally responsible to Him. That is true in my own experience. After I had preached a sermon on the necessity of being burning and shining lights like John the Baptist, I was stricken by my own need. When I read in the Word of God of the faith, as well as the failures of others, I am stricken in my own heart and know that I have heard the voice of God. The voice of the Lord always creates responsibility. As you read these words you may hear the Lord speak. He may not speak in an audible voice, though He can certainly do so; but if we sense in our own hearts a conviction of sin, it is not of our own making. When that happens, in the Name of the Lord, respond!

We must then face a decision: **we have the freedom to respond positively or negatively to the voice of God.** We are urged not to harden our hearts when we hear His voice. The assumption is that we have the ability to obey or resist. God has given us the "risky gift of free will" and we cannot avoid personal responsibility when He speaks. No one can take this obligation for us.

In most of life's decisions we are given adequate time to carefully weigh the facts and, therefore, make correct choices. But a **sure warning** is suggested by the word "**today.**" Obedience to God must not be delayed; it is an urgent matter. If we are contemplating marriage or deciding on our future vocation we must give those decisions plenty of careful consideration and earnest prayer. Usually there is little need for haste. If we, however, are going to San Diego we needn't spend time considering whether we should go south from Los Angeles. We will go south or we will not go. No amount of thinking will change the geographical facts; no seminar or conference will alter the matter. So it is in our response to Jesus Christ. There is no other way to God and Glory (Acts 4:12). All the careful individual and collective opinions on this subject will not change one iota the way to God and heaven. The tragedy of taking undue time is suggested by the word "**today.**" Time may run out on us while we are simply thinking about it! If we hear the voice of God today we need to respond today. "But," someone may argue, "This may call for a complete reorganization of my plans, indeed, my whole life." Then, let it be! Don't, for one moment, delay obedience. Delayed obedience is disobedience. More souls are lost in this way than perhaps any other. They may not be antagonistic toward the Lord God, nor would they admit that they think response to Him is unimportant or unnecessary. But they do feel it can be postponed. Many have lost their souls by presuming on the grace of God and not giving their immediate attention to this matter.

William H. Hinson tells us why animal trainers carry a stool when they go into a cage of lions. They have their whip, of course, and a pistol at their side. But invariably they will also carry a stool. Hinson says that it is the most important tool of the trainer. He holds the stool by the back and thrusts the legs toward the face of the wild animal. The animal tries to focus on all four legs at once and a kind of paralysis overwhelms it causing it to become tame, weak, and disabled; all because its attention is fragmented.[5] When God speaks to us we must give Him our undivided attention. Otherwise, we will miss His directives.

Even if a space of time is allowed for response, there is, nevertheless, another peril in such delay. When God speaks and we do not hear, do not obey, then **the voice of God grows dim to our hearing.** This is surely not because God speaks less intensely, but because we lose our ability to hear Him. Amos, the prophet, called this "a famine for the Word of God," one of the most horrible judgments recorded in the Bible. Judgment cannot be diverted if the voice of the Lord cannot be heard. Our Lord said, "He that has an ear to hear, let him hear," a proverb born because this terrible judgment was so common. If we fail to obey the voice of God when He calls we risk the possibility that we may not be able to hear if He calls again.

A young lady, although raised in the godly atmosphere of a church parsonage, with no regret walked away from all she and her family had held dear. Things once believed sacred she now laughed at. Hardness set in and her heart, once soft and pliable, was now a heart of steel. What caused this? It was her failure to hear the voice of the Lord. The word **"today"** urges immediate obedience, and suggests great peril in delay.

Finally, there is **a suggested gospel** in the word, **today.** Immediate response to the voice of God is possible because there is no need to consider any other gospel than the gospel of Jesus

Christ. Cultic teachings rising from the New Age Movement and eastern mysticism are no substitute for the Christian gospel!

The word "**today**" encourages us to come to Jesus Christ just as we are! No preparation necessary! No indoctrination is required to be accepted by Him. He calls us to Himself, not to an ecclesiastical organization, not to a religious system, but to Him!

Some may not respond for fear that they may not be able to obey Him. Be encouraged! The same Jesus Who calls you to Himself empowers you for the road ahead. He does not call us in order to mock our weakness. As surely as He is our Light and Salvation, He is also the Strength of our lives (Ps. 27:1).

Hear Him today! We can listen to others so closely that we miss hearing **His** voice. To delay hearing Him **now** may deaden capacity to hear Him **later.** Right now He may be saying to you, "Come unto Me." He may be saying more, but that is surely His message to those not walking with Him.

It is to our own detriment that we try to escape His voice. In 1981, a car was stolen in Southern California. Police staged an intense search for the vehicle and the driver, even placing announcements on local radio stations to the thief. On the front seat of the car, unknown to the thief, sat a box of crackers laced with poison, which the owner of the car intended to use as rat bait. The police were more interested in saving the life of the thief than recovering the car. [6]

God calls us, not because He is simply trying to recover what He has lost. His great concern is that we do not self-destruct.

Beware, brethren, lest there be in any of you an evil heart of unbelief in departing from the living God; but exhort one another daily, while it is called "Today," lest any of you be hardened through the deceitfulness of sin. For we have become partakers of Christ if we hold the beginning of our confidence steadfast to the end, while it is said: "Today, if you will hear His voice, do not harden your hearts as in the rebellion." For who, having heard, rebelled? Indeed, was it not all who came out of Egypt, led by Moses? Now with whom was He angry forty years? Was it not with those who sinned, whose corpses fell in the wilderness? And to whom did He swear that they would not enter His rest, but to those who did not obey? So we see that they could not enter because of unbelief.

Hebrews 3:12-19

CHAPTER 7

Sin's Deceitfulness

(Study No. 7 in the Book of Hebrews)

Hebrews 3:13 is one of the most serious warnings given in Scripture. It has a word in it which, in our day, has lost much of its meaning—the word "sin," a word that has been so compromised that for many it has little current significance.

With the word "sin" there are two other words to consider— hardened and deceitfulness. The words "**hardened** by the **deceitfulness** of **sin,**" when properly understood, send a chill through the soul.

More than any other New Testament book, the Book of Hebrews is filled with warnings. The warning in our text is particularly appropriate to our day, for it has to do with a common malady—hardness. The cause of this hardness is clearly given.

When we encounter hardness in others we often ask, "What could possibly have caused such a condition?" Usually we follow that question with, "I knew him/her when they were so open and pliable. What a change!" The writer of Hebrews had no problem discerning the cause of this terrible malady. Hardened! How? "By the deceitfulness of sin."

Basketball star Pete Maravich died on a basketball court in Pasadena. The heart problem which claimed his life had escaped everyone's notice, and was only discovered by autopsy. Spiritual hardness of heart is a common and deadly problem today. Seldom do those afflicted by it realize its presence.

Consider **the risk of hardness, the road to hardness, and the root of hardness.** To study the **risk of hardness** is to see its danger. By studying **the road to hardness** we will understand if we are moving toward this ailment. To discover **the root of hardness** is to uncover the origin of this dreaded disease.

"Lest any of you be hardened" speaks of **the risk of hardness,** but also suggests that they were not already hardened. There is, then, a process involved. Though they were not hardened, they were in danger of becoming so. Some of us by nature are more pliable than others, but no child was ever born hardened. Tenderness and pliableness are universal qualities in children.

We live in an age that frowns on tenderness and labels it weakness. The T.V. "Marlboro Man" is presented as an image to be imitated, but all the while Jesus insists, "Unless you become as little children..." It takes more strength of character to live righteously than to "go with the flow." God save us from hardness! A few years ago I prayed with a young lady who was weeping profusely. When I asked if there was some way I could help, her response was, "Pastor, it has been so many years since I have wept that I have almost forgotten what it is like." She needed to be left alone while her heart softened once again.

Our values may be so distorted that we imagine strength to be weakness and weakness to be strength. Isn't it strange that so-called "tough guys" usually do their mischief after dark? Tough guys afraid of daylight! Why is it that they use guns and knives and usually travel in gangs instead of alone? Strength is not shown by grabbing an elderly lady's purse, by escaping reality through drugs, by taking advantage of the weak. These cowardly but destructive activities show how weak so-called tough guys really are.

Consider how a person becomes hardened. What are the steps taken along **the road to hardness?** Since we are not born hardened, how do we reach the state where tears no longer flow and conscience is seldom troubled? The ultimate answer is found in the word **sin**, and sin in this letter is **unbelief**. The **sin of unbelief** hardens the heart.

My father was a man who expected his children to behave in church although he did not attend regularly himself. He was, in a sense, a "believer," yet he was not a Christian until just before his death. He intellectually accepted the truth of the Bible, the reality of the Person and claims of Christ, and yet he had not committed his life to Christ. His intellectual belief was not sufficient. Belief does not become saving faith until we commit our lives to those truths we believe.

Many "believers" intellectually accept Biblical teachings, but it takes commitment to those truths to result in salvation. Until that time of surrender, no matter how religious we are or how faithful we are to an ecclesiastical system, we are bound by the sin of unbelief. Even though I believe that Jesus Christ died for my sins, if I refuse to submit my heart to Him, then, though I may believe with my mind, my heart remains full of unbelief. Unbelief rules when we are not committed to the gospel truth.

If I only intellectually acknowledge Him to be Savior, then that truth, instead of freeing me, binds me. Jesus said, "If you abide in My word, you are My disciples indeed. And you shall know the truth and the truth shall make you free" (Jn. 8:31, 32). These verses must never be separated. Disciples are both dominated and freed by the truth they know! Knowing to do good and refusing to do it is sin. Refusing to be governed by that which we know to be true is sin; and sin hardens.

What can possibly be **the root of such hardness?** The answer is found in the word **deceitfulness**. Deceitfulness suggests misrepresentation, deception, fraud, guile, delusion, trickery, treachery. Sin does all that and more.

"Therefore, to him who knows to do good and does not do it, to him it is sin" (Ja. 4:17). Have you wondered, "If I know to do right then **why do I not do what is right?**" If I have a road map but refuse to follow it, you will question my reasoning. If, then, the way to God is clearly in the Person of Jesus Christ, why do some refuse to follow Him as He leads the way home?

The answer is **deceitfulness.** Deception causes us to believe that there must be another way or that there must be more time. A young man on death row recently said on a newscast, "Yes, I knew that it was wrong to kill, but I had gotten away with so many crimes that I didn't think that I would ever be caught." He was deceived.

Drug addicts often claim they can stop using drugs any time they want. They are deceived. Society about us, our lustful flesh, and the devil himself promises that no one will ever know about that sexual fling, that we are only doing "what comes naturally." We are deceived.

Sin offers a false argument. The devil is a liar. He tells you there is no way that you can live for God and still find fulfillment in this life. He lies! He says that you have far too much to give up by becoming a Christian. He lies! God Almighty will never, in your entire Christian experience, ask you to give up anything that is good for you.

In some cities they are now offering free needles to drug addicts to prevent AIDS. The whole drug culture is based on deception! The suggestion that life cannot be experienced to its fullest without an outside stimulant is one of the most blatant lies the devil ever laid on mankind.

"But," someone may argue, "I just don't feel good. I need a fix." Remember, most of the work done in this world is done by people who don't feel good! The Christian feels better when he feels bad than he used to feel when he felt good!

God grant that we will never experience the hardness produced by deception. If the desire to be pliable is in your soul thank God for it! That longing to be pliable, plastic, to be clay in the Potter's hand, indicates that our hearts are not hardened. Thank God for a continued sensitivity to His touch!

A favorite story about Helen Keller concerns her first introduction to the gospel. When Helen, who was both blind and deaf, learned to communicate, Anne Sullivan, her teacher, decided that it was time for her to hear about Jesus Christ. Anne called for Phillips Brooks, the most famous preacher in Boston. With Sullivan interpreting for him, he talked to Helen Keller about Christ. It wasn't long until a smile lighted up her face. Through her teacher she said, "Mr. Brooks, I have always known about God, but until now I didn't know His name." [1] Without ability to hear or see Helen Keller still had a sensitive spirit. God grant that we, with all our faculties, will have tender hearts before the Lord. God forbid that we will ever know what it means to be "hardened by the deceitfulness of sin."

Therefore, since a promise remains of entering His rest, let us fear lest any of you seem to have come short of it. For indeed the gospel was preached to us as well as to them; but the word which they heard did not profit them, not being mixed with faith in those who heard it. For we who have believed do enter that rest, as He has said: "So I swore in My wrath, 'They shall not enter My rest,'" although the works were finished from the foundation of the world. For He has spoken in a certain place of the seventh day in this way: "And God rested on the seventh day from all His works"; and again in this place: "They shall not enter My rest." Since therefore it remains that some must enter it, and those to whom it was first preached did not enter because of disobedience, again He designates a certain day, saying in David, "Today," after such a long time, as it has been said: "Today, if you will hear His voice, do not harden your hearts." For if Joshua had given them rest, then He would not afterward have spoken of another day. There remains therefore a rest for the people of God. For he who has entered His rest has himself also ceased from his works as God did from His. Let us therefore be diligent to enter that rest, lest anyone fall according to the same example of disobedience.

Hebrews 4:1-10

CHAPTER 8

The Rest that Offers Contentment

(Study No. 8 in the Book of Hebrews)

The difficulties these early Hebrew Christians encountered after embracing Jesus as Messiah meant, for many of them, separation from friends and family and a turning away from things held sacred for generations.

In 1871 when archaeologists uncovered a piece of wall that divided the inner and outer temple in Jerusalem, they found this Greek inscription: "No man of another race is to proceed within the partition and enclosing walls about this sanctuary; and anyone arrested there will have himself to blame for the penalty of death which will be imposed as a consequence."[1] We can understand how hostility built up on either side of such a wall. The Jews viewed the Gentiles as dangerous pagans and the Gentiles saw the Jews as self-righteous bigots.

Walls are easily built between people. In 1800 John Adams sought a second term as President of the United States, but was defeated by his Vice President, Thomas Jefferson. Their friendship was severed. They disagreed sharply on foreign and domestic issues. Both these knowledgeable and talented men had helped draft the Declaration of Independence. Adams was blunt and spent much of his career in the shadow of others. Jefferson had greater gifts but was perplexing and many-sided. Forgiveness eventually reunited these two men.

Their correspondence to each other over the last 14 years of their lives adds much to understanding the birth of our nation. On July 4, 1826, the 50th anniversary of the Declaration of Independence, both men died within hours of each other. They had broken down the wall of hostility and division between them. [2] Walls must come down if we are to be reconciled to God and others.

Paul alludes to what these Jews, like himself, had given when he wrote, "But what things were gain to me, these I have counted loss for Christ...I have suffered the loss of all things, and count them but rubbish, that I may gain Christ" (Phil. 3:7, 8). Others did not respond to their losses as positively. Persecution had brought a sense of disillusionment. Instead of experiencing great blessing they were enduring trials, tests, and oppression. Under these circumstances, they reasoned, why not simply return to Judaism?

Making important or hasty decisions on the basis of current circumstances is risky, but how prone we are to do that very thing. Some make decisions by checking the latest poll, making judgments on the basis of popular consensus. This happens when we are adrift, with no set standards. Thank God, "We have an anchor..."

The writer explains that Jesus Himself, Who went through suffering, temptation, and death, was able to help them through their trials (Heb. 2:18; 4:15, 16). All tests and trials will not cease, but in the midst of any situation we can have **rest**, rest which has nothing to do with fatigue! It is **God's rest** and is, therefore, eternal. But it is an experience that can be ours perfectly and forever, not only in eternity, but here and now.

With much gravity the writer warns, "Let us therefore fear, lest..." Our Christian walk is one of **faith** but it also includes walking in the **fear** of God. Hebrews 11:7 says, "By faith Noah, being warned of God of things not seen as yet, moved with fear, prepared an ark." How can he speak of **faith** and **fear** in the same breath?

When **faith and fear have to do with God they are not contradictory.** "The fear of the Lord is the beginning of wisdom" (Prov. 1:7). Paul warns in Romans 11:20, 21: "...because of unbelief they (the Jews) were broken off, and you stand by faith. Do not be haughty, but fear. For if God did not spare the natural branches, He may not spare you either." If the Gentiles did not continue "in His goodness" they, too, would be cut off (v. 22). Is being "cut off" a real and present danger today?

Philippians 2:12,13 puts the sovereignty of God and the free will of man together: "Work out your own salvation with fear and trembling; for it is God Who works in you both to will and to do for His good pleasure."

Christians for centuries have argued over Calvinism and Arminianism which, among other things, have to do with whether or not a person can lose his salvation after having been genuinely converted. Godly, intelligent people disagree on this subject. "Work out your salvation with fear and trembling" seems to say that the responsibility lies solely with us, while "For it is God Who works in you both to will and to do for His good pleasure" seems to indicate that it is God alone Who bears the responsibility for our salvation. Those who think they are saved one day and lost the next need to study Calvin. Those who think that they are so secure that their personal behavior doesn't matter need to study Wesley. And both extremes need to study the Bible! Someone said "Calvinists are so sure that they can't be lost that they are afraid that they are not saved; while Arminianists are so afraid that they are going to be lost that they doubt that they are saved." Recall that these warnings in Hebrews are given to "holy brethren, partakers of the heavenly calling" (3:1).

The ancestors of these Hebrews offer a good example of what happens to those who turn away from God. They had come under God's wrath. The writer of Hebrews repeatedly pleads with his readers not to imitate their forefathers. He urges them to be both **consistent** and **persistent**.

To that person who determines by the grace of God to be both **consistent** and **persistent** there comes the **rest of God.** Because it is "God's rest" He alone can bestow it. We cannot conjure up this rest, but we certainly may have it. We must not consider this an optional matter.

In the midst of problems, trials, heartaches, when family and friends may not understand or sympathize, we have a choice to make. We can throw our faith away; we can cast away our confidence and return to what we were before; or, we can lift our eyes above the current circumstances, lift our voices in praise to God, lift our hands to glorify His Name, and begin to worship and praise our dear Savior. If that is the course we take we will enter into God's rest. His rest has nothing to do with circumstances. It has everything to do with making Christ the center and circumference of life.

These Hebrews were not advised to "get some rest." They are not introduced to rest as a verb, but as a noun. They are not "to rest" but to "enter into His rest."

Verse eight tells us that Joshua could not provide this rest. G. Campbell Morgan writes, "Moses led them out but could not lead them in. Joshua led them in but could not give them rest. Jesus leads us out and leads us in and gives us rest."

Galveston, Texas, was built on a barrier island. After a big storm on August 20, 1886, people began to talk about the need for a sea wall. On September 8, 1900 at 7:32 p.m. a tidal wave 12 feet high came over the island. Six thousand people were lost. After the tragedy the people worked for four years building a sea wall and raising the ground level by pumping in sand. In 1911, this sea wall withstood, not a 12 foot high wave as in 1900, but a 14 foot tidal wave in another great hurricane. [3] Imagine the rest the people of Galveston had in 1911 as compared with what they previously had. There is rest for all of us, but it is only in Jesus Christ, *God's Final Answer!*

For the word of God is living and powerful, and sharper than any two-edged sword, piercing even to the division of soul and spirit, and of joints and marrow, and is a discerner of the thoughts and intents of the heart. And there is no creature hidden from His sight, but all things are naked and open to the eyes of Him to Whom we must give account.

Hebrews 4:12, 13

CHAPTER 9

The Word that Brings Conviction

(Study No. 9 in the Book of Hebrews)

༒

This text is often committed to memory. Speaking of memorization, I have read that at Al-Azar University in Cairo, Egypt the 21,000 students are required to quote the Koran from memory. The Koran is about the length of the New Testament and it takes three days to recite it. We Christians should be challenged by that kind of commitment.

These verses mark one of the high points of the Word of God for they openly declare that the Lord God communicates Himself to mankind. He is not an "absentee landlord." He can and does speak. In doing so He is not simply seeking fellowship; He expects His speaking to bring about a desired result in our lives.

God's Word expresses His mind to us. Jesus said of His Father's Word, "Your Word is truth" (Jn. 17:17). We cannot disregard the Word of God without eternal consequences. A generation of Israelites died in the wilderness because of this sin. We cannot separate fellowship with God from obedience to His Word.

Ted Koppel of ABC said in a speech at Duke University, "We have actually convinced ourselves that slogans can save us. Shoot up if you must, but use a clean needle. Enjoy sex whenever and with whomever you wish, but wear a condom...The answer is, 'No'! Not because it isn't cool or smart or because you might end up in jail or dying in an AIDS ward; but because it is wrong. Because we have spent 5,000 years as a race of rational human beings trying to drag ourselves out of the primeval mud by searching for truth and moral absolutes. In its purest form, truth is not a polite tap on the shoulder, it's a howling reproach. What Moses brought down from Mt. Sinai were not the Ten Suggestions."[1] How true!

This text defines the Word of God! First, it is **alive!** The word for alive (Q*uick* in our King James Version) is not used today except in reference to "quick" flesh, as "the pin pricked my finger down into the quick." "Quick" flesh is living flesh. We usually use the word "quick" to indicate rapid movement. Someone said that there were only two kinds of pedestrians in Los Angeles...the quick and the dead! The Word of God is never a "dead letter." It is spiritually alive and able to impart life. Concerning the Scriptures Martin Luther said, "They are not dead words; they are living creatures, and have hands and feet."

Efforts have been made to destroy the Word of God and if it were not alive its influence would have been destroyed long ago. The fact that it speaks to all ages and cultures indicates that it is the living Word of God. More books have been written about the Bible than any other book! Peter writes that we have been "born again, not of corruptible seed, but of incorruptible, by the Word of God, which **lives** and abides" (1 Pet. 1:23).

The Word is not only alive, it is **powerful!** A little girl in the third grade chose to investigate electricity for her class project and wrote the General Electric Company, "I'm trying to get all the information I can about electricity. Please send me any booklets and papers you have. Also would it be asking too much for you to send me a little sample of electricity?"[2]

God's powerful Word is available to us but we need more than "samples!" Powerful means **energetic!** No book dominates the world more in the moral realm than the Bible. What other book could speak of itself as a "fire," a "hammer," or a "sword?" Isaiah says God's Word does not return void (Isa. 55:11). It does what it sets out to do! When God speaks something happens! God spoke and the universe came into being. God spoke and the rains came and washed sinful man from the earth. God spoke and Abram left

Ur of the Chaldee, not knowing where he was going, but going nevertheless. God spoke saying, "Let My people go," and mighty Pharaoh obeyed. God spoke and the sea swallowed up Pharaoh's army. God spoke and Israel became a nation. God spoke and Israel went into captivity. God spoke and Cyrus released them. God spoke and a little Jewish handmaiden gave birth to the Son of the Most High. God spoke and an old rugged cross was lifted up between heaven and earth. God spoke on that first Easter morning and the stone was rolled away revealing an empty tomb. God spoke and the Holy Spirit fell upon and empowered waiting believers. Someday, we believe soon, He will speak again, a trumpet will sound, and the dead will be raised in incorruptible bodies!

God still speaks! He speaks today to all who have ears to hear Him! And He will always have the last word! What a privilege to proclaim a Word that is powerful and eternal! His Word is not only alive and powerful, it is also **sharp...**"sharper than a double-edged sword." The Word of God has never met a barrier in the soul or spirit of man that it could not penetrate. It can cut through to a person's need quicker than a sharp knife cuts through hot butter! It is written, "Out of His mouth went a sharp two-edged sword" (Rev. 1:16).

As a sword the Word can be used defensively and offensively. Indeed, it is the only offensive weapon in the Christian's armor. This sword was used both correctly and incorrectly in the temptation of Jesus. Satan misused this sword and Jesus used it correctly. One needs to know it to use it correctly. It should never be abused for personal benefit.

It is surely a serious matter to stand week after week before God's people and declare, "Thus saith the Lord." The following thoughts came to my mind as I thought upon the fact that I have stood before those who have gathered to worship God for so many times over decades of ministry. It is certainly no light thing to stand before God's people and proclaim His Word.

THIS SWORD IN MY HAND

Here I am again, Lord, Among Your people, wielding the Sword; a living, sharp, two-edged blade. And I must choose: Do I carry it confidently, yet remain awed by its absolute authority, its infinite *dimensions; or do I come to believe that **I** am the authority, that my understanding of the Sword is conclusive?*

Like any reliable weapon, it has power to defend or destroy. It penetrates. Am I, as a sensitive surgeon, careful and incisive; or like a brutal butcher, slashing and mutilating?

Because I have, by academic and actual experience, been schooled to understand it better than some, am I ever dominated by pride, the evil power it seeks to ruin?

Am I ever delighted when either enemy or friend is stricken by the power of this blade? Do I believe, even for one brief moment, that the God Who used Balaam's steed, could not have used even a weaker vessel in my stead?

Have I, this day or any other, deferred the use of the Sword, considering my own words to be less (or more) offensive; have I, in wanting to spare those I love from pain, merely delayed their cure?

Lord, let me never believe that years of study and experience can diminish my amazement at its simplicity or its depth. Lord, may my doubts never be so severe that I am tempted to shake this Sword in the face of its Author.

Above all, let me never believe that this Sword in my hand is mine to use; rather, let me ever be convinced that I am its servant.

Amen. (8/1/88)

Peter, the fisherman, proved that he was a poor "swordsman" in Gethsemane! When we try to **use** the Bible to win an argument, or substantiate some questionable doctrinal position we are in danger of twisting the Scripture. Using this two-edged sword requires care, for there are no dull edges! I often leave the pulpit being wounded myself by the Sword of the Spirit.

Some people use the Scripture like a young mother used a play pen. She said, "I sit down in it and the children can't get to me for hours." The Sword of the Spirit must never be mistaken as simply a defensive weapon.

Besides being alive, powerful, and sharp, the Word is also **piercing**, so piercing that it divides between the soul and spirit and joints and marrow. Not only does the Word divide the soul from the spirit, it also divides the spirit itself and the soul itself. It not only cuts **to** the bone, it cuts **through** the bone. No problem remains beyond its reach!

The Word has an edge like a sword and a point like a needle. Some hearts are so hard that no instrument can penetrate them except the Word of the Lord. The Word works its way into the heart revealing secret sins. It pierces, not to kill, but to heal; and it penetrates like a surgeon's knife, opening and exposing, then cleansing and healing.

Only the piercing Word of God can deal with both the soul **and** spirit of man. We are not disembodied spirits. We **are** a spirit but we **have** a soul and a body. Eternal spirits made in God's image still have physical and soulish needs. Jesus paid the price for the redemption of our total personality...intellect, emotions, and will. We have problems distinguishing the soul from the spirit, but the Word knows how to do it!

This living, powerful, sharp, piercing Word is also **discerning**. We may try to pass judgment on it, but it surely passes judgment on us! Such judgment is not to make us miserable, but to cleanse us. Jesus said, "You are clean through the Word which I have spoken unto you" (Jn. 15:3).

Convictions born out of the Word of God help us to discriminate in our choices. Some psychologists thought that the fence around a playground was too restrictive, so they took it down and gave the children total freedom...no boundaries, no fences. But a strange thing happened. When the fences were removed, the children refused to run the length and breadth of the playground as they previously did. Instead, they huddled insecurely in the middle of it. As soon as the fences were replaced, their sense of security and freedom was renewed. [3] God's Word provides necessary standards.

Though hearts can be desperately wicked, the Word of God can discern desires and motivations. It constantly probes, making us uncomfortable with our shortcomings. When the Holy Spirit uses the Word to reveal our sinfulness we often want to hide as our father Adam did; but the Word that convicts us is that same loving voice that called Adam back into fellowship. The Word only convicts that it may cleanse.

May God help us, by His Word, to be a discerning people. John Morley once traveled from England to Canada to address a university graduating class. He began by saying, "I have traveled 4,000 miles to tell you that there is a difference between right and wrong."[4] That difference today is "fuzzier" than ever to those who are not guided by the Word.

After giving five characteristics of the Word of God **the purpose of that Word** is stated: "And there is no creature hidden from His sight, but all things are naked and open to the eyes of Him to Whom we must give account" (v. 13). This statement is at once both terrible and majestic. The word "open" is used only here in the New Testament. It suggests literally grasping someone about the neck so that they are forced to look up. God's Word grips us in such a way that we must look up into His face. This same word is used of skinning animals. We are bare before Him. It is also applied to a criminal who cannot lower his head while walking to his execution. He has a dagger placed beneath his chin and cannot avoid the people's gaze. This compels him to look upon those "to whom he must give an account."

So the Word of God exposes our unbelief. It lays us open before the Lord. There is no cover from His sight. This is altogether bad news until we realize that the Word only penetrates so we might see our exceeding sinfulness and cry for His cleansing.

Ed Beck, a former basketball player, is a minister who serves as a part-time chaplain to the U.S. Olympic team. Ed was watching the running of the Special Olympics which features the physically and mentally limited persons of all ages, races, and backgrounds. He noticed eight of these special Olympians lined up for the 100 yard dash. At the sound of the gun they charged from the starting line. Suddenly a small-framed boy fell to the asphalt and began crying. What happened next was a beautiful thing. The other seven stopped and returned to help. One girl bent down, kissed his hurt knee, and said, "That will help it feel better." Then all eight joined hands and walked to the finish line to the roar of the crowd. [5] This soul-searching Scripture makes us feel like that young man. The good news is that our great High Priest has come to where we are and is now walking with us to the finish line!

Seeing then that we have a great High Priest who has passed through the heavens, Jesus the Son of God, let us hold fast our confession. For we do not have a High Priest who cannot sympathize with our weaknesses, but was in all points tempted as we are, yet without sin. Let us therefore come boldly to the throne of grace, that we may obtain mercy and find help in time of need.

Hebrews 4:14-16

CHAPTER 10

The Priest Who Provides Mercy

(Study No. 10 in the Book of Hebrews)

The original readers of this letter were suffering misunderstanding and persecution. They experienced such alienation that they were about to abandon their faith. Because they had no visible gods the Romans considered them dangerous atheists, while the Jewish community thought it strange that they had no temple, sacrificial system, or priesthood. How could those who called themselves Christians be true worshipers of God without these necessary elements? Why couldn't they come back home to their old religion which provided these things? The orthodox Jews refused to believe that the priesthood, the sacrificial system, and the temple were fulfilled in Jesus Christ. Today we cannot imagine bleating of sheep or shedding of blood associated with worship. The average Hebrew of that day could not conceive of worship without these things.

But these Hebrew Christians **did** have a Great High Priest Who represented the people to God and God to the people. Concerning this High Priest the author writes of the holiness of His life, the value of His sacrifice, and the influence of His intercession. There is an enormous difference between **priesthood** and **priestcraft**. This text is about priesthood which honestly and faithfully carried out those duties assigned by the Lord. Priests are to be faithful in both small and large matters. But priestcraft, often practiced by professional religionists, takes advantage of God's people. Such people, who preach one thing and live another, are accountable to no one. If we are familiar with true priesthood we will avoid priestcraft.

After studying the probing and cutting power of the Word, it is comforting to come to this portion of the Word which has to do with our compassionate Great High Priest, the Lord Jesus Christ. Our purpose is to consider **five truths about this High Priest** and **how His Priesthood should affect us.**

First, this Great High Priest has "**passed through the heavens**" (v. 14). Aaron, the Old Testament priest, entered once a year into the Tabernacle, through the blue curtain, and into the Holy of Holies. Our Great High Priest, after offering Himself up as the Final Sacrifice, passed through the blue sky into the heaven of heavens where He now sits at the right hand of God! From that position of power He will continue to reign until all His enemies are made His footstool! Satan, the "prince of the power of the air," saw his kingdom torn asunder as the Risen Jesus passed **through** it in order to forever reign **over** it!

Second, His Name is "**Jesus the Son of God**" (v. 14). "Jesus"... He is human! "Son of God"...He is divine! Since He is human He identifies with us; since He is Deity He has the power to meet our needs. In Christ God stooped to become Man, and a Man was exalted to Deity. What mystery! What comfort!

Third, "**He sympathizes with our weaknesses**" (v. 15). "He Himself took our infirmities and bore our sicknesses" (Matt. 8:17). What amazing grace that He, from highest heaven, enters earth's sorrows. Unlike the mythical Greek gods, who were above feeling, Jesus enters into our grief. He is "touched with the feeling of our infirmities" (v. 15). No one can adequately sympathize with a sufferer unless he himself has suffered; and no one ever suffered as our Lord.

As Head of the Church He is its "**Nerve-Center.**" Anyone who touches one of His people touches "the apple of His eye." He asked the persecutor, "Saul, Saul, why are you persecuting Me?" (Acts 9:4) Anyone who persecutes one of God's children persecutes the Lord Himself. How intimately and sensitively He identifies with His people!

It is conceivable that a physician may be impersonal and mechanical in treating his patients, offering no personal concern or cheering word. One may only be a "heart problem" or a "cancer case" to him. Jesus not only manifested power in bringing Lazarus out of the tomb, He was strong enough to weep with the grieving sisters. He is not only the **Son of God** Who has all power; He is also the **Son of Man** Who fully sympathizes with our sorrows.

Fourth, He was tempted as we are (v. 15). He conquered temptation by the power of the Spirit. He went into the wilderness "led by the Spirit" and returned from the wilderness "full of the Spirit." Clearly His greatest temptation must have been Gethsemane, where He "trod the wine press alone." There the Pure Gold went into the furnace to manifest its purity.

Not only was He tempted by the devil, He was also tried by loneliness of spirit. None on earth, not even His mother, could understand Him. He must have been deeply tried by the ingratitude of those He served.

Fifth, He did not sin (v. 15). In the school of temptation He took the entire curriculum and graduated as no one ever had or will...with a perfect grade! There is mystery here. The question is often asked how Jesus Christ, being the Son of God, could possibly sin by yielding to temptation. This question is not one to be answered glibly, but there could have been no temptation without the possibility of yielding. Although His temptations were real, no inclinations to sin ever defiled His pure heart. The lust of the flesh, the lust of the eyes, and the pride of life found no place in Him. He found sin repulsive, never enticing.

These five facts declare our Lord Jesus to be as far above ordinary man as heaven is above hell. Thank God for the purity and power of His Person! But **how do these truths affect us,** especially as we go through trials? **Three responses** should be made as a result of these truths concerning our High Priest.

First, we should **hold fast our confession** (v. 14). We must "cling to what we confess." We are to hold fast our inward faith and, in spite of opposition, openly express our confession before others. Criticism and mistreatment had caused these saints to shy away from sharing their faith. Because they had no temple, sacrifice, priesthood, or visible god, their faith seemed cultic to some. They had allowed these circumstances to intimidate them.

How can we openly witness for our Lord if we are embarrassed or afraid? In our nation today the enemy uses embarrassment more than fear to silence believers. Some Christians have been embarrassed because, in recent years, they have unintentionally made idols of certain Christian leaders, and these leaders have fallen. The Church of Jesus Christ needs to cry out as the people in Elijah's day, "The Lord **He** is God! The Lord **He** is God!" I said to a pastor friend, "If God ever sees that you are going to publicly embarrass Him and His Church I pray that the Lord will take you home first." He agreed to pray the same for me!

Our profession, or confession, must not be tied to any human being. It is forever linked to the unfailing Christ. Holding fast to our confession demands that we cleave to Jesus and persevere in fellowship with His people. How can some say that they love walking with the Lord Jesus but seldom gather with others to worship Him? If we walk with Jesus we will want to walk with others who are also walking with Him.

Second, we should **come boldly to the throne of Grace** (v. 16). Jesus, our High Priest invites us to take His hand and allow Him to usher us into the very Presence of God! This is an allusion to the Old Testament priest, in fear and trembling, approaching the mercy seat with the blood of a sacrificed animal. None of us, I suspect, would have accepted an invitation to accompany a priest into the Holy of Holies! As he made his annual entrance through the veil into the Holy of Holies, if the priest had sin in his life he would be stricken dead in the Presence of God. In such a case, tradition says the priest had a rope tied to his leg so his body could be pulled out for burial. Thank God, there is no fear in our hearts concerning the perfection of our Great High Priest! Boldly and gratefully we accept His invitation to come before the Father's throne.

Our entrance, however, is not an arrogant one. We are coming for mercy...mercy for past sins, and grace for present weaknesses. We enter freely, without fear, into the very throne room of an accessible God. Were His throne one of justice alone we would not enjoy such liberty. It is, however, a throne of mercy, rather than merit! All are accepted equally. None are more welcome than others at

His throne! We enter the throne room with a Man, the Man Christ Jesus! This Man, perfect Mediator between God and man, stands in the Presence of God in our very nature. We are "at home" with Him. Entrance is not based on any personal claim to God's favor, for our sin forfeited any right to it. Our hope rests in His mercy which He freely gives.

To all who do not know God this throne is one of **judgment.** But those seeking forgiveness find it a throne of **grace.** The redeemed, coming to a throne of **majesty,** worship Him. What a contrast to the thunder of Mount Sinai and the dreaded annual entrance behind the veil!

Third, we come to Him **in the time of need** (v. 16). When are these "times of need"? There are times when **temptation** is particularly intense. For some these times come when they are alone; for others, when they are with a crowd. Whatever the situation, He is able, as we come to Him, to meet the need.

A man said to his doctor, "Doc, I'm ready to end it all. I have nothing to live for anymore." The doctor asked, "What do you mean you have nothing to live for? Your house isn't paid for. Your television isn't paid for. Your furniture isn't paid for. You haven't paid me for this visit. What do you mean that you haven't got anything to live for?"[1] When **we** think life is meaningless others may be hoping we'll hold on!

Financial needs can be distressing. Some are tempted by a lack of this world's goods, while others are tempted by **prosperity.** If we are tempted to steal because we have little, or tempted by false security because we have much, these are times of need.

When we are **verbally or physically abused** this, too, is a time of need. Such trials draw us nearer to God or drive us further away. Like Job, we will either "curse God and die" or "come forth as pure gold."

Physical **sickness** is another need. Jesus Christ heals the sick; yet there are those who, for reasons we do not understand, are not healed. Whatever the circumstances we dare not allow doubts or bitterness to cloud confidence in our Living Lord. We must talk to Him openly and honestly...and listen as well as talk. Time before the throne is meant for dialogue, not monologue.

Some are reluctant to admit needs. John Madden says that some professional football players won't have an injury treated when others are around. Quarterback Kenny Stabler was like that, as was the legendary Jim Brown. Instead of going into the trainer's room after the game, Brown treated himself at home so no one would know he was hurt. He figured that if even the trainer knew, then somebody on the other team might hear about it. If the other team knew, their tacklers might try to re-injure him. [2] But in the Christian family we must freely express our needs, for together we can take our problems to One Who heals.

In the midst of need we require three things: **strength to stand the strain, consolation which will encourage us, and deliverance at the right time.** All these needs are met in our High Priest, Jesus Christ. He gives us **strength by His Word.** He supplies **consolation by the Spirit.**

Finally, He **rebukes the cause of the suffering.** We are strengthened to stand until, in His time, our need is met. As our Mediator, Christ **reconciles** us to God. As Advocate, He **restores** us after sin and as Priest He **sustains** us.

Though he was in the swimming pool the little three-year-old boy felt secure, for he was in his father's arms. But, then dad began walking slowly toward the deep end, gently chanting, "Deeper... deeper...deeper. As the water rose higher and higher on the child his face registered increasing panic, and he held all the more tightly to his father who, of course, easily touched bottom.

Had the little boy been able to analyze his situation, he would have known that there was no reason for fear. The water's depth in **any** part of the pool was over his head. Without his father he would have drowned even in the shallowest part of the pool. His safety **anywhere** in the pool depended upon his dad. At times we feel we are in over our heads. We panic as if we've lost control. The truth is, whether we admit it or not, we are **always** in over our heads! Our Father is forever holding us up. God is never in "over **His** head" and, if He takes us deeper and deeper, we are still safe in the security of His arms! [3]

Without fear of rejection we can come boldly to the throne of grace. And the invitation comes from the One Who sits on the throne!

For every high priest taken from among men is appointed for men in things pertaining to God, that he may offer both gifts and sacrifices for sins. He can have compassion on those who are ignorant and going astray, since he himself is also subject to weakness. Because of this he is required as for the people, so also for himself, to offer sacrifices for sins. And no man takes this honor to himself, but he who is called by God, just as Aaron was. So also Christ did not glorify Himself to become a High Priest, but it was He who said to Him: "You are My Son, today I have begotten You." As He also says in another place: "You are a priest forever according to the order of Melchizedek"; who, in the days of His flesh, when he had offered up prayers and supplications, with vehement cries and tears to Him who was able to save Him from death, and was heard because of His godly fear, though He was a Son, yet He learned obedience by the things which He suffered. And having been perfected, He became the author of eternal salvation to all who obey Him, called by God as High Priest "according to the order of Melchizedek," of whom we have much to say, and hard to explain, since you have become dull of hearing.

Hebrews 5:1-11

CHAPTER 11

Jesus...Perfect Priest Forever

(Study No. 11 in the Book of Hebrews)

What a marvelous text! Since every word in this passage is so full of meaning how tragic that the readers were "dull of hearing" (v. 11).

In answer to the claim that Christianity, because it had no High Priest, was inferior to Judaism the writer sets forth Jesus Christ as their High Priest. He claims that the Lord Jesus not only meets all the qualifications for this high office, His Priesthood is vastly superior. Three factors are mentioned: **the qualifications for priesthood, how Christ met those requirements, and the proper response to His Priesthood.**

As to the **qualifications for priesthood,** first, **the priest had to be a human being,** a partaker of our common human nature (v. 1). The Hebrews believed strongly in the ministry of angels and, perhaps to some, it seemed logical for God to use angels in this important office. If angels were mediators we would have no concern about sinful behavior on their part; but the priest had to be an identifiable human being.

Furthermore, **the priest was to be appointed and ordained as a representative of the people** (v. 1). His work was to be vicarious, for when he stood before God he represented all the people, not merely himself.

He must also **offer both gifts and sacrifices** (v. 1). "Gifts" refer to bloodless offerings, such as meal offerings, while "sacrifices" have to do with blood sacrifices. A high priest must also **have compassion on the ignorant and straying** (v. 2). An angel could not qualify, but a priest, since he shared their same nature, could compassionately identify with the failures of the people. He dare not use his position to condemn, for he understands and wrestles with human frailty and weakness himself.

Why is the priest expected to have pity on the ignorant and wayward? The Old Testament speaks of sins of ignorance (Lev. 15:22-29) which result from a lack of knowledge. Waywardness implies neglect. Sins of ignorance are treated with more understanding than premeditated sins presumptuously committed.

We may become impatient with those who lack knowledge and are, therefore, careless in their walk. If we are impatient and uncaring, ultimately some failure in our own lives will remind us that we are ourselves "also subject to weakness." No high priest could make a fitting atonement for the sins of the people if he was unforgiving and indignant toward them. He must have the same attitude as Moses who went before God in intercession for Aaron and the people who had sinned against both him and the Lord. Effective intercession is made for the weak by those who acknowledge their own vulnerability.

Because of his human frailty the priest **must be aware of his own weakness** (v. 2) and offer sacrifices for his own sins. The weakness of Aaron the priest is seen in his agreement to make a golden calf, a sin that brought judgment upon all the people. Caiaphas, one of the high priests in the New Testament, was a wicked, vicious, and ungodly man. The writer does not say, "If you want to see how terrible the Hebrew priesthood really is then look at its failures in your own history. Consider the awful sins of Caiaphas! How can you continue in a religion such as that, a system that produces such priests as Aaron, Eli, Amaziah or Caiaphas?" He does not attempt to prove the weakness of the Hebrew religion by attacking their priests. Rather than attack their leaders he exalts the Lord Jesus Christ! What a lesson for us today! God help us not to be judgmental toward others, unmindful of our own imperfections, too harsh or too indulgent.

Every priest is also **called by God** (v. 4). Aaron served as high priest, not because he was an honorable man, or inherited the position, but because he was personally called by God. These six qualifications for priesthood demonstrate the superiority of Jesus Christ in His Great High Priesthood. Consider how our Lord not only **meets, but surpasses all these requirements for priesthood.**

First, **He became a Man** (v. 1). Though He came from Deity and remains Deity, He is also Man. Paul writes, "For there is one God and one Mediator between God and men, the **Man** Christ Jesus" (1 Tim. 2:5). He identifies with both God and man. "The days of His flesh" does not suggest that His manhood had been terminated. He is today, and will forever remain, the God-Man.

Second, **He was appointed and ordained as a representative of man** (v. 1). Christ "did not glorify Himself to become High Priest." God called Him! Since Jesus was of the tribe of Judah rather than the tribe of Levi this would normally mean that He could not serve as a high priest. However, as God had done in other cases, **He** called a priest Who was not of the priestly tribe. Our Lord's priesthood was "according to the order of Melchizedek" (v. 6), an eternal priesthood.

Third, rather than offer gifts and sacrifices **He offered Himself** (vv. 7, 8) once and for all! These verses speak of the terrible agony of Gethsemane, a suffering perhaps greater than that of the cross. It was there in the garden that all His anguish came into focus. All our sins, with their accompanying guilt, were placed upon the sinless Son of God. Our sin and guilt justly merited the wrath of God, but in Gethsemane that wrath was focused on the Lord Jesus. It was there that this issue was dealt with. Who can fathom the anguish He must have known as He cried, "If it is possible let this hour pass from Me"? (Mk. 14:35)

Consider the words "prayers and supplications" (v. 7). The word "prayers" suggests need or desire based on a sense of insufficiency. "Supplications" was originally used for carrying an olive branch as a symbol of humbleness and earnestness. These prayers and supplications were offered with "vehement cries and tears." "Crying" suggests a loud cry, as the noisy, hoarse cry of a raven or an inarticulate cry from pain or distress.

When Adlai Stevenson lost his bid for the presidency, the reporters pushed a microphone into his face and asked him how he felt. His reply was, "I'm too big to cry, and it hurts far too much to laugh." Where did we get the idea that the more mature we are the less we are apt to shed tears? Jesus did not teach that by word or example. He offered Himself and the dreadful cost was beyond human comprehension.

Who can doubt the fourth truth—that **He has compassion on the ignorant and erring** (vv. 2, 7, 8)? He endured agony more intense than any other and, at the same time prayed, "Father, forgive them. They know not what they do" (Lk. 23:34). This compassionate High Priest walked knowingly with a traitor for three years without exposing him! His mercy not only allows enemies to live, but offers them forgiveness and restoration rather than what they justly deserve! He remains the same today!

Jesus was "exceedingly sorrowful," or "sore amazed," in Gethsemane as He took upon Himself the vileness of our sin. "Exceedingly sorrowful" means "to render immovable" and is associated with terror and astonishment. Who can imagine the anguish that came to the Holy Son of God, Who had never experienced the slightest stain of sin, as He took upon Himself all the sin of the world—past, present, and future!

How could the very Lord of Heaven fulfill the fifth qualification of priesthood, that of **being aware of His own weakness** (vv. 2, 7, 8)? He had to voluntarily lay aside His omnipotence and take upon Himself the form of man. He was no stranger to hunger, pain, and rejection. Even His family did not understand Him: no, not even His mother.

Crying, tears, and fears often indicate weakness, but when used of Christ they show He fully identified with us. As the Son of God He did not need to learn; but as the Son of Man He "learned obedience by the things that He suffered." As God, He never knew temptations, trials, or tests, but as Man, He "learned" all these things. As King of Kings He knew no limitation, but as the Suffering Servant He went to Gethsemane, the whipping post, and the cross. He was not **taught** obedience; He **learned** it in the school of suffering. He was tempted and overcame as a Man by using God's Word and power.

The words "having been perfected" (v. 9) do not suggest any previous imperfection, but His being "fully qualified" to serve as our Great High Priest. He is both perfect Priest and perfect Sacrifice.

Sixth, **He was appointed by God** (v. 10). It was **God** Who offered the cup to Christ. Peter, mistaking the whole event in the garden, drew his sword and tried to defend his Lord. Jesus responded, "Put your sword into the sheath. Shall I not drink the cup which My Father has given Me?"(Jn. 18:11) The loving Father sent His Son to drink the cup for us! The Lord Jesus' appointment as High Priest was made by the Father Himself.

If Satan could have had Mary stoned when she was found with Child, Jesus would not have fulfilled His divine appointment. If Herod could have slain Him in the slaughter of the innocents, He would not have realized His Priesthood. The crushing load in Gethsemane was so severe our Lord could have died, but He prayed "to Him that was able to save from death" and was, therefore, able to fulfill His priestly calling.

How should we respond to His High Priesthood? Since we believe in the priesthood of all believers we should fulfill, by the grace of God, the demands of our own priesthood. We must realize our personhood, know that we are appointed by God, offer our sacrifice of praise and worship, have compassion on the ignorant and erring, be aware of our own weaknesses, and know that our ultimate responsibility is to God Himself.

Those who read the writer's words found them hard to understand because they had become "dull of hearing." A preoccupation with our own problems can diminish our hearing capacity. Attention on self causes difficulty in hearing others. Their problem was not a lack of intelligence, but an inability to hear. Only those who have an ear to hear, hear. When the Word of God is presented some hear while others listen politely but fail to comprehend.

A new fire engine station was built in Tennessee. When it opened the firemen gathered in full uniform along with people from the community to celebrate. During the festivities the station's first fire call came, but the firemen were so busy celebrating that another station had to answer the call! [1] Preoccupation with self also deadens the voice of God.

The curse which Amos describes as a "famine for the Word of God" occurs when people are dull of hearing. It may be the most devastating of all judgments. Famines are caused by an absence of food, but can you imagine people starving while food is plentiful all around them? Thus it is with a famine for the Word of God. God continues to speak but dullness of hearing often prevents response. God grant that we will be quick to hear and respond for we have been given *God's Final Answer!*

For though by this time you ought to be teachers, you need some-one to teach you again the first principles of the oracles of God; and you have come to need milk and not solid food. For everyone who partakes only of milk is unskilled in the word of righteousness, for he is a babe. But solid food belongs to those who are of full age, that is, those who by reason of use have their senses exercised to discern both good and evil. Therefore, leaving the discussion of the elementary principles of Christ, let us go on to perfection, not laying again the foundation of repentance from dead works and faith toward God, of the doctrine of baptisms, of laying on of hands, of resurrection of the dead, and of eternal judgment. And this we will do if God permits.

Hebrews 5:12-6:3

CHAPTER 12

Spiritual Anorexia

(Study No. 12 in the Book of Hebrews)

S everal years ago I went to minister to a family and as I entered the house I was stunned by an unforgettable sight. Twin boys about three to four years old were crawling like animals about the house. These frail, thin children had never been properly fed. When they cried for food the mother, instead of offering them solid food, simply gave them a bottle. Their little bodies were so malnourished their very lives were endangered. This situation, thank God, was soon changed.

Today some people suffer from anorexia, a life-threatening condition. The person simply has no appetite, or loses their food after eating. Is it possible for a person to suffer **spiritual anorexia**?

Paul used a commonplace analogy when he said, "And I, brethren, could not speak to you as to spiritual people but as to carnal, as to babes in Christ. I fed you with milk and not with solid food; for until now you were not able to receive it, and even now you are still not able" (1 Cor. 3:1, 2).

Hebrews was addressed to people who were stunted in their spiritual development and at the same time were threatened by a hostile society. To complicate the situation, they had no appetite for the only "food" that would promote spiritual growth and provide the strength they needed.

Having no completed New Testament as we have today, they relied on the Old Testament and the living voices of those who spoke God's message. Their inability to teach, though they should have been teaching by now, was both a loss to themselves and to fellow Christians.

Spiritual immaturity cannot be casually accepted. Everybody loves a baby—but not a 40-year-old baby! How heartbreaking that some Christians never grow up! This unnatural condition must be taken seriously, for immaturity can lead to apostasy. Consider these three truths: **the reasons for spiritual anorexia, the cure for this dreadful disease,** and **the conditions for the cure.**

What are **the reasons for spiritual anorexia?** First, **there was spiritual weakness among them.** If a person has been on a diet of milk for a prolonged period it is difficult to take strong food. Enough opportunities for growth and development had been given to these Hebrew believers that they should have been teachers, but they had retrogressed! All of us grow at a different pace, but we all **must** grow!

Second, **they were intellectually prejudiced.** They became selective about the truths they were willing to receive. Some who wanted to return to Judaism looked for any excuse to discount the Christian faith. Nothing produces blindness more surely than that prejudice which chooses from inspired truth that which it will believe. This is why the writer says, "We have much to say, and hard to explain, since you have become dull of hearing" (v. 11).

If we ignore those challenging portions of the Word we crowd God's will out of our lives. The Bible then becomes a closed book that we may admire and discuss, but refuse to obey. If we insist on having our own way we will resist any word from God that challenges our inflexibility.

The third reason for spiritual anorexia is **willful inattentiveness to the Word of God.** Lack of attention to the Word breeds an inability to discern between true and false doctrine and behavior (v. 14). This lack of discernment causes the Bible to become a sealed book to us and thus we forfeit the nourishment it provides.

Thank God, **there is a cure for this terrible affliction** (6:1-3). First, we must **leave the foundational truths,** and second, we are to **go on to maturity** (v.1).

In almost every field of endeavor there must be an **abandonment of the present** and a **commitment to the future.** When I graduated from college I thought it was wonderful that I could at last have some relief from books. What a mistake! Any minister who does not read and study will become repetitious and hinder maturity in the church as well as in himself. This is especially true of ministers who travel from place to place repeating the same messages. It is not surprising when such teachers fall into failure. Their message may be a blessing even while their personal lives deteriorate. The Christian life is like riding a bicycle—you go forward or fall.

Movement is not always discernible. Winona and I were flying into Los Angeles and just as we crossed the mountains and started our descent, the sound of the jet motors grew so quiet that the plane seemed suspended in the night air. An elderly lady whispered to us, "Have we stopped?" As surely as an airplane cannot stop in mid air, neither can we "stop" in our Christian walk.

When we move forward some things are left behind and new things emerge. We are to move beyond six elementary truths: **repentance, faith, baptisms, laying on of hands, resurrection of the dead and eternal judgment.** These six doctrines, though important, are never stopping places. If we do not move beyond these truths, we will experience stagnation and ultimate failure. The writer assumed that these immature believers knew these doctrines, and he did not ask that they abandon them, but simply move beyond them. They were foods which once nourished but could not sustain forever.

Two words, **principles** and **perfection**, indicate growth. We are to **leave** the principles and **go on** to perfection (maturity). We do not **abandon** the principles, but build on them as a structure is built on its foundation. We leave the elementary principles just as a tree "leaves" its roots without forsaking them. If roots are removed the tree dies. Roots are necessary to the tree as a foundation is to the building.

It is tragic to lay a good foundation and fail to erect the building. These six principles could be well known without producing growth. This is why we must be exposed to the whole Word of God rather than our favorite themes. Time spent in the Word is imperative. David wrote, "Your word have I hidden in my heart, that I might not sin against You...Your word is a lamp unto my feet and a light to my path" (Ps. 119:11,105). Nothing can replace the Word.

Some have categorized the first two of these six principles (repentance and faith) as acts of mind and heart, the second two (baptisms and laying on of hands) as ordinances, and the third two (resurrection of the dead and eternal judgment) as eschatology. Repentance and faith are **inward experiences**, baptisms and laying on of hands are **outward ceremonies**, and the resurrection of the dead and eternal judgment are **future events**. The first two speak of the **beginning** of our Christian walk, the second two of the **present**, and the final two of the **future**. Consider each of them.

Repentance suggests "a change of mind." It is far more than remorse. Though he was not repentant Judas felt remorse...and hanged himself. The rich young ruler felt remorse as he went away from the Lord's presence, but was unrepentant. **Repentance is feeling as God does about your sin.** "Godly sorrow produces repentance leading to salvation" (2 Cor. 7:10a).

The prodigal son was repentant. He recognized his circumstances ("He came to himself."), admitted he had sinned, and confessed his unworthiness, but none of these things got him out of the hog pen. It took an act of his will. **He** had to say, "I will arise and go to my father." Repentance always involves an act of the will. The text speaks of "repentance from dead works," a reference to justification by works rather than by faith in the finished work of Calvary.

Faith toward God refers to a belief that God hears the prayer of a repentant sinner. Repentance and faith are essential to salvation. Paul wrote, "But to him who does not work but believes on Him Who justifies the ungodly, his faith is accounted for righteousness" (Rom. 4:5). "If you confess with your mouth the Lord Jesus and believe in your heart that God has raised Him from the dead, you will be saved" (Rom. 10:9).

The doctrine of baptisms has to do with putting away the old life and living the new. The word "baptisms" is plural. Many baptisms are spoken of in the Bible: Jewish baptisms or washings, John's baptism, and Christian baptism. John's baptism was a baptism of repentance and remission of sins (Matt. 3:11). Paul speaks of being "baptized into Christ Jesus" (Rom. 6:3) and of being "baptized into one body" (1 Cor. 12:13). Jesus commanded us to baptize in water (Matt. 28:19). Water baptism expresses outwardly what has transpired inwardly. We are dead to the old life and risen to newness of life in Jesus Christ.

Laying on of hands includes the transference of guilt. The priest laid his hands on the scapegoat as the sins of Israel were confessed, and the goat was led away into the wilderness never to return. Jesus did the same with our sins. They are gone, and He never reminds us of them! (Lev. 16: 21, 22) Laying on of hands also suggests spiritual blessings or authority, showing that a person was set aside for special responsibility. (See Gen. 48:13, 14: Heb. 11:21: Num. 27:15, 16, 18-20, 22, 23)

The resurrection of the dead was also an Old Testament doctrine, just as all six are, but it was brought into great clarity by the resurrection of Jesus Christ. Jonah's experience in the great fish typified the death and burial of our Lord. Job said, "For I know that my Redeemer lives, and He shall stand at last on the earth; and after my skin is destroyed, this I know, that in my flesh I shall see God" (19:25,26).

There are some Old Testament insights into immortality, but it remained for the New Testament to boldly declare that Jesus Christ was alive, the "firstfruits of them that slept" (1 Cor. 15:20). Paul wrote that "Jesus Christ abolished death and brought life and immortality **to light** through the gospel" (2 Tim. 1:10). In apostolic sermons the resurrection is always central. God is the Author of life on both sides of the grave! We have two worlds to consider. Though aliens in this present life, we are destined for eternity! We are on our way somewhere!

It is fitting that **eternal judgment** follows the doctrine of the resurrection. Of course, God is **more** than a judge, but He **is** Judge. Ask Adam and Eve, Sodom and Gomorrah, Ananias and Sapphira and all will confess that God judges sin. John writes, "And I saw a great white throne and Him Who sat on it, from Whose face the earth and heaven fled away. And there was found no place for them. And I saw the dead, small and great, standing before God, and books were opened. And another book was opened, which is the Book of Life. And the dead were judged according to their works, by the things which were written in the books. And anyone not found written in the Book of Life was cast into the lake of fire" (Rev. 20:11, 12, 15).

These six doctrines are called **elementary!** Consider that! "Elementary," he says, and yet some teachers confine themselves to only one or two of them. Many teachers today write or speak consistently on faith alone. No wonder some in the Body of Christ are anemic and stunted. Those who follow such selective teaching are even led to believe they are hearing the deep things of God! These first-century Christians already knew these six doctrines and yet were apt to apostatize.

It is never proper to have spiritual weaklings teaching spiritual weaklings. If every teaching the writer refers to "milk," where is the "strong meat" today?

To some today **repentance** mistakenly means crying when you get caught. Others believe that **faith** is a means to get everything you can out of God. **Baptisms** may have to do only with water and power, but never with suffering. **Laying on of hands** may be done without regard to character or giftedness. Ordinations may be given without proper qualifications. When empty hands are laid on empty heads, the whole body of Christ suffers! We hear little about the **resurrection of the dead** though it was central in apostolic preaching. Obsession with this present world precludes consideration of the next. Our present-day conception of God does not allow us to think of Him as a **Judge** Who punishes sin. If the writer of Hebrews wrote to the Church today he might well say that even our milk is skim milk! God help us to have an adequate diet!

Today a congregation's health is often measured by size or money. If that were true, then a man who weighed 1000 pounds would be the healthiest of men, and drug dealers who make millions from their contemptible trade could be judged immanently successful. God never measures success by size or wealth!

If we want to be free from **spiritual anorexia** the healing depends on two issues. The Bible says: "And this we will do if God permits" (6:3). "This we will do" refers to our will. We must determine to eat the correct spiritual diet. This can be settled by an act of the will. The world, flesh, and the devil cry out against such a determination, for this means an exposure to the Word of God on a regular basis. We **must** partake of the Word privately as well as gather with God's people to study, pray, and worship. Hebrews urges us not to "forsake the assembling of ourselves together as the manner of some is."

My parents had seven children. I am embarrassed to recall how often my mother had to call more then once to get us to the table after preparing the best meals you can imagine. How privileged we are to be invited to the Lord's table. Come without delay. The Father, as well as the family, misses you when you are not present. A healthy appetite and an act of the will assure your presence.

We end with a sobering and unsettling statement. We **can** be mature saints of God, grown up in every way, only **if God permits** (6:3), i.e., God's will conditions every determination we make. The writer is not questioning God's will as to whether or not we should be mature. No doubt about that. He is considering **the absolute sovereignty of God.** Since our times are always in His hands we ought to say, "If the Lord wills, we shall live and do this or that" (Ja. 4:15).

God could call us home in the next hour. A popular bumper sticker says, "Today is the first day of the rest of your life," but today could be our last day before we meet the Lord face to face. Our good intentions amount to precisely nothing if not carried out when we have the opportunity.

For it is impossible for those who were once enlightened, and have tasted the heavenly gift, and have become partakers of the Holy Spirit, and have tasted the good word of God and the powers of the age to come, if they fall away, to renew them again to repentance, since they crucify again for themselves the Son of God, and put Him to an open shame. For the earth which drinks in the rain that often comes upon it, and bears herbs useful for those by whom it is cultivated, receives blessing from God; but if it bears thorns and briers, it is rejected and near to being cursed, whose end is to be burned. But, beloved, we are confident of better things concerning you, yes, things that accompany salvation, though we speak in this manner. For God is not unjust to forget your work and labor of love which you have ministered to the saints, and do minister. And we desire that each one of you show the same diligence to the full assurance of hope until the end, that you do not become sluggish, but imitate those who through faith and patience inherit the promises. For when God made a promise to Abraham, because He could swear by no one greater, He swore by Himself, saying, "Surely blessing I will bless you, and multiplying I will multiply you." And so, after he had patiently endured, he obtained the promise. For men indeed swear by the greater, and an oath for confirmation is for them an end of all dispute. Thus God, determining to show more abundantly to the heirs of promise the immutability of His counsel, confirmed it by an oath, that by two immutable things, in which it is impossible for God to lie, we might have strong consolation, who have fled for refuge to lay hold of the hope set before us. This hope we have as an anchor of the soul, both sure and steadfast, and which enters the Presence behind the veil, where the forerunner has entered for us, even Jesus, having become High Priest forever according to the order of Melchizedek.

Hebrews 6:4-20

CHAPTER 13

The Peril of Apostasy

(Study No. 13 in the Book of Hebrews)

⚜

This is perhaps the most challenging passage in Hebrews. It has been interpreted in many ways. Commentaries on this passage remind one of a sign hanging over the old ironsmith's shop: "All kinds of fancy twistings and turnings done here." May the Holy Spirit give us light on the warning as well as inspiration from the promises of this text.

The writer had fellowship earlier with these Hebrews and wanted to visit them again (13:19, 20). Obviously they needed encouragement, for no book in the New Testament is given more to encouragement and exhortation. Of Hebrews' 303 verses 160 are given to exhortation. The author alternates from exalting Jesus to exhorting the saints. He warns them repeatedly of the peril of falling away. No book in the Bible is so filled with warnings about the danger of departing from the faith. Holding fast to the faith is its main thrust.

Paul cautions, "Let no one deceive you by any means; for that Day will not come unless the falling away comes first..." (2 Thess. 2:3). When the writer asks, "How shall we escape if we neglect so great a salvation...?"(2:3), he is warning that our security rests upon a continuing relationship with Christ.

Those to whom he is writing are identified by these five characteristics: (1) they were once enlightened; (2) tasted the heavenly gift; (3) partakers of the Holy Spirit; (4) tasted of the good word of God; (5) and tasted of the powers of the world to come. In order to defend their doctrinal position, some will say that these people were not Christians, but had only "tasted" the Christian experience. However, the same word, "tasted," is used of Christ in Hebrews 2:9, "...that He, by the grace of God, might **taste** death for everyone." He experienced death to the ultimate!

The apostasy referred to is real, not hypothetical. Other translations read "and then fell away" (ASV), "and after this have fallen away" (NEB), "and then have fallen by the wayside" (Wms.). It is not a conditional or imaginary situation. Some had **already** fallen away. But he is confident of better things concerning those who received his letter (v. 9).

The writer is deeply concerned about this issue. It is not a light matter that these to whom he refers as "holy brothers" and "beloved" are considering departing from the faith. He did not believe that one religion was just as good as another. His heart was breaking as he saw these believers growing colder toward the Lord Jesus Who had bought them with His own blood. What would he write to the Church today or to us personally?

Consider first, **the danger of apostasy**, and second, **God's provision for victory**. It is possible to fall away from the faith. The question is not whether or not a person **can** fall away, for some had already fallen away. Our concern is whether people **can ever recover** from such a state.

Why does the writer say it is impossible, since they have fallen away, to renew them again to repentance (v. 6)? How does this relate to 1 John 2:1, 2, "If any man sin we have an Advocate with the Father?" The writer describes people who had once walked with the Lord but had now renounced their faith in Him. They were of such a mind that, if asked, they would say, "Yes, He should have been crucified, and if I had been there I would have wanted Him executed" (v. 6). If they turned back to their old religion, their Jewish friends would not accept them unless they completely renounced their faith. Nothing other than a complete rejection of Jesus as Messiah would ever satisfy the old crowd. Jews today who accept Jesus as their Messiah are often considered as non-persons. This is one of the reasons why the land of Israel is a difficult place for people to respond freely to the gospel of Christ.

It was impossible for these Hebrew Christians to be accepted in the synagogues unless they utterly broke with Christianity. They would, in such a case, continue to crucify the Son of God and expose Him to open contempt. These verbs are in the continuous sense. Because apostates by their actions are **constantly** crucifying Jesus and **constantly** holding Him up to public ridicule, they are unable to find forgiveness. In such an instance it is impossible for someone to receive forgiveness, for they cannot sincerely ask for it while their whole lifestyle argues against it. The possibility of forgiveness is, therefore, canceled.

A drunkard cannot be changed unless he is willing to quit drinking. A drug addict cannot be cured if he continues using drugs. An adulterer cannot be freed from debauchery as long as he insists on practicing it. Those who kill unborn children cannot be guiltless until they stop it. Too blunt? Should I say that an alcoholic cannot recover from his illness unless he is helped to taper off; that the person who is beset with chemical abuse is simply a product of society and must be educated until his appetite goes away; that the person who has an "alternate lifestyle" must be assured that to be "sexually active" is acceptable as long as the parties are mutually agreeable?

We will never be free from destructive sins until we call them what they are—**sin**, and repent of them. Education will never solve the problem. We already have the smartest criminals in the world! The people who flood our cities with deadly drugs and filthy pornography are not ignorant people. Those with venereal diseases are not ignorant people. We will not be healed until we are willing to change how we live and acknowledge unchanging, absolute standards.

One of our senators said that we must educate our young people who are involved in drugs and violence. The campaign to get young people to simply say, "No," is commendable, but many lack the conviction, or the ability, to "just say no." It is said that Napoleon III could speak four languages but could say "No" in none of them. When tempted he would twirl his mustache and yield. His wife threatened to cut off his mustache unless he learned to say "No."

The text speaks of "tasting the heavenly gift." We are all invited to "taste of the power of the world to come," a power that enables us to live triumphantly.

God provides certain guidelines to life and if we violate them we suffer. He sent His own Son to offer us power over sins which kill and destroy. His power enables us to abandon destructive lifestyles. Forgiveness cannot be experienced when one, by his lifestyle, continues to crucify the Savior. Notice that the soil mentioned in the text continued to bear thorns and thistles. As long as that is the case, there can not be forgiveness, for this suggests a deliberate, consistent hostile attitude toward Jesus Christ. The American Standard Version reads, "It is impossible to renew them again unto repentance, **while** they crucify to themselves the Son of God afresh and put Him to an open shame." Williams translates verse eight, "But **if it continues** to yield thorns and thistles, it is considered worthless and in danger of being cursed, and its final fate is burning." Hebrews 10:26, 27 is a serious warning: "For if we sin willfully (or willfully persist in sin; a purposeful and continuous apostasy, not a single act of unbelief but a state of condition) after we have received the knowledge of the truth, there no longer remains a sacrifice for sins, but a certain fearful expectation of judgment, and fiery indignation which will devour the adversary."

The writer mentions two types of response from soil. One soil drinks in the rain, has a good harvest, and is blessed of God. The other soil has the same rainfall but bears thorns and briars, is worthless, and burned. The emphasis here concerns the harvest, the fruit of our lives.

The readers would remember that their fathers forfeited entrance into the Promised Land because of unbelief. Perhaps, some might have reasoned, if they were less aggressive about their faith they could be readmitted into the synagogue; if a bit less bold in their testimony, the Romans might better tolerate them. But believers are not called to compromise.

These Hebrews were painfully aware of the prophecy in Isaiah chapter five where Israel is compared to a vineyard in which the Lord worked. But when harvest time came the vineyard only produced sour grapes. The Lord promised that the vineyard would be burned, trampled down, the walls broken down, briars and thorns would come up, and even the rains would stop. The author hoped this prophecy would get their attention and awaken them to their hazardous circumstance. The choice however, is not between fruit or no fruit. The choice is either fruit or thorns and thistles.

Three positive assurances follow this serious warning. First, **God does not forget** (v. 10); second, **God does not lie** (v. 18); and third, **our anchor holds** (vv. 19, 20).

What a comfort to know that **God never forgets!** These Hebrews continuously "ministered to the saints" (v. 10). God sees! Others forget, but God, never! He sees when good works are done in secret, when others fail to notice or take for granted. Someday, when it really matters, He will openly reward properly motivated good deeds. When that day arrives for God to reward some will say, "Lord, when did I do that?" (Matt. 25:37-39) Good deeds, forgotten by those who did them, are those most likely to be rewarded by our Lord. God, Who never forgets our pure works, always forgets our confessed sins! Heaven's records are not kept for fear that God may forget.

God can choose to forget or remember, but "It is **impossible for God to lie**." It is "great consolation" to remember that whatever God has promised He will do. God promised to bless Abraham personally, nationally and internationally...and He did! These blessings were fulfilled in a promised son, just as God's promises to us were fulfilled in His Son!

The watchword is **patience** (v. 15)! Patience prevents discouragement and, therefore, is an answer to the peril of apostasy (vv. 4-8). Faith is **never** a substitute for patience. Impatience insists on telling God how and when to answer prayer. This is not faith, but presumption. We have no more right to say "Now" to God than we have to say "No" to Him.

Third, **we have an anchor** which is our hope (vv. 19, 20). This hope is sure for it is based on "two immutable things" (v. 18), **His promise and His oath**. What an encouraging word! We can understand man taking an oath, but why should God condescend to take an oath? As a concession to our weakness God, Who cannot lie, takes an oath that we might more easily believe! He, as always, goes beyond what is anticipated!

This hope, which is our anchor, grips the Solid Rock! An anchor must cling to something solid and unmovable. Our anchor is fastened securely to Jesus Christ Who has entered into the very

Presence of God. One end of the chain is attached to our hearts and the other to our Lord. All who are anchored to human beings will be disappointed; but those anchored in Jesus will never be moved!

No earthly priest could be a "forerunner" as Christ is said to be. A "forerunner" is not simply someone out front, but one who shows the way, and demonstrates how to travel it. If any high priest had said to the people, "Follow me," as he prepared to enter behind the veil, no sensible person would have accepted his offer. If the priest had unconfessed sin in his life he was stricken dead as he entered the Holy of Holies.

By that example God teaches an important truth. Trust in man and you will be disappointed and ultimately destroyed, for the only Man you can follow without fear is Jesus Christ. There is a photograph of a cat and dog sitting side by side in unusual harmony. The caption over their heads reads, "A Couple of VIP's." In fine print are the words, "What makes them important is who owns them." We should never be "owned" by any other than Jesus Christ! We go into God's Presence only if we go in with Him!

Be patient with the work God is doing in you. If He is at work, and He is, you can surely know He is doing something beautiful. It may not appear at the moment, but His every touch on your life is a touch of love, a touch by a nail-pierced hand. We have a choice: patience or apostasy!

A young soldier, Lt. John Blanchard, took basic training in Florida during World War II. One evening he wandered into the Army library to find a book. As he worked his way through the book he became impressed, not with the book but with the notes penciled in the margins; the feminine handwriting showed insight and understanding as well as tenderness. He flipped to the front of the book and found the name of the previous owner, a Miss Hollis Maynell.

Blanchard noticed that she had a New York address and wrote to her. The following day he was shipped overseas. For thirteen months the two corresponded, opened their hearts and realized that they were falling in love. He asked her to send a picture, but she refused, saying that if he really loved her it wouldn't matter what she looked like.

Finally the day came when they were to meet. They arranged to meet at Grand Central Station in New York at 7:00 p.m. She had written, "You'll recognize me by the red rose I'll be wearing on my lapel."

At one minute to 7:00 the lieutenant straightened his uniform as he entered Grand Central Station, his heart pumping with anxiety as he anticipated the long-awaited meeting. Here is how he describes it:

"A young woman was coming toward me, her figure was long and slim, her blond hair lay back in curls, her eyes were blue as flowers, her lips and chin had a gentle firmness, in her pale green suit she was like springtime come alive. I started toward her entirely forgetting that she was not wearing a rose. As I moved a small provocative smile curved her lips: 'Going my way, sailor?' she murmured. Almost uncontrollably I made one step closer to her, and then I saw Hollis Maynell.

"She was standing almost directly behind the girl. A woman well past forty, she had graying hair tucked under a worn hat. She was more than plump. Her thick-ankled feet were thrust into low-heeled shoes. But she wore a red rose on the rumpled brown lapel of her coat.

The girl in the green suit was quickly walking away. I felt as though I was being split in two, so keen was my desire to follow her and yet so deep was my longing for the woman whose spirit had truly accompanied me and upheld my own. And there she stood. Her pale, plump face was gentle and sensitive. Her gray eyes had a warm and kindly twinkle. I did not hesitate. My finger gripped the small, worn, blue leather copy of the book which was to identify me to her. This would not be love, but it would be something precious, something perhaps even better than love, a friendship for which I had been and must be, grateful.

"I squared my shoulders, saluted, and held out the book to the woman; but even while I spoke I felt choked by the bitterness of my disappointment. 'I'm Lt. John Blanchard, and you must be Miss Maynell. I am so glad you could meet me; may I take you to dinner?' The woman's face broadened in a tolerant smile. 'I don't know what this is about, son,' she answered, 'but the young lady in the green suit who just went by, she begged me to wear this rose on my coat. And she said if you were to ask me out to dinner I should tell you that she is waiting for you in the big restaurant across the street. She said it was some kind of test!'"[1]

Lt. Blanchard passed the test. Do others know that you are a believer? What evidence is there of our commitment? These Hebrews were being tempted to turn back because circumstances were difficult. But our faith does not depend on circumstances; it is anchored in Jesus, *God's Final Answer!*

For this Melchizedek, king of Salem, priest of the Most High God, who met Abraham returning from the slaughter of the kings and blessed him, to whom also Abraham gave a tenth part of all, first being translated "king of righteousness," and then also king of Salem, meaning "king of peace," without father, without mother, without genealogy, having neither beginning of days nor end of life, but made like the Son of God, remains a priest continually. Now consider how great this man was, to whom even the patriarch Abraham gave a tenth of the spoils. And indeed those who are of the sons of Levi, who receive the priesthood, have a commandment to receive tithes from the people according to the law, that is, from their brethren, though they have come from the loins of Abraham; but he whose genealogy is not derived from them received tithes from Abraham and blessed him who had the promises. Now beyond all contradiction the lesser is blessed by the better. Here mortal men receive tithes, but there he receives them, of whom it is witnessed that he lives. Even Levi, who receives tithes, paid tithes through Abraham, so to speak, for he was still in the loins of his father when Melchizedek met him. Therefore, if perfection were through the Levitical priesthood (for under it the people received the law), what further need was there that another priest should rise according to the order of Melchizedek, and not be called according to the order of Aaron? For the priesthood being changed, of necessity there is also a change of the law. For He of whom these things are spoken belongs to another tribe, from which no man has officiated at the altar. For it is evident that our Lord arose from Judah, of which tribe Moses spoke nothing concerning priesthood. And it is yet far more evident if, in the likeness of Melchizedek, there arises another priest who has come, not according to the law of a fleshly commandment, but according to the power of an endless life. For He testifies: "You are a priest forever according to the order of Melchizedek." For on the one hand there is an annulling of the former commandment because of its weakness and unprofitableness, for the law made nothing perfect; on the other hand, there is the bringing in of a better hope, through which we draw near to God. And inasmuch as He was not made priest without an oath (for they have become priests without an oath, but He with an oath by Him who said to Him: "The LORD has sworn and will not relent, 'You are a priest forever according to the order of Melchizedek,'" by so much more Jesus has become a surety of a better covenant. Also there were many priests, because they were prevented by death from continuing. But He, because He continues forever, had an unchangeable priesthood. Therefore He is also able to save to the uttermost those who come to God through Him, since He always lives to make intercession for them. For such a High Priest was fitting for us. who is holy, harmless, undefiled, separate from sinners, and has become higher than the heavens; who does not need daily, as those high priests, to offer up sacrifices, first for His own sins and then for the people's, for this He did once for all when He offered up Himself. For the law appoints as high priests men who have weakness, but the word of the oath, which came after the law, appoints the Son who has been perfected forever.

Hebrews 7:1-28

CHAPTER 14

The Only Perfect High Priest

(Study No. 14 in the Book of Hebrews)

We were having breakfast together but neither of us was enjoying our food. Our purpose for meeting was enough to cause loss of appetite. His marriage was ready for the divorce court. For years he had been cheating on his wife and all the while concealing his infidelity by religious activity. Now she knew all about it. The children had to be told. He quietly wept as we talked about all that he was about to forfeit— his family, his reputation, his friends. All were being sacrificed on the altar of his own lusts. I said, "Notwithstanding the vows you made to your wife when you married her, it just simply doesn't make sense to do what you are doing. There is no way that a few moments of sensual pleasure can compensate for the losses you are going to experience." We prayed together there in the restaurant, and I am pleased that this story has a fortunate ending. There was a lot of grief to work through, a lot of adjustments to be made in their marriage, but they are together serving God today. The deceptive power of sin is astonishing.

The Hebrew Christians to whom this book was written were considering leaving the lovely Lord Jesus and returning to their old religion. The writer must have been more perplexed by the cooling of their love for Jesus than I was over my friend's readiness to abandon his wife and family. Neither he nor these first-century

Hebrews were acting responsibly. What a tragedy to lose so much by making such a foolish mistake.

The writer of this letter compared the supreme goodness of Jesus Christ to what they were going back to. To forsake Jesus, the "merciful and faithful High Priest" and go back to the old system would be utter folly. He urged them not to apostatize, as some of their friends had already done.

He explained that Jesus, their Great High Priest, had entered into the very Presence of God as their "Forerunner" (6:20). As "Forerunner" Jesus says to the Father, "They are on their way! They're coming, Father! My brethren are coming!" Jesus had said, "No man comes to the Father but by Me" (Jn. 14:6). How disturbing that these Hebrews were thinking they could get to God by some other way. If a person abandons **this Way** he forsakes **the only way to God.**

After Richard Petty, the stock car driver, had run his first race, he rushed home to tell his mother. "Mama!" he shouted, "There were 35 cars that started and I came out second in the race." His mother said, "You lost." Petty pleaded, "But Mama, don't you think it's pretty good to come in second in my first race—especially with so many starters?" His mother looked him in the eye and said, "Richard, you don't have to come in second to anybody!" Richard Petty went on to win more money in stock car racing than any racer in the history of the sport. [1] To have "the second best way to God" means losing out altogether!

All agree that man needs a priest to reach God. These Hebrews knew that the Levitical priesthood was ordained by God so His people could approach Him. The priesthood of Melchizedek was also acknowledged as God-ordained. In this chapter the writer demonstrates the preeminence of Christ as High Priest by proving that these two ways, blessed by God in earlier times, were perfectly fulfilled in Jesus Christ.

Three truths are made clear by the text: first, **Jesus is greater than Melchizedek;** second, **Jesus is greater than the Levitical priesthood;** third, **Jesus is the only ideal, perfect Priest.**

How is Jesus a **greater Priest than Melchizedek?** Both Melchizedek and Abraham lived in Canaan amid an idolatrous and immoral population. Two of its cities, Sodom and Gomorrah, were particularly corrupt. Abraham is called "a friend of God" and Melchizedek, "king of righteousness." These men stand as a rebuke to those who insist that they can only worship God in a clean and wholesome society. Our lights really shine when they are **turned on in dark places!** If we want people to know that we are friends of God we must **walk among His enemies.** Through Abraham and Melchizedek God claimed that degenerate territory. Salem would later become Jerusalem. God's plan is to take what is available and change it, to move from chaos to creation, to turn sorrow into joy, to exchange ashes for beauty. Don't look for God in holy isolation or as an escape from the reality of society. God lives among His people. If Abraham, the friend of God, lived in our city, you would find him among God's enemies, trying to change their minds about God. If Melchizedek lived today this king of righteousness would live uprightly in the midst of perversity. This king of peace would be making peace out of trouble. Jesus' blessing for peacemakers would rest upon him!

It is amazing that Salem, an evil society, could become Jerusalem, City of God. But it is also incredible that Jerusalem would ultimately turn treacherous and crucify the Son of God. Perhaps God does not intend that those who name His Name should congregate together too long in one place. Is it possible that Christians hang around with each other too much? Let the salt be salt. Too much salt in one place spoils the food! The New Jerusalem, a city built by God to remain forever, belongs to a future day.

Since Jesus is greater than Melchizedek, He is greater than Abraham, for Abraham paid tithes to Melchizedek. Abraham, returning from war, met Melchizedek, priest of the Most High God (Gen. 14:18-20). The priest brought forth bread and wine, typical of the Word and the Spirit, and blessed Abraham. At that time Abraham had a revelation of God as El Elyon, the Most High God, possessor of heaven and earth. The King of Sodom offered Abraham all the spoils of his recent victory but Abraham refused, saying, "... I will take nothing, from a thread to a sandal strap, and that I will not take anything that is yours, lest you should say, 'I have made Abram rich'" (Gen. 14:23). Instead of receiving from the heathen king, Abraham gave a tithe to Melchizedek, priest of the Most High God.

If we truly know that God is **the Most High God, all-sufficient,** then two consequences follow. First, **we have confidence in His ability to supply our needs.** Second, **we will not be fearful of tithing.** Some need to learn that double-edged truth. If you do not tithe it may be that you are new in the faith and have not learned the Biblical teaching of giving one tenth of your income to the Lord. But if you know that truth and do not practice it, then your disobedience may be based on fear—fear that God will fail to supply your needs. We need to know Him as Abraham learned to know Him, as the Most High God, the All-Sufficient One. If we trust the "king of Sodom" he will ultimately fail us. Our dependence is on the All-Sufficient One to "make us rich."

We rule our pocketbooks or they rule us! When we worship by giving we should say, "Lord, here's my tithe. What else can I do for You?" Tithing should be as natural as breathing for the child of God. For us, "rendering unto Caesar" annually should be more difficult than rendering unto God each week! Someone said, "Death and taxes may always be with us, but at least death doesn't get any worse." Arthur Godfrey once said, "I feel honored to pay taxes. The thing is I could probably feel just as honored for about half the price."

Melchizedek is shrouded in mystery. Verse three simply means we have no recorded genealogy of this man. It is clear that he is a type of the perpetual priesthood of Christ. Since Melchizedek is a type of Christ and Abraham tithed to him, how can we do less in relation to the Lord Jesus?

The writer then shows that **Christ's priesthood is greater than the Aaronic priesthood of the Levitical order.** Unlike the sons of the tribe of Levi who became priests because their genealogies were clearly known, Melchizedek's priesthood did not rest on a known genealogy. Only Aaron's lineage could qualify for priesthood. Since there is no record of Melchizedek's death, he typifies Christ's priesthood as "a priest continually." A Levite's priesthood was terminated by death and necessitated a successor. No one need seek a successor for the Lord Jesus!

The Levitical priest had to be concerned not only about his background, but his mental and physical qualifications as well. Believers, who today are "priests and kings" can thank God that He is not concerned about their lineage. New creatures in Christ never need worry about their background! It cannot qualify them. Indeed, our past must be forgiven.

If God ordained the Levitical priesthood why would He choose a priest from the tribe of Judah? The old priesthood pointed to another One to come. God's perfect plan was never realized through the Old Testament priesthood. Sacrifices under the old economy were made continuously; Jesus' sacrifice was "once and for all." Our need was not for another Aaronic priest, but for a completely different order.

The old order was superseded because it failed. Not only the people, but the priests themselves, were in need of sacrifice. The old transitory system, being feeble and inefficient, had to be canceled. This was done by virtue of two facts: first, God superseded the law in that Christ was from the tribe of Judah, rather than Levi. Second, Christ's priestly appointment had to do with "the power of an endless life" (v. 16). Jesus' appointment was made by God, for "Christ did not glorify **Himself** to become High Priest" (Heb. 5:5). God's wrath is upon those who try to usurp the office of priesthood. God smote King Uzziah with leprosy because he did not maintain the sanctity of the office of the priesthood (2 Chron. 26:18-21).

Our Priest, the Lord Jesus, needs no successor for His priesthood is based on the "power of an endless life," undisturbed by death. Having offered Himself as the perfect Sacrifice, He was raised from death by the power of God.

When Thomas Edison died in 1931, a committee met to plan a proper tribute to this great man. The committee at first thought that the most dramatic salute would be for President Hoover to order all the power companies to shut off their power for one minute. The plan, however, was abandoned. Modern society, even in 1931, was so dependent on electricity, that to shut off its flow for even one minute would be a national catastrophe. [2] Think of the catastrophe that would occur if the Lord God for one second shut off the flow of His power to this planet. Without the power of Christ's endless life the Church cannot function even for one moment.

Though He took no oath at the introduction of the Levitical or Melchizedek priesthoods, God established the priesthood of Christ with an oath (vv. 20, 21). By establishing the unending priesthood of His Son by an oath, God made the priesthood of Christ superior to any other. It "continues forever" (v. 23).

The conclusion is that **Jesus is the only perfect High Priest,** a deduction that rests on the contrasts between the old and the new. The Aaronic priests had to offer sacrifices continuously, but Jesus offered Himself once and for all. The Old Testament priests sinned and were subject to death. Augustine, a great Church father, was a rowdy youth before he met the Lord. He tells of slipping with a group of boys into a vineyard and taking a huge load of pears—not to eat, but to throw to the pigs. "We ate just enough," he said, "to have the pleasure of forbidden fruit." He added, "They were nice pears but it was not the pears that my wretched soul coveted, for I had plenty and better at home. I picked them simply to be a thief."[3] Perhaps all of us can identify in some way with that story. The Old Testament priests needed sacrifices for their own innate sinfulness.

But Jesus Who was perfect in every way lives forevermore. The priests had no power, but Christ has all power and authority. The priests were not of royalty, but Jesus is King of Kings and Lord of Lords. The priests lacked compassion, but Jesus is a merciful High Priest Who makes intercession perpetually (v. 17).

This High Priest is "able to save to the uttermost those who come to God through Him" (v. 25). He blots out our transgressions and cleanses our lives from the forces which ruin us.

They said as He died, "He saved others; Himself He cannot save" (Matt. 27:42). What a lie! He could have saved Himself. He could have called an angelic rescue squad, but He chose to offer Himself as the one perfect Sacrifice. Thus He identified with sinners like you and me as He took our place on Golgotha.

A man who needed spiritual guidance wandered into a church. The pastor asked him about his religious background. He said, "I went to Sunday School when I was a child, but the only scripture I can remember is John 3:16: 'God so loved the world that He gave His only *forgotten* Son that whosoever believeth in Him should not perish, but have everlasting life.'" The man had substituted the word "forgotten" for the word "begotten." The sensitive pastor asked the man, "Do you know why God forgot His Son?" The man replied, "No." The minister said, "It was because He wanted to remember you."[4]

The writer does not contradict Jesus' identification with us when he says that Christ was "separate from sinners" (v. 26). He was separate as far as character was concerned, for He is "holy, harmless, undefiled, separate from sinners, and has become higher than the heavens" (v. 26). He is "separate from sinners" in His absolute purity.

He could not free us from sin unless He was free from it Himself. Neither can you and I help someone from the mire of sin if we are stuck in it ourselves. Jesus was separate from sinners, yet He loved them with an everlasting love; and because of His fellowship with them He forfeited His reputation in the eyes of the religious community. The companions we keep often predict what sort of person we will be. Not so with Christ! He contacted the worst of sinners and loved them into relationship with Him. He so identified with sinners that Luke wrote, "He was numbered with the transgressors..." (Lk. 22:37), and yet He was so pure that He was "separate from sinners" (v. 26). O glorious paradox!

Each day we face choices. Today may be such a time for you. These Hebrews had to choose law or grace—the old way or the Jesus way. Would they choose the rich way, the accepted way, the established way, the way of national identity, or would they choose the poor way, the rejected way, the new way, the way that promised persecution, loss of prestige, rejection by family and friends, and perhaps, even death itself?

There is a price to pay for anything you hold dear. The parents of Elizabeth Barrett objected so strongly to her marriage to Robert Browning they disowned her. Elizabeth wrote regularly to tell them that she loved them. After a silence of ten years, she received a large box from them containing all the letters she had written. None were opened. [5] Declare your love for the Lord Jesus and you, too, may experience rejection.

If you are opting for **religion** choose whatever appeals to you at the moment, but if you are reaching for **truth** you will find it only in Christ. Melchizedek and Aaron both fail in the final hour. Aside from Christ "all other ground is sinking sand."

No one can choose Jesus **and** Aaron, or Jesus **and** Melchizedek. The Judaizers of that day were telling these Hebrews that they had to be circumcised and keep ceremonial rituals. But on Calvary Jesus cried, "It is finished," and He meant it! The old ceremonies and rituals that pointed out our sins and pointed us to the Savior had served their purpose. The Lord, Who cleansed the Temple of sacrificial animals and then offered Himself on Golgotha's altar, declared that there was no other way to the Father.

Just as Abraham, representing the entire Hebrew people, knelt before Melchizedek and received blessing, every one of us should kneel before the only perfect High Priest and ask for His touch upon our lives. He wants none of us to be excluded from His benediction.

The papers reported the death of 78 people in New Delhi, India. A bus carrying two castes of Indians was in an accident. A man tied a rope to a tree, and all 11 of the so-called "untouchables" climbed out to safety. But 78 other Indians died because they would not use the same rope used by the "untouchables."[6] Jesus Christ knows no "untouchables." No one is beyond the love and concern of this compassionate High Priest, *God's Final Answer*.

Now this is the main point of the things we are saying: We have such a High Priest, who is seated at the right hand of the throne of the Majesty in the heavens, a Minister of the sanctuary and of the true tabernacle which the Lord erected, and not man. For every high priest is appointed to offer both gifts and sacrifices. Therefore it is necessary that this One also have something to offer. For if He were on earth, He would not be a priest, since there are priests who offer the gifts according to the law; who serve the copy and shadow of the heavenly things, as Moses was divinely instructed when he was about to make the tabernacle. For He said, "See that you make all things according to the pattern shown you on the mountain." But now He has obtained a more excellent ministry, inasmuch as He is also Mediator of a better covenant, which was established on better promises. For if that first covenant had been faultless, then no place would have been sought for the second. Because finding fault with them, He says: "Behold, the days are coming, says the LORD, when I will make a new covenant with the house of Israel and with the house of Judah—not according to the covenant that I made with their fathers in the day when I took them by the hand to lead them out of the land of Egypt; because they did not continue in My covenant, and I disregarded them, says the LORD. For this is the covenant that I will make with the house of Israel after those days, says the LORD: I will put My laws in their mind and write them on their hearts; and I will be their God, and they shall be My people. None of them shall teach his neighbor, and none his brother, saying, 'Know the LORD,' for all shall know Me, from the least of them to the greatest of them. For I will be merci-

ful to their unrighteousness, and their sins and their lawless deeds I will remember no more." In that He says, "A new covenant," He has made the first obsolete. Now what is becoming obsolete and growing old is ready to vanish away.

Hebrews 8:1-13

CHAPTER 15

The Ministry of the Perfect Priest

(Study No. 15 in the Book of Hebrews)

A writer may conclude his work by saying, "Let me summarize." But when this writer says in verse one, "Now of the things which we have spoken this is the sum," he is saying, "The chief point is this..." (ASV). He then makes three contrasts: the old tabernacle with the new, the old gifts and sacrifices with the perfect sacrifice offered by Jesus Christ, and the old covenant with the new or better covenant. This is one of the high peaks in the book.

Hebrews 1:4 says that the Lord Jesus has a "more excellent Name," and this chapter teaches that He also has a more excellent ministry than any other. Since Hebrews is the supreme commentary on the priesthood of Jesus Christ we can see in it how His priestly ministry excels all others.

First, Jesus our High Priest, ministers where no other priest has ever ministered. **He ministers in heaven** where He **sits at the right hand of God.** He is in authority at the right hand of Majesty! Sitting suggests that He is both Priest and King. Old Testament kings were not to confuse their role with that of the priests. God was not pleased when King Saul usurped Samuel's priestly role by offering the sacrifice. The separation of church and state is not some clever idea our founding fathers dreamed up. It is rooted, like many of the truths our nation was built on, in Scripture.

We have no record of either Jesus or others referring to Him as a priest while He ministered on earth. He was urged to take political power, but steadfastly refused. During His triumphal entry into Jerusalem the ecstatic crowd referred to Jesus as "the King of Israel." A few days later Pilate had a multi-lingual inscription fixed to the cross above His head—"the King of the Jews," a title that incensed the Pharisees. They might tolerate Him as Teacher or Prophet, but they could not bear hearing Him referred to as "King." Upon hearing Him addressed as King, they insisted on His disciples quieting the crowd.

Although the Old Testament separates monarchy and priesthood, they merge in Jesus Christ. He is both Priest **and** King. As a teacher He had less trouble with His enemies, but when they thought He was moving toward political power, there was great disturbance among the Pharisees. It is the same today. The world, flesh, and the devil care little if we "act religious." The enemy is actually pleased for one to simply be "religious," for ritualistic religion can inoculate against the real thing. Submission to His Kingship sets all hell against us. Don't be surprised when that happens. It is commonplace.

We cannot help but worship Him for He has won that high throne of authority through His finished work on Calvary! Earthly priests inherited their position, but our Lord **won** His. A son of missionary parents spent some time with Dr. Albert Schweitzer as he treated the people in his hospital at Lambarene in Africa. A friend asked him, "Do you think those people ever realized what a great man Albert Schweitzer was?" The missionary's son answered, "No, they probably didn't. They knew a man, full of compassion, who simply loved them. That made him great in their eyes." Only those who knew what Schweitzer gave up to minister to his patients could appreciate his greatness. [1] Consider all Christ gave up to save us!

Earthly priests annually entered the Holy of Holies taking with them the sacrificial blood of a slain animal. They offered that blood before the mercy seat and directly left that sacred place. Our High Priest entered the Presence of God, not with the blood of a sacrificed animal, but with His own precious blood. And He did not immediately withdraw from that awesome Presence, but sat down in the very light of God's holiness. Until this very hour He remains there making intercession for us!

What consolation for those first-century Hebrews who received this letter! Their High Priest was not ministering in some wilderness tabernacle, but in the very Presence of the Living God! What encouragement that we are at this very moment represented by such a Mediator!

Through the centuries Israel witnessed notorious failures in its priesthood. Some priests were much further from God than the people they served. The prophets, at times, called the priests to repentance. Our High Priest Who sits in the Presence of God **cannot fail** in any way.

There are so many who seem unable to say "No" to temptation. According to *Newsweek* a sting operation in New York uncovered graft and corruption among public officials. The sting involved 106 public officials. U.S. Attorney Rudolph Giuliani made the following statement: "On 106 occasions bribes were offered or discussed. On 105 of these occasions, the public officials accepted the bribe. On the other occasion the public official turned it down because he did not think the amount was large enough."[2] Our confidence rests only in our High Priest, the Lord Jesus! He never disappoints!

This High Priest ministers in the true tabernacle made by God (v. 2). God Himself designed the Old Testament tabernacle. Every color, thread, tent stake, ritual, and vessel spoke of God's relationship to His people. He cautioned Moses to follow carefully the building instructions which He had given. Nothing was left to Moses' creative ability in erecting the tabernacle. Every God-given detail was to be followed. Even the men who constructed the tabernacle were to be Spirit-filled men (Ex.25:8, 9; 31:2-6).

Do you suppose that the same God Who gave such minute details about the construction of the tabernacle can give His children directions on how to build their lives? Yes! The same Holy Spirit Who supervised Moses helps us in ordering our lives. We also have a marvelous book at our disposal, and with the touch of His Spirit, the "Instruction Manual" comes alive.

The Lord asked the Israelites to donate materials for the building of the tabernacle. Every person was to give willingly, or their gifts were not accepted. So overwhelming was the response that Moses had to restrain the people from any further giving (Ex. 36:5-7). What a far cry from employing professional fund-raisers! God grant that more of us will have to be cautioned about giving too much!

The wilderness tabernacle was also a type of the humanity of Christ. John says that Christ "...became flesh and dwelt (tabernacled) among us, and we beheld His glory, the glory as of the only begotten of the Father, full of grace and truth" (Jn. 1:14). God *tabernacled* among us for 33 years. He Who was high, holy and undefiled walked among the ungodly. Though He healed their diseases and cast out demons, He was misunderstood and experienced rejection.

Can we appreciate the fact that Jesus is at this very moment in the heavenly tabernacle interceding for us? Consider the price He paid to be our Priest before God. Before Israel's priests could enter the Holy of Holies they had to offer a blood sacrifice, but Christ offered Himself as the one perfect Sacrifice, removing forever the barrier between God and man. No other priest could have offered such a sacrifice, for all were imperfect. None other than Jesus Christ could be Priest **and** Sacrifice.

The ministry of our High Priest is better for many reasons. First, **He mediates a better covenant.** How marvelous to have a Mediator Who perfectly **understands** both parties and can be totally **trusted** by both parties!

The word "covenant" suggests an agreement between two parties. Jesus, being both human and divine, can mediate such a covenant. No other party ever could. The new covenant exceeds the old in many ways. To go back to Judaism would be like going from sunlight to candlelight.

Second, **the old covenant was not without fault** (v. 7). Stephen reminded some who wanted to keep the old covenant that though their fathers had received the law by the direction of angels they had not kept it (Acts 7:53). The Apostle Peter candidly asked the gathered assembly in Jerusalem, "Why do you test God by putting a yoke on the neck of the disciples which neither our fathers nor we were able to bear?"(Acts 15:10)

How is it that we can speak of the old covenant as being "faulty" if it was made by God? Did He make the law imperfect? No. The purpose for the old covenant was to bring us to the new one. The first would have been acceptable had it not been for human inability to perfectly keep it. The weakness was in sinful man, not in the law itself (Rom. 8:3). Even in its weakness the old covenant taught the holiness of God, how He felt about sin, and how He was to be approached. All this was necessary for man to be a worshiper. We dare not be casual in our approach to the Almighty. He is more than simply "The Man Upstairs."

When theologian Karl Barth stood before students and faculty during the Princeton Lectures a student asked: "Sir, don't you think that God has revealed Himself in other religions and not only in Christianity?" Barth stunned many when he thundered, "No, God has not revealed Himself in **any** religion, including Christianity. He has revealed Himself in His Son!"[3] If we know God as He is revealed in Christ we will reverence His high and holy Name.

Jeremiah writes about sinful Israel, "For my people have committed two evils: they have forsaken Me, the fountain of living waters, and hewn themselves cisterns—broken cisterns that can hold no water" (Jere. 2:13). These two sins forever accompany each other. Man simply **must** have a deity. When we forsake the True God we add to our sin by fashioning a facsimile, and thus get further from Him. The English explorer, William Perry, and his crew were on an icy vessel exploring the vast nautical wasteland of the Arctic Ocean. They felt that their investigation would best be served by heading further north, so they charted the stars and started their treacherous journey northward. Marching across ice floes, they crept along for hours. Finally, almost totally exhausted, they stopped. Hastily, they took another bearing on the stars and were astonished to find they were further south than when they had started walking! How could it be? They found that they had been walking on an ice flow which was traveling south faster than they had been walking north.[4] The more we try to save ourselves the further we distance ourselves from God!

Third, Christ's ministry is better because of **the power and glory of the better covenant.** Jeremiah said a day would come when God's law would be written upon the hearts and minds of His people (Jere. 31:31-34). The Holy Spirit would, in that new day, not only say, "This is the way, walk in it," but also, "I have come to empower you to walk in the Lord's way." Hebrews teaches us that this day has now come (vv. 8-13). He makes possible what He commands. Paul refers to this ability, "For the law of the spirit of life in Christ Jesus has made me free from the law of sin and death" (Rom. 8:2). If this is true, then what of our boasting? We have not freed ourselves! Christ has released and empowered us! To Him be all praise.

How thankful we are for this universal promise, "All shall know Me, from the least to the greatest of them" (v. 11). Here is an open door for everyone! Never mind background, social status, educational or financial state, for **all** can now approach Him.

There is no better news in all the Bible than verse 12, "For I will be merciful to their unrighteousness, and their sins and their lawless deeds I will remember no more." How is this possible? The answer is found in the death and resurrection of Christ which saves us, and offers peace and hope. "For He (God) made Him (Christ) Who knew no sin to be sin for us, that we might become the righteousness of God" (2 Cor. 5:21). We sing of such grace as "amazing" for it is beyond our comprehension! I have given up understanding electricity, but I know that things beyond my poor understanding work whether I comprehend them or not. I do not know everything about God's plan of salvation, but when I trusted Him as Savior and Lord something greater than the creation of light happened within me. Jesus said, "For the Son of Man did not come to be served, but to serve, and to give His life a ransom for many"(Mk. 10:45). He ransomed me! What joy when a person experiences that Ransom personally!

There is a beautiful love story about the courtship of Moses Mendelssohn, the grandfather of the great German composer. Moses Mendelssohn was a small man with a misshapen, humped back. One day he visited a merchant in Hamburg who had a lovely daughter. Though Mendelssohn admired her greatly, she avoided him, seemingly because of his handicap.

On the last day of his visit he went to tell her good-bye. Her face beamed with beauty, but when he entered she cast her eyes to the floor. Mendelssohn's heart ached. After some small talk, he slowly drew to the subject that filled his mind. "Do you believe that marriages are made in heaven?" he asked. "Yes," replied the young woman. "And do you?" "Of course," Mendelssohn answered. "I believe that at the birth of each child the Lord says, 'That boy shall marry that girl.' But in my case the Lord also added, 'But alas, his wife will have a terrible hump.' At that moment I called, 'Oh Lord that would be a tragedy for her. Please give me the humped back and let her be beautiful.'" The young woman was so moved by these words that she reached for Mendelssohn's hand and later became his wife. [5]

Our loving and faithful High Priest, the Lord Jesus, still bears in His body the marks of suffering which you and I should have borne. Such love "demands my life, my soul, my all."

Then indeed, even the first covenant had ordinances of divine service and the earthly sanctuary. For a tabernacle was prepared: the first part, in which was the lampstand, the table, and the showbread, which is called the sanctuary; and behind the second veil, the part of the tabernacle which is called the Holiest of All, which had the golden censer and the ark of the covenant overlaid on all sides with gold, in which were the golden pot that had the manna, Aaron's rod that budded, and the tablets of the covenant; and above it were the cherubim of glory overshadowing the mercy seat. Of these things we cannot now speak in detail. Now when these things had been thus prepared, the priests always went into the first part of the tabernacle, performing the services. But into the second part the high priest went alone once a year, not without blood, which he offered for himself and for the people's sins committed in ignorance; the Holy Spirit indicating this, that the way into the Holiest of All was not yet made manifest while the first tabernacle was still standing. It was symbolic for the present time in which both gifts and sacrifices are offered which cannot make him who performed the service perfect in regard to the conscience—concerned only with foods and drinks, various washings, and fleshly ordinances imposed until the time of reformation. But Christ came as High Priest of the good things to come, with the greater and more perfect tabernacle not made with hands, that is, not of this creation. Not with the blood of goats and calves, but with His own blood He entered the Most Holy Place once for all, having obtained eternal redemption. For if the blood of bulls and goats and the ashes of a heifer, sprinkling the unclean, sanctifies for the purifying of the flesh, how much more shall the blood of Christ, who through the eternal Spirit offered Himself without spot to God, cleanse your conscience from dead works to serve the living God? And for this reason He is the Mediator of the new covenant, by means of death, for the redemption of the transgressions under the first covenant, that those who are called may receive the promise of the eternal inheritance.

Hebrews 9:1-15

CHAPTER 16

The Priesthood, Sacrifice, and Tabernacle

(Study No. 16 in the Book of Hebrews)

The writer now deals with three essential elements in the Mosaic Covenant, the **priesthood, the sacrifice, and the tabernacle.** All three had served as a foundation for the relationship between God and Israel, and all are perfectly fulfilled in Jesus Christ.

Hebrews 8:1, 2 teaches that Jesus Christ is our **great High Priest.** But Peter, writing to believers, said, "**You** are a chosen people, **a royal priesthood,** a holy nation..." (1 Pet. 2:9). John agreed that Christ "... has made us kings and priests to His God and Father" (Rev. 1:6). Although we **have** a High Priest, we ourselves **are** priests.

We have no further need of a **sacrifice.** Verse 14 tells us, "How much more shall the blood of Christ, Who through the eternal Spirit offered Himself without spot to God, cleanse your conscience from dead works to serve the living God?" Verse 26 adds, "He put away sin by the sacrifice of Himself." Paul pleads, "I beseech **you** therefore, brethren, by the mercies of God, that you present your bodies a living sacrifice, holy, acceptable to God, which is your reasonable service" (Rom. 12:1). Although He is our Sacrifice we are urged to offer ourselves as living sacrifices.

A worker in an inner city mission gave many years to a most discouraging ministry. A friend came to him one day and said,

"Why don't you leave this job before you are broken by its inhuman burden? Why don't you run away from it all?" The man replied, "There are times when I would very much like to leave it all. But there is a strange, loving Man on a cross Who won't let me."[1] The sacrifice of our Lord inspires us to personal sacrifice.

The third element, **the tabernacle,** is also fulfilled in our Lord. "But Christ came as High Priest of the good things to come, with the greater and more perfect tabernacle not made with hands, that is, not of this creation" (v. 11). John also tells us that "the Word became flesh and dwelt (tabernacled) among us" (Jn. 1:14). In the days of His flesh on this planet He was that Tabernacle; today, the church is "the Body of Christ."

Since all these elements—the tabernacle, the sacrifice, and the priesthood—are all perfectly fulfilled in Jesus Christ, they are, therefore, unnecessary today. When the early Church learned that they were freed from any certain location (tabernacle), from certain professional religious leaders (priesthood), and from a repetitious sacrificial system, they, spiritually, **conquered the Roman Empire!**

We are free from these Old Testament types and shadows which pointed to the actual. Some have forgotten this truth and returned to the concept of sacrifice, believing that doing good deeds somehow pleases the Father. Others hire professional religious leaders to do their praying and witnessing, while some build great cathedrals thinking that God will live in their costly buildings as He dwelt in the wilderness tabernacle. Why try to please a God Who is already pleased? Why leave worship and service as the responsibility of professional religionists, while God seeks personal worship and service? Why look for Him in masonry and wood when He lives inside His people?

When God said, "Let them make Me a sanctuary, that I may dwell among them" (Ex. 25:8), it was His intention that the tabernacle be a sign of His Presence. Since God could not live fully in the hearts of the people because of their sins, He gave to Moses intricate details concerning the construction of the tabernacle (Ex. 26:30).

For centuries the Presence of God dwelt in the tabernacle and for a season in the Temple, but then God dwelt inside His own dear Son, the Lord Jesus. Today He lives in the hearts of His people. Jesus promised that His Spirit would dwell with us and in us (John

14:17). Both He and the Father, Jesus promised, would make Their home with us (Jn. 14:23). Furthermore, Paul defined the Church as "a dwelling place for God in the Spirit" (Eph. 2:22).

In the Old Testament tabernacle, God dwelt among His people. They had to **go where He was.** Today He lives in our hearts and never forsakes us. We do not come to a church building to meet God. He is wherever His people gather to worship Him or wherever they go to serve Him. Ball teams may play better at home but none of them rise to championship unless they can win on the road. It is good for the church to meet on its own "turf," but what happens outside the church building is even more significant.

The Old Testament tabernacle was distinct and different from the temple. Solomon's temple was stationary. How strange to build a stationary, solid, unmovable building and house in it the mobile Ark of the Covenant! This is comparable to building a boat in your basement! The tabernacle and the Ark of the Covenant witnessed that God was forever apt to move. Though God is forever the same in His character, He is diverse in His dealings. C.S. Lewis said the one single prayer God would probably never answer is represented by the word "encore." Israel served a dynamic God Who was always doing new things, and the tabernacle reflected that fact. It could be easily taken down, dismantled and moved. This creative idea did not originate with Moses; it came from God...and He hasn't changed!

The Israelis **had** to have a portable tent, for they were always moving during the 40 years in the wilderness. God initiated that journey from Egypt to Canaan and the events the Israelis experienced were to serve as examples for us. We, too, are pilgrim people, "traveling through Emmanuel's ground to fairer worlds on high." The God Who travels with us cannot be limited to our conceptions of Him or our creedal statements about Him.

Consider Numbers 9:17-23 (NIV): "Whenever the cloud lifted from above the tent, the Israelites set out; whenever the cloud settled, the Israelites encamped. At the Lord's command the Israelites set out, and at His command they encamped. As long as the cloud stayed over the tabernacle, they remained in the camp. When the cloud remained over the tabernacle a long time, the Israelites obeyed the LORD'S order and did not set out. Sometimes the cloud was over the tabernacle only a few days; at the LORD'S command they would encamp, and then at His command they would set out. Sometimes the cloud stayed only from evening till morning, and when it lifted in the morning they set out. Whether by day or by night, whenever the cloud lifted, they set out. Whether the cloud stayed over the tabernacle for a few days or a month or a year, the Israelites would remain in the camp and not set out; but when it lifted, they set out. At the LORD'S command they encamped, and at the LORD'S command they set out. They obeyed the LORD'S order, in accordance with His command through Moses."

It might have been disconcerting to move at a moment's notice, but it surely was better than staying in the desert after the cloud had left! What an important teaching for the Church today!

About 500 years after the settlement in Canaan a desire arose to build a permanent temple, a desire that did not originate with God, but man. David was apologetic because he dwelt in a beautiful house while the ark of God was in a tent. When he purposed to build the temple God's word to David was, "Would you build a house for Me to dwell in? For I have not dwelt in a house since the time that I brought the children of Israel up from Egypt, even to this day, but have moved about in a tent and in a tabernacle. Wherever I have moved about with all the children of Israel, have I ever spoken a word to anyone from the tribes of Israel, whom I have commanded to shepherd My people Israel saying, 'Why have you not built Me a house of cedar?'" (2 Sam.7:5-7)

God often allows us to have our own insistent way, but we suffer for such stubbornness. It was never God's idea that Israel should have a king, but He permitted the monarchy when they clamored to be ruled like other nations. From this monarchy, which they had outside the will of God, came the idea for a temple. Had they not had a king it is doubtful that they would have had a temple. God gave lengthy directives concerning the building of the tabernacle but, in sharp contrast, we read of all that Solomon *did* in the building of the temple. Though its blueprints did not come from God, He honored the temple with His Presence for a season; but, just as He promised, He moved out when the people proved unfaithful. God, Who had communicated through the tabernacle, now had to speak by prophets and through judgment.

One of the problems in having a temple was the tendency of the people to believe that if the temple were simply there, as long as organized, institutional religion functioned, nothing could go wrong. If this temple was the temple of the Lord, how could their enemies conquer them? Surely God would never allow such a thing to happen! Never mind how they lived, if the temple stood, they thought it offered security.

A PEANUTS cartoon shows Schroeder, that piano-loving intellectual, being interrupted, as he often was, by his infatuated admirer, Lucy. Lucy asked, "Schroeder, do you know what love is?" Schroeder abruptly stopped his piano playing, stood to his feet and said precisely, "Love: noun, to be fond of, a strong affection for or an attachment or devotion to a person or persons." Then he resumed playing his piano. Lucy sat there stunned and murmured sarcastically, "On paper, he's great."[2] Institutional religion centered in the temple could also "look good on paper."

This is why Jeremiah cried out, "Do not trust in deceptive words and say, 'This is the temple of the Lord, the temple of the Lord, the temple of the Lord!'" (Jere.7:4 NIV) These words nearly cost Jeremiah's his life. The first Christian martyr lost his life for preaching on this very subject. These were Stephen's last words before he was martyred: "Our fathers had the tabernacle of witness in the wilderness, as He appointed, instructing Moses to make it according to the pattern he had seen, which our fathers, having received it in turn, also brought with Joshua into the land possessed by the Gentiles, whom God drove out before the face of our fathers until the days of David, who found favor before God and asked to find a dwelling for the God of Jacob. But Solomon built Him a house. However the Most High does not dwell in temples made with hands, as the prophet says: 'Heaven is My throne, and the earth is My footstool. What house will you build for Me, says the Lord, or what is the place of My rest? Has not My hand made all these things?'"(Acts 7:44-50) Saul, who heard that message, was later converted and went from place to place telling the church that **we** are the dwelling place of God! Wherever believers are the Church is, for God lives in His Church!

This is why we can sing to other believers, "I can see **in you** the glory of my King." We refuse to look for God in stone, mortar, and wood for He dwells inside His people, people who are called "the temple of the Holy Spirit!" Let us be done with looking for "holy places" for, as the chorus says, "**This** is holy ground. We're standing on holy ground; for the Lord is present and **where He is, is holy.**" This is as true on the job as it is in a church building!

The enemies of Israel thought if they could capture the Ark of the Covenant or destroy the temple they would destroy the nation. A nation can be held together by its religion. Even a bad religion can be a cohesive force. Tyrants may destroy churches and kill Christian leaders, but faith in Jesus Christ can never be diminished by destroying buildings or killing believers. Persecution, instead of hindering, serves to spread the gospel! When Christians gather like bees in a hive, God sees to it that the hive is shaken and the "honey" is spread all over! The Church is salt, but not a salt block out in the pasture to be licked occasionally. This salt is to be spread over the earth, not stored up. The Church is also light, but Jesus did not call us the light of the church building, but the light of the world! We do not come together to discover who is shining brightest. God's people stagnate when they settle down. We can justify using church buildings because they are convenient places to meet. We meet to **worship** and go out to **serve.** A lady who visited a small Quaker congregation asked as they were sitting in silence, "When does the service begin?" The answer was, "As soon as the meeting is over."[3]

I often hear people say, "Now that he/she is a Christian we must give them something to do in the church." Thus Christian service is often linked to a building. Service to the Lord is to be done primarily on the job, in the home, and on the streets. We sometimes have the peculiar notion that the only place the gifts of the Spirit operate is in a church building. The gifts of the Holy Spirit freely flowed out of the lives of our Lord and His disciples though they had no church buildings. They went into the market place and homes and found God among His people...at a wedding, by a pool, in a home, on a ship, in an open field, at a funeral procession, at a dinner party.

I have had self-appointed prophets tell me, "I went to such-and-such a church with this message that God gave me and they wouldn't hear me. The leadership of that church is out of touch with God. Now I have come here to tell you..." Such souls, rather than hearing from heaven, seem to be looking for an audience. 1 Samuel

3:20 says "all Israel from Dan to Beersheba knew that Samuel had been **established** as a prophet of the Lord." There is a place for the gifts of the Spirit in the gathering of the saints, but the Biblical record puts the gifts primarily in service rather than worship. If gifts are used only when we gather they are limited to a few hours per week, generally on Sunday. God forbid!

In his book, *People-Centered Evangelism*, John Havlik says: "The Church is never a place, but always a people; never a fold but always a flock; never a sacred building but always a believing assembly. The Church is you who pray, not where you pray. A structure of brick or marble can no more be a Church than your clothes of serge or satin can be you." Believing that, the early Church covered their world.

Do you know that you are a "living sacrifice" unto Him? That you are a priest of God? That you are the dwelling place of Deity? Therapist, Richard Bandler, tells about dealing with a man who insisted that he was Jesus Christ. "Are you Jesus?" Bandler asked. "Yes, my son," the man replied. Bandler said, "I'll be right back in a minute." This left the man a bit confused. Within minutes Bandler came back holding a measuring tape. Asking the man to hold out his arms, Bandler measured the length of his arms and his height from head to toe. After that, Bandler left. The man became a little concerned. Bandler returned with a hammer, some large spiked nails, and long boards. He began to pound them into the form of a cross. The man asked, "What are you doing?" As Bandler put the last nails into the cross, he asked, "Are you Jesus?" Again the man answered, "Yes, my son." Bandler said, "Then you know why I am here." Suddenly the man had a remarkable recovery and yelled, "I'm not Jesus. I'm not Jesus!"[4] He knew immediately who he **really** was. Do we?

As the people of God we must be on the move. We cannot stand still. God help us to respond to His leading. Whether a cloud by day or a fire by night, "if Jesus goes with me (and He will) I'll go anywhere." If He leading you right now you can be sure that you are on your way home, for He is *God's Final Answer.*

Then indeed, even the first covenant had ordinances of divine service and the earthly sanctuary. For a tabernacle was prepared: the first part, in which was the lampstand, the table, and the showbread, which is called the sanctuary; and behind the second veil, the part of the tabernacle which is called the Holiest of All, which had the golden censer and the ark of the covenant overlaid on all sides with gold, in which were the golden pot that had the manna, Aaron's rod that budded, and the tablets of the covenant; and above it were the cherubim of glory overshadowing the mercy seat. Of these things we cannot now speak in detail.

Hebrews 9:1-5

CHAPTER 17

The God Who Lived In a Tent

(Study No. 17 in the Book of Hebrews)

During the 40 days that Moses spent on the mountain with God he received the pattern for the tabernacle (Ex. 25-31). Coming down from the mountain with the Commandments and the plans for the tabernacle he found the Israelis lapsed into gross idolatry. Instead of erecting the tabernacle as planned, Moses pitched a temporary tent outside the camp. Thus, one might say, Moses "excommunicated" the entire nation! What a dark time in Israel's history! (Exodus 32-34) It was a happy day when, at last, the tabernacle was completed as directed and set up among the tribes (Exodus 35-40).

The description of the tabernacle and its furniture held little excitement for me until I saw in it a type of our Lord and the redemption which He graciously provides. No less than seven times in Scripture we read of Moses being solemnly charged to "make all things according to the pattern shown him on the mountain." God was not concerned with impressive architecture. His purpose in the tabernacle was to convey a message to His people.

The total structure was in three parts—the Outer Court, the Holy Place, and the Holy of Holies. The Outer Court had one entrance called "**the gate**" (Ex. 27:16). The entrance into the Holy Place was called the "**door**" (Ex. 26:36), and the entrance into the Holy of Holies was called the "**veil**" (Ex. 26:31). The gate, the door, and the veil all opened toward the east. In each case there was only **one way** available. God has never given options in approaching Him. There is yet only One Way to the Father (Jn. 14:6).

The Outer Court was 75x150 feet (using 18 inches as a cubit), the tabernacle itself 15x45 feet, and the Holy of Holies 15x15x15, a perfect cube. Later, when the temple replaced the tabernacle, the size of the Holy of Holies was increased to 30x30x30 feet. Revelation 21:16 says that the city which comes down from God out of heaven will also be foursquare—the length, breadth, and height being equal. The cube, because of its symmetry, was the symbol of perfection among the Hebrews. Turned any way it appears the same, each side a perfect square and all six sides equal. A city whose Builder and Architect is God Himself must be gloriously perfect! Paul may have alluded to such perfection when he wrote of the "width and length and depth and height" of "the love of Christ which passes knowledge" (Eph. 2:18, 19). Though it is exciting to think of it, it will be more wonderful to experience it!

The Holy of Holies served as a dwelling place for God among His people. Never before had God dwelled among His people. He **walked** with Adam, **spoke** to the patriarchs, **visited** Abraham, but He had never dwelt among His people. What grace that He should choose to live among us, first in a tent and then in the temple. In the New Testament we read, "the Word (Christ) became flesh and dwelt (tabernacled) among us" (Jn.1:14). Though our Lord returned to His Father's side, He refused to abandon His children. Today the Church is a "holy temple...a dwelling place of God in the Spirit" (Eph. 2:21, 22). With all its faults, the Church remains the dwelling place of God until that day when "the tabernacle of God is with men, and He will dwell with them, and they shall be His people. God Himself will be with them and be their God" (Rev. 21:3). History teaches that God is not content unless He is with His people. There is never a moment when we are out of His mind or beyond His reach!

Of all the truths about the Holy of Holies one stands above all others—its **sacredness.** The people were only allowed in the outer court. The Holy Place was for the priests alone. Only the High Priest, on special occasions and with careful preparation, was allowed into the Holy of Holies.

It is impossible to worship the Eternal God without being aware of His holiness. Nothing will separate our hearts from sin like the knowledge of a holy God. Without holiness His love could be sentimentality, His wrath vindictiveness, and His wisdom cleverness. May the Lord God awaken our hearts to His holy character! A pastor's wife noted a number of people chuckling when her husband announced that in the interest of time they would sing only one verse of "Take Time to Be Holy."[1] An awareness of His holiness, God's distinct "otherness," promotes worship.

Significant truths are foreshadowed in the seven pieces of **furniture in the tabernacle.** The number seven suggests completeness. Let us enter through the gate which opens toward the east. If we look over our shoulders we see the encampment of the Tribe of Judah from which our Lord came.

The first of the seven pieces is **the brazen altar** for animal sacrifice. Sinful man cannot approach God without atonement. The sacrifice speaks of our sinfulness and God's satisfaction by atonement. Thank God for Calvary!

Then we come to **the brass laver.** Those who ministered in the tabernacle had to first be cleansed. Both hands and feet were to be washed; both **conduct** and **walk** must be sanctified for man to serve God acceptably. What my hands **do** and where my feet **go** may disqualify me from service. David properly prayed "wash me" (Ps. 51:2).

We need constant cleansing! Bob Stamps, a faculty member at Oral Roberts University, has a good sense of humor. He is also bald. One night he and his wife hired a babysitter and went out to dinner. The babysitter got interested in a television program and wasn't carefully watching the children. Their little boy, Peter Andrew, got his father's electric shaver and cut a big landing strip right down the middle of his head. When his father came home he was furious and said, "Peter Andrew! I told you never to play with my shaver. Now you are going to get a spanking you will never forget!" Peter Andrew looked up at him and said, "Wait until you see sister!" Bob Stamps said he was horrified. He went into the next room and there was his little four-year-old daughter, looking like a skinned rabbit, her hair shaved off just like her brother's. He grabbed Peter Andrew and said, "Now you really are going to get it." Just as he lifted his hand, Peter Andrew looked up at him and with tears in his eyes said, "But Daddy! WE WERE JUST TRYING TO LOOK LIKE YOU!" Instead of a spanking that night, Peter Andrew got a big hug. [2] Our master passion must be to "look like" our Heavenly Father.

Passing through the "door" into the sanctuary, we enter the Holy Place. On our right (to the north) is the **table of showbread** with its food and drink. Our spiritual life needs to be sustained, even as the physical. The Word and the Spirit meet our daily diet for growth. The Holy Place is like a garden dining room.

The **seven-branched candelabrum** on the left speaks of our need for spiritual illumination. We are not meant to be spiritual illiterates. Knowledge of God issues in a right relationship with Him. Hosea claimed that the root of Israel's waywardness was a lack of "the knowledge of the Lord" (Hos. 6:6). Knowledge of the Lord has to do with the heart more than the head.

Immediately in front of the veil which separates the Holy Place from the Holy of Holies, we see **the golden altar of incense**. The rising incense reminds us of the need of prayer, supplication, and praise.

Before entering the **Holy of Holies** the High Priest remembered that to enter this holy place with sin in one's heart could mean instant death. Inside is the gold-covered chest called **the Ark of the Covenant.** The covenant reminds us of the relationship that God initiated and sustains with His people. On top of the ark is the **mercy seat** with two golden cherubim facing each other, their wing tips touching. There is a strange glow in this place where the High Priest, on special occasions, sprinkled sacrificial blood. This Shekinah-lit mercy seat speaks of the imparted presence of God. Thank God for the bold entrance we now have into His holy Presence!

There is a remarkable parallel between the order of the furniture in the tabernacle and the order in the Gospel of John. John, in his first chapter, takes us to **the brazen altar** when he declares twice, "Behold! The Lamb of God Who takes away the sins of the world" (Jn. 1:29, 36). Jesus—our Perfect Sacrifice!

At **the laver** for cleansing we hear our Lord saying, "Unless one is born of water and the Spirit, he cannot enter the kingdom of God" (Jn. 3:5). Praise God for His constant sanctifying touch!

At **the table of showbread** we remember that Jesus said, "I am the Bread of Life. He who comes to Me shall never hunger, and he who believes in Me shall never thirst" (Jn. 6:35). The woman at the well heard Him say, "Whoever drinks of the water that I shall give him will never thirst. But the water that I shall give him will become in him a fountain springing up into everlasting life" (Jn. 4:14). "Come and dine," the Master calleth!

The golden candlestand characterizes the way our Lord dealt with the woman taken in adultery. To this woman, disgraced and living in darkness, He said, "I am the Light of the world. He who follows Me shall not walk in darkness, but have the light of life" (Jn. 8:12). When Jesus ministered to the man blind from birth, He said, "I am the Light of the world" (Jn. 9:5). Think of it—the people of God have come from seven flickering candles in a tent to the Sun of Righteousness Who has arisen with healing in His wings! O God, may we let that Light shine!

Those priests, who for centuries made their supplications before **the altar of incense,** never knew the joy of coming boldly to the throne of grace. They did not know Him Who said, "Whatever you ask in My Name, that will I do, that the Father may be glorified in the Son. If you ask anything in My Name, I will do it" (Jn. 14:13, 14). That precious Name is dear to the heart of God. We breathe that Name to Him in prayer!

John 17 has been called the New Testament **Holy of Holies**, for that chapter gives a glimpse of our Great High Priest interceding for us before the Father. In the Holy of Holies He is not only High Priest, but He is **Ark** and **Mercy Seat** as well. Our covenant relationship with the Father is secured through Him. John 20:17 declares, "I am ascending to My Father and your Father, and to My God and your God." **His** Father is **our** Father, and **His** God is **our** God! How close is such a relationship!

John 20:22 adds, "Receive the Holy Spirit." We are now standing on holy ground and the Shekinah of God shines all about us! The very life of God becomes ours as the Holy Spirit is imparted upon us. "Spirit of the Living God, fall afresh on me!"

The tabernacle embraces both Calvary and Pentecost. The same God Who lived in the Old Testament tent now lives in His people through the Presence of the Spirit. God will have a home. If you have shut Him out of your life, open the door to Him. **"Behold, I stand at the door and knock. If anyone hears My voice and opens the door, I will come in to him and dine with him, and he with Me" (Rev. 3:20).**

How much more shall the blood of Christ, who through the eternal Spirit offered Himself without spot to God, cleanse your conscience from dead works to serve the living God?

Hebrews 9:14

CHAPTER 18

The Cleansing Blood

(Study No. 18 in the Book of Hebrews)

Receiving Jesus Christ as Savior not only saves us from the penalty of sin, it brings to our hearts a desire for purity. In the Old Testament economy there was a "sin offering" and a "sins offering." The sin offering had to do with a person's nature, while the sins offering dealt with actual sins, known and unknown, sins of commission and omission. When we are genuinely converted there is born within us a desire for wholeness, for constant cleansing. Sinful acts are simply a manifestation of our common affliction, the disease of sin. We are all aware of sin's power, and try as we might, the struggle against sin is too challenging for our mortal strength. Nevertheless, pardon by the cross provokes within us a desire to live pleasing to our dear Redeemer.

All are sinners by birth. Those who deny their sinnerhood are either deceived or are lying about this common problem. In all of us there is a desire to do what is right, but that desire must contend with a power which would prevent us from being all we ought to be.

The message of the cross deals with that double consciousness and meets the deepest need of our lives. We cannot measure the blessed joy of knowing that, through God's grace, our names are written down in glory. Thank God for that assurance! But what can be done about the power and poison of sin that throbs within the hearts of even the redeemed? No need proving that Christians have problems with temptation. Tragic failures in the Body of Christ leave no doubt that the battle with temptation often has been fought and lost. We often cry as David did over Saul and Jonathan, "How the mighty have fallen!" How tragic that Saul never prayed, as David, "Create in me a clean heart, O God." Is there an answer to such a prayer? Hebrews 9:14 gives us the answer.

When David said that he "was born in sin and shaped in iniquity" He meant that there is an inherited inclination to do wrong. In the face of that conviction we believe one of two things. First, that this dual consciousness will forever be with us and we must handle it as best we can; or, secondly, that the redemption which comes through Christ's death on Calvary touches, not only **sin,** but the **sins** that grow out of our defiled natures. Jesus provided victory over habitual sinfulness by His perfect redemption.

No, this is not a "sinless perfection" doctrine. When the Holy Spirit convicts us that an action is wrong He is supremely able to provide victory over that sin. He would never reveal any behavior as sinful simply to emphasize how miserably we are failing the Lord. Christ, through the **eternal** Spirit, cleanses our consciences from dead works that we might serve the living God. The word "eternal" is not limited to the future. Redemption is not only long, it is broad and high and deep. It deals with today just as it does with our yesterdays and tomorrows.

Consider the two expressions in our text—**conscience** and **dead works**. We generally think of the word "conscience" as the ability to determine right and wrong, but this word includes "consciousness," much more than simply a discernment between good and evil. Having a "good conscience" requires more than simply distinguishing good from evil. One who has a "good conscience" has a "good consciousness," that is, a true understanding and awareness.

For instance, our consciousness of people or situations determines how we react to those people or situations. Conduct toward others is evidence of our consciousness of them. To illustrate, if I am in the presence of a large sum of money I remember that it is wrong to steal. But if I am truly conscious of the small value of money as opposed to the great value of my own character, then I will not steal. Knowing that stealing is wrong may not deter me from stealing, but having the correct consciousness or true understanding toward material things dictates response. The biggest thief in town may believe that "honesty is the best policy," but he does not have a good conscience.

If I have a German Shepherd and a Mexican Chihuahua, and feed both of them at the same time, the German Shepherd may eat all his food at one swallow and then eat the Chihuahua's too. After I have disciplined him for eating the Chihuahua's food he may reluctantly behave himself, but his behavior is not altered because he has been "born again." He will continue to covet the other dog's food, but his behavior is acceptable. He fears punishment and governs his behavior even though his nature remains unchanged. If he had a good "consciousness" toward the smaller dog their relationship could be on a higher plane.

The consciousness of men toward their wives affects their conduct toward them. A man knows it is wrong to cheat on his wife. But knowing what is right and what is wrong does not always keep a person from sin. Having a good conscience toward your wife means you are aware of her as God's gift to you. A wife may say of her husband, "He doesn't pay attention to me. He doesn't know that I exist?" If we are unaware of a person we place little value on them. Having a good conscience toward a spouse means proper behavior toward her/him. A good consciousness toward any man or woman means we will never take advantage of them, not even with their consent.

This applies to our children. Why is it difficult to get people to teach in our Sunday School or Children's Church? Is limited value placed on our little ones? Remember that consciousness affects conduct. Why was Jesus angry with those who wanted to send the children away? He saw the value of the little ones while others did not. When Jesus said that if we offend one of these little ones it is better that a millstone were hanged about our neck and we were drowned in the depth of the sea, He was not speaking of what we commonly call child abuse. He was referring to the attitude that says, "We don't have time for them. Send them away."

What will create within us the proper attitude toward children? As you look at them think all the while, "At this very moment this child's angel is beholding the face of the Heavenly Father" (Matt. 18:10), and your conscience toward the children will be purer. Seeing children in the light of those words elevates our consciousness of them.

This same concept will govern every relationship of life if we allow it. It solves racial problems. We will not see black, white, red, brown, or yellow people; we will see God's handiwork in all the many colors, customs, and languages. I asked a missions representative for advice concerning a ministry trip to another country. He said that some people make a very common blunder in assuming that the natives of that land, who live very near the earth, with soil on their bodies, are "dirty." He said, "Don't think that they are dirty simply because they have soil on them." He was conveying, "Have a good consciousness and true understanding of them as the people of God, the redeemed of God. Don't think less of them because they are not like you." May God give us a cleansed consciousness of others who are unlike us!

What does he mean by **dead works?** Conscience may be defiled, or spoiled, by dead works. Here is the reason some have made shipwreck of their Christian testimony. It takes little discernment to see the dead, corrupt works in the **physical, mental, and spiritual life** of many today. Concerning the **physical,** today we see a blatant inclination to self-indulgence and sensuality among Christians. In the **mental** realm there is much woolly-minded, so-called "deep spiritual teaching" today. There is much dishonesty in the pulpit. A preacher peddling his booklets on TV suddenly stopped and said, "Right now God is speaking to me and telling me that He is telling someone out there to write to me and get this book. This book will tell you how to get God to do miracles for you." Such manipulation is grieving. The gifts of the Holy Spirit are real, but we do not believe that they only work when someone is raising money or adding names to a mailing list. It is embarrassing that on some occasions it has taken the secular media and the inside squabbling of television preachers to bring such hypocrisy to light. How sad that the Christian Church is so quiet, so "loving" (sentimental), so passive, that when we discern dishonesty in the ministry we fail to deal with it! One of the "dead works" is dishonesty in failing to tell the truth.

In relation to the **spirit** of man, there is often a proneness to lethargy and laziness. Though we can know the difference between right and wrong, compromise can still blur our discernment. We cry out, not simply for the forgiveness of sin, but for a consciousness cleansed by His blood. Our text teaches us that the blood of Jesus not only offers forgiveness, but cleansing as well!

The standing problem of the Church is that many have experienced forgiveness but do not experience constant cleansing. If you are longing for such cleansing, how may you have it?

First, **it will not come by simply trying to do better.** Temptation to lie, steal, or lust will never be overcome by our efforts alone. The disciples who wanted to send the children away could not change their attitude toward children by saying, "From now on we are going to act differently around children." They had to see little children as their Lord saw them.

Second, if you are tempted to sin under certain circumstances, **change the circumstances.** For instance, if tempted to use drugs around certain people, don't fellowship with those people. If tempted to lust by looking at certain books or magazines, burn them. Paul wrote, "Therefore, having these promises, beloved, let us **cleanse ourselves** from all filthiness of the flesh and spirit, perfecting holiness in the fear of God" (2 Cor. 7:1). What promises is he writing about? They are found in the previous verses—"I will be their God and they shall be My people." "I will dwell in them and walk among them." "I will be a Father to you, and you shall be My sons and daughters." (2 Cor. 6:16-18)

When we read, "Let us cleanse ourselves," we are not dealing with a contradiction. We cannot change ourselves, but there must be a conscious putting away of those things that trip us up, coupled with a dependence upon the precious promises of God. Trusting Him gives the ability to do what we could never do on our own.

Finally, we must **hand over our lives just as they are to the Lord Jesus.** This is what we say to people who have never accepted Jesus Christ, who have not even begun to walk the Christian pathway, but it is also the message that the Risen Lord gave to the Ephesian Church after they had lost their first love. What must they do? "Repent, and do the first works" (Rev. 2:5). Yes, we come for **purity** just as we come for **pardon.** Two old hymns illustrate: "Nothing in my hand I bring" suggests we cannot change ourselves, while "All to Jesus I surrender; all to Him I freely give" speaks of absolute surrender to Christ.

Burn some bridges this very day; drive down some stakes at this point in time, and say to the Lord Jesus, "Since You have cleansed me by Your precious blood I stop my pitiful striving and, relying on your promises, I believe my life from now on will be different for I have accepted *God's Final Answer*."

And for this reason He is the Mediator of the new covenant, by means of death, for the redemption of the transgressions under the first covenant, that those who are called may receive the promise of the eternal inheritance. For where there is a testament, there must also of necessity be the death of the testator. For a testament is in force after men are dead, since it has no power at all while the testator lives. Therefore not even the first covenant was dedicated without blood. For when Moses had spoken every precept to all the people according to the law, he took the blood of calves and goats, with water, scarlet wool, and hyssop, and sprinkled both the book itself and all the people, saying, "This is the blood of the covenant which God has commanded you." Then likewise he sprinkled with blood both the tabernacle and all the vessels of the ministry. And according to the law almost all things are purified with blood, and without shedding of blood there is no remission. Therefore it was necessary that the copies of the things in the heavens should be purified with these, but the heavenly things themselves with better sacrifices than these. For Christ has not entered the holy places made with hands, which are copies of the true, but into heaven itself, now to appear in the presence of God for us; not that He should offer Himself often, as the high priest enters the Most Holy Place every year with blood of another—He then would have had to suffer often since the foundation of the world; but now, once at the end of the ages, He has appeared to put away sin by the sacrifice of Himself. And as it is appointed for men to die once, but after this the judgment, so Christ was offered once to bear the sins of many. To those who eagerly wait for Him He will appear a second time, apart from sin, for salvation.

Hebrews 9:15-28

CHAPTER 19

The Purpose of His Coming

(Study No. 19 in the Book of Hebrews)

Two things are emphasized in this portion of Hebrews. First, **there is no further need for the Old Testament sacrificial system.** Second, **through Jesus Christ we have access into fellowship with a holy God.** Indeed, the first system not only made way for, it demanded the second. The writer concludes: "And as it is appointed for men to die once, but after this the judgment, so Christ was offered once to bear the sins of many. To those who eagerly wait for Him, He will appear a second time, apart from sin for salvation" (vv. 27, 28).

Consider three truths from this text. **First, Jesus came the first time in order that He might come again.** Not only was He, in His first appearance, fulfilling Old Testament prophecies concerning Himself, but He was also preparing for that day when He would once again return to Planet Earth.

All the things that Jesus came to do are not yet done. He came to destroy the works of the devil, but they are not yet destroyed. He came to abolish sin and death, but we still contend with these forces. Hebrews 2:8 explains, "For in that He put all in subjection under him, He left nothing that is not put under him. **But now we do not yet see all things put under Him.**" So the first coming of the Lord demands a second coming. Without it the first is not complete; something more is needed. The first coming was preparatory. The Bible teaches that His second appearance will be just as genuine, personal, and positive as His first.

Notice the certainty in verse 28, "He **will** appear a second time." Some take this statement in a spiritual manner, that Christ will not come physically and literally, but in some sort of mystical way to those who believe in Him. If we believe that Jesus Christ actually came the first time, then, unless we handle the text dishonestly, we must agree that He will come again. The second coming of the Lord is taught throughout the entire New Testament. No serious person can doubt that the writers of the New Testament firmly believed that the Lord would come again **just as He had gone away.**

Although sincere Christian people may disagree as to **how** and **when** the coming of Christ will occur, the angels' statement in Acts 1:11 is clear enough: "Men of Galilee, why do you stand gazing up into heaven? This same Jesus, Who was taken up from you into heaven, will so come in like manner as you saw Him go into heaven." We choose to believe that the angels were telling the truth!

Paul wrote, "For the Lord Himself will descend from heaven with a shout, with the voice of the archangel, and with the trumpet of God. And the dead in Christ shall rise first. Then we who are alive and remain shall be caught up together with them in the clouds to meet the Lord in the air. And thus we shall always be with the Lord" (1 Thess. 4:16, 17). This firm conviction strongly influenced the early Christians. They lived fearlessly and died heroically believing that Jesus' coming was imminent. They saw themselves as pilgrims, strangers, and aliens, passing through a foreign land, and believed the Lord might interrupt their journey at any moment by His return. If we believed as strongly as they did that Jesus was coming again our lifestyles would be different and our evangelism more effective.

One tactic of the devil is to get the eyes of Christians on this present world. He is delighted with the teaching that Jesus Christ is supremely interested in blessing His followers with money and other pleasantries. The Bible does not teach that Christians must be poor; but there is too much emphasis today on materialism. Some rejected the Jesus People Movement because these young people turned their backs on the idea that happiness depended on having things. Today the pendulum has swung so far in the other direction that some judge a person's spirituality by their health or wealth.

What would it mean if we lived in the anticipation our Lord's second advent? If we no longer look for our Lord we will amass things as though planning to be here forever. How embarrassing when Jesus comes looking for fruit to only have material things to show Him, things of no interest to Him.

The **second truth** is that **the second coming will be different than the first.** Notice that "He will appear a second time, **apart from sin,** for salvation." The writer draws a contrast between the first and second coming. His first coming was necessary for the second coming, but the second coming will be "apart from sin."

Consider the American family and you will agree that we still deal with sin today. An estimated 365,000 to 500,000 young people attempt suicide each year. Another million run away from home. Twelve million teenagers regularly take some form of alcohol and drugs. Five million children live in broken homes. Four million are beaten, molested, or otherwise abused by parents. [1]

John the Baptist cried, "Behold! The Lamb of God Who takes away the sin of the world!" (Jn. 1:29) In His first coming Jesus dealt with sin. By His spotless purity He aroused hell's hatred and brought conviction to all who had to do with Him. No one can be neutral about Him. We must love Him or loath Him, cling to Him or despise Him. Herod's wrath was so kindled toward the Baby Jesus that all the male children under two years of age were slain. Satan used every arsenal at his disposal against the Lord Jesus. He was misunderstood by His family and hated by home-town neighbors. All His friends forsook Him and one turned traitor. The civil and religious rulers, collaborating in His death, crucified Him as Public Enemy Number One. So, in His first coming, He dealt with sin in all its cleverness and cruelty.

Today "sin" is a word that many have stricken from their vocabulary. A man came home drunk after a night of carousing in a number of neighborhood bars. His wife helped him up to the bedroom, helped him to undress and get into bed. She knelt at his bedside and whispered, "John, do you want me to pray for you?" He nodded and she began to pray, "Dear Lord, I pray for my husband who lies here before You drunk..." Before she could continue, he interrupted with, "Don't tell him I'm drunk; just tell Him I'm sick."[2] Calling sin "sickness" doesn't make it so!

Christ was "offered" to bear the sins of many. "God so loved... that He gave." God sent Christ to "bear" our sins. He got under the load of sin and carried it away. Isaiah writes, "Surely He has borne our grief and carried our sorrows." Sickness, poverty, loneliness- all these, He bore for us. Look behind them and you will discover sin's power. Of course, all sick, poor, or lonely people are not sinful. Multitudes of sinners are both healthy and rich. Poverty may come from laziness or oppression. When our Lord got under the load of sin it was written of Him, "Though He was rich, yet for your sakes He became poor that you through His poverty might become rich" (2 Cor. 8:9). The weight He bore when taking our sin away caused that unspeakable cry, "My God, My God why have You forsaken Me?" (Mk. 15:34)

Finally, unlike the first coming, **His second appearance will be total victory.** Sickness, sorrow, sighing, and death will end. The old song says, "We'll soon be done with troubles and trials." How true!

When He came the first time there was no room for Him in the inn, no place for Him to lay His head. But when He comes again the whole world will make room, plenty of room, for Him! He will not be holding a reed in mockery, but the scepter of universal rulership! He is not coming to atone for our sins; He is coming to administrate the affairs of earth.

Notice the parallelism: "It is appointed unto man to die once." Jesus Christ came to this earth and did just that—He died once, "But after this the judgment." That will happen when He comes the second time, He will come to judge, to administrate.

All of us have an inescapable appointment with death. None know exactly **why** we die. Scientists who excel in the mysteries of life cannot tell us exactly what causes our physical death. Our bodies renew themselves every seven years. My wife and I have served Angelus Temple for so long that there is not a single part of us here now that was here when we came! White Laboratories stated that more than 98% of the atoms in our bodies were not present one year ago today. Why do we constantly grow mentally and spiritually while our bodies deteriorate? There is no other answer—

"The wages of sin is death" (Rom. 6:23). We all will die unless our dear Lord comes first. The mortality rate among both believers and unbelievers is still 100%!

On the other side of death there is an appointed judgment. But mercy, rather than judgment, is in store for those who have accepted Jesus Christ. Christians look back at a time when they **were** saved. They know that they are **now being saved** and will some day **experience complete** salvation.

How sad that some look for fulfillment outside of Christ. Headlines mourned the death of the handsome, talented, super-successful 30-year-old Andy Gibb. He was barely 19 and fresh from Australia when his first single, *I Just Want to Be Your Everything*, hit the top of the charts. He was nominated for two Grammys and made nearly $3,000,000. He was the only solo performer to have his first three singles top the charts, and he sold some 15 million records worldwide by the time he was 21. Then, as easily as the money came, it went—much for cocaine.

Gibb sought treatment and by all accounts put drugs behind him. But by that time his fortune was gone, and he filed for bankruptcy. His debts totaled $1.5 million. Now he is dead.

The official cause of death was listed as heart failure. A small amount of cocaine can permanently damage the heart. What happened to Andy Gibb? Friends said he had a great emptiness within. [3]

Someone may think it is too late to find new life in Christ. In his book, *First Do No Harm: the Making of a Neurosurgeon*, J. Kenyon Rainer, M.D. recalls an incident as a senior medical student. He was working in an emergency room when an unconscious 12-year-old boy with a stab wound in his heart was wheeled in. The cardiac monitor showed a straight line. The boy's skin was cold and his pupils didn't react to light, indicating the brain was not functioning. Rainer looked to the nurse and said, "He's dead, turn off the monitor." Just then a doctor came in, felt the wound on the dead boy, grabbed a needle and stuck it into the boy's chest. Immediately the boy's heart began to beat; a few hours and an operation later he was moving his legs and mumbling. Rainer said, "I left the room and wandered down the hall, discouraged. I had just pronounced a boy dead who had been saved seconds later while I watched."

Someone reading this might have said of himself, "It's too late." But the Great Physician can come to you, touch you, and give you new life—life that is available to all who come to the Him, *God's Final Answer.*

For the law, having a shadow of the good things to come, and not the very image of the things, can never with these same sacrifices, which they offer continually year by year, make those who approach perfect. For then would they not have ceased to be offered? For the worshipers, once purified, would have had no more consciousness of sins. But in those sacrifices there is a reminder of sins every year. For it is not possible that the blood of bulls and goats could take away sins. Therefore, when He came into the world, He said: "Sacrifice and offering You did not desire, but a body You have prepared for Me. In burnt offerings and sacrifices for sin You had no pleasure. Then I said, 'Behold, I have come—in the volume of the book it is written of Me—to do Your will, O God.'" Previously saying, "Sacrifice and offering, burnt offerings, and offerings for sin You did not desire, nor had pleasure in them" (which are offered according to the law), then He said, "Behold, I have come to do Your will, O God." He takes away the first that He may establish the second. By that will we have been sanctified through the offering of the body of Jesus Christ once and for all. And every priest stands ministering daily and offering repeatedly the same sacrifices, which can never take away sins. But this Man, after He had offered one sacrifice for sins forever, sat down at the right hand of God, from that time waiting till His enemies are made His footstool. For by one offering He has perfected forever those who are being sanctified.

Hebrews 10:1-14

CHAPTER 20

What a Fellowship!

(Study No. 20 in the Book of Hebrews)

Man is a spirit made in the image of God. He was created to live in a house of muscle and bone, endowed with a free will and made for fellowship with God. As the offspring of God man had access to God, communion with God, and could cooperate with God in carrying out His designs. But when sin entered the picture man was cut off from God, no longer had communion with God, and could no longer cooperate in fulfilling God's purposes for his life.

The redemptive message of the Bible offers hope to those who want to walk in communion with God. It is for sinners, not the righteous, as Jesus said. So we are not hopeless; there is a Way back!

A wise woman of Tekoa said to David concerning his son, Absalom, "God devises ways so that a banished person may not remain estranged from Him" (2 Sam. 14:14 NIV). What ways has God devised? The first verse of Hebrews tells us that God first spoke to this need for renewed fellowship through the prophets in different ways, but in these last days He has spoken to us through the revelation of His Son. God's earlier methods were suggestive, illustrative, while His final method was so clear and concise that none need misunderstand.

The sacrifices of the old economy were "shadows" of the Perfect Sacrifice which was to come. Consider the **five sacrifices** in the old system—**the Burnt Offering** was a symbol of total dedication to

God; the **Meal Offering**, a symbol of dedication to the service of God. The **Peace Offering** was a symbol of fellowship with God as a result of dedicating the life and service to God. The **Sin Offering** opened up a way for fellowship and cooperation with God, while the **Trespass Offering** dealt with the actual sins of man

All these sacrifices were "shadows" of the good things to come (v. 1). No one can be saved by a "shadow;" but shadows suggest substance. There was more than feasting and fasting to these Old Testament sacrifices. God was revealing what He would do about the sin of man. "For by one offering He has perfected forever those who are being sanctified" (v. 14). We who were outcasts, excluded from the Presence and approval of God, have been given a Way back home to our Father! God devised a plan! It was "by one offer-ing"—His dear Son.

"We have been sanctified through the offering of the body of Jesus Christ once for all," a body which God prepared for His Son. The Son then **offered** that body which God had given Him to be our Sacrifice.

Our Lord, by **offering** His body, taught us how to view our own body. It should be an expression of the spirit within. The body was never meant to master, but to serve. The spirit is meant to dominate, the body serving as its instrument. When the appetites and desires of the body are in control, the total person is in jeopardy. The Lord Jesus never experienced defeat by a sinful body. He is unique in that He won the struggle over the desires of the flesh. His Spirit domi-nated His flesh. Alexander Solzhenitsyn writes that some people are outraged if someone gives his soul as much attention as his groom-ing!

Alexander the Great, the most powerful general of his time, approached a great walled city with only a handful of soldiers and demanded its surrender. The people inside laughed and said, "Why should we surrender? You've only got a handful of soldiers out there." By way of an answer Alexander lined his men up single file and ordered them to march toward a nearby steep, treacherous cliff. One by one they marched to their deaths as the people of the city watched in horror. At a certain point Alexander halted the march and ordered the rest of the men to his side. They responded without any sign of fear, relief, or panic. When the residents of the great walled city saw the loyalty that Alexander commanded they realized that their defeat was inevitable and surrendered. [1] Our renewed spirit should, without question, dominate.

The uniqueness and perfection of Jesus was also seen in the measure of pain He experienced in the presence of sin. The pain we feel when we are exposed to evil is a good indication of our spiritual state. If we can co-exist with evil without pain and shame, we should be concerned about our spiritual state.

Instead of being pained by evil we are sometimes embarrassed by virtue. A certain wife went to lunch with eleven other women. One rather bold type asked, "How many of you have been faithful throughout your marriage?" Only one lady raised her hand. That evening one of the ladies related the incident to her husband. When she admitted she was not the one who raised her hand, her husband looked crest-fallen. "But I've been faithful to you," she quickly assured him. He asked, "Then why didn't you raise your hand?" She answered, "I was ashamed."[2] Ashamed of being faithful!

Because Jesus was uniquely the Son of God, His sacrifice brought us back into perfect relationship with the Father. Such a relationship allows us to have no secrets from the Father. He knows everything about us. After many years of marriage I have to say less and less about the way I feel to my wife. She knows how I feel before I express my feelings. Such a relationship produces contentment and rest. What an awkward thing to express feelings to someone who does not know or care about you. With God there is no such agony. "All things are naked and open to the eyes of Him to Whom we must give account." That truth frightens those who do not know God's forgiveness; but it is a great comfort to the soul resting in Christ.

By offering Himself, He has perfected forever those who are being sanctified. God looks upon us as perfect, but not yet perfected. Our standing before God is perfect, but we have not realized that perfection experientially. Our claim to perfection is based upon the Perfect Sacrifice, the Lamb of God! He is our **only** Perfection. We dare not put our confidence in anything else; not in our good deeds, our giving, our praying, or in any thing other than Jesus' complete and final sacrifice. A motorist was lying in the street having been badly injured in a traffic accident. As the crowd gathered, a woman rushed to the victim. Instantly she was pushed aside by a man who said, "Please step aside and let me do this. I've had a course in first aid." Attentively the woman watched. In a few minutes she said, "When you get to the point in your training where it says to call a doctor, I'm already here."[3] Some of us have to exhaust our pitiful resources before we finally turn to the Great Physician Who has been there all the time. When we acknowledge Him as the only Source of help we enter into peace.

Dr. E. V. Hill was pastor of Mount Zion Baptist Church in the Watts area of Los Angeles. During the burnings, lootings, and community rioting Dr. Hill did a very painful thing. He denounced his neighbors who were destroying property and stealing. During the worse part of the rioting, his preaching brought threats to him and his church. However, the worse the rioting became the more publicly he condemned the rioters.

One night his telephone rang and his wife noticed how solemn he was. "What was that all about?" she asked. "Oh nothing," replied Dr. Hill. But his wife pressed him until he told her, "They have threatened to blow up our car with me in it."

Late in the night they discussed how impossible it would be to protect their car 24 hours a day from wire-bombing. Next morning, Dr. Hill noted that his wife was not in the house. Neither was his automobile in the carport. A few minutes later he saw his car roll into the driveway with his wife at the wheel. She had driven the car around the block to make sure it was safe for her husband! "From that day," said Dr. Hill, "I have never asked my wife if she loves me." He saw love in action. [4]

We never need to ask if Jesus loves us. He has done all that He could do... all that will ever be necessary!

But the Holy Spirit also witnesses to us; for after He had said before, "This is the covenant that I will make with them after those days, says the LORD: I will put My laws into their hearts, and in their minds I will write them," then He adds, "Their sins and their lawless deeds I will remember no more." Now where there is remission of these, there is no longer an offering for sin.

Hebrews 10:15-18

CHAPTER 21

The Nature of the New Covenant

(Study No. 21 in the Book of Hebrews)

The writer of the Book of Hebrews was a knowledgeable student of the Old Testament. In our text he quotes Jeremiah 31:33, 34 showing that these words are fulfilled in the Christian gospel. This same prophecy appears in Hebrews 8:8-12 in its entirety. (See Study No. 15) "Behold, the days are coming, says the Lord, when I will make a new covenant with the house of Israel and with the house of Judah—not according to the covenant that I made with their fathers in the day when I took them by the hand to lead them out of the land of Egypt; because they did not continue in My covenant, and I disregarded them, says the Lord. For this is the covenant that I will make with the house of Israel after those days, says the Lord: I will put My laws in their mind, and write them on their hearts; and I will be their God, and they shall be My people. None of them shall teach his neighbor, and none his brother, saying 'Know the Lord,' for all shall know Me, from the least of them to the greatest of them. For I will be merciful to their unrighteousness, and their sins and their lawless deeds I will remember no more."

When Jeremiah gave this word he had just awakened: "My sleep was sweet to me" (Jere. 31:26). Coming out of "sweet sleep" he gave the only prophecy in his book that is full of consolation.

Looking ahead with prophetic foresight, he saw the coming of a beautiful day of everlasting victory. This prophecy applies both to Israel and the Church, individually and collectively.

This covenant, referred to as a "better" covenant (7:22), a "second" covenant (8:7), and a "new" covenant (9:15), promises the people of God an understanding of His will without human mediation. His promise, "I will put My laws in their mind and write them on their hearts," is a knowing of the will of God, a personal knowledge of God that is associated with the putting away of sin.

When we consider this wonderful promise from **cause to effect** we see a cleansing from sin and how this cleansing results in knowing God and understanding His will.

Our purpose is to consider the following benefits of the three-fold covenant. First, **the covenant promises spiritual discernment.** Second, **it provides fellowship with God** and third, **it offers forgiveness of sins.**

Consider the **spiritual discernment** promised in the new covenant—"I will put My laws in their mind and write them on their hearts; and I will be their God, and they shall be My people. None of them shall teach his brother, saying, 'Know the Lord.'" Jeremiah foresees a coming day when those who want to follow the Lord will have the law of God written in their individual hearts. This law is not the Mosaic law or any written code, but the purposes of God for our individual lives.

To people who lived under such strict disciplinary practices this promise must have seemed unrealistic. Jeremiah was predicting a day when God would communicate personally, continually, and clearly with every person who wanted to know Him. What a day that would be! This would be a day when God, through His Spirit, would communicate His will to those who walked with Him. The consequence of this condition is this: "I will be their God, and they shall be My people."

Many "gods" are available to us today; but more than one god is too many! Gurus claiming special insight abound on every side. Beware of people who always have some "inside revelation," some esoteric information that "God has given only to them." The ultimate end of such claims is often wealth, acclaim, or control. God can and will reveal Himself to us and He consistently does so through His Spirit and His Word. Nothing else is as authoritative.

Mill Valley, California with its prestigious residences priced at millions of dollars, is one of the most desirable suburban communities in the United States. Driveways display a sparkling array of Porsches, BMWs, and Winnebagos. Schools are equipped with state-of-the-art computers, lab equipment, and video units. And every Christmas looks as if the department store blew up in the living room. But recent research shows a very different side of Mill Valley. Those fabulous dream homes mask one of the highest levels of drug and alcohol abuse in the nation. Teen suicide and family breakups are critical problems. [1] Some think that affluence will fill the emptiness in our lives. Only Jesus Christ can do that!

Former Nixon "hatchet-man" Chuck Colson, in an interview in the *Christian Century*, tells how he found this out: "I had arrived at everything I had ever dreamed about as a kid. I was 41 years old, had a healthy six-figure law practice, clients at the door, a yacht in the Chesapeake Bay, a limousine and a driver, was a friend of the president, and had all kinds of people working for me and others dying to come into my firm. And I never felt more rotten in all my life." Mr. Colson felt like so many others without Christ in their lives.

The promise, "I will be their God," is followed by, "and they shall be **My** people." Pastors should never claim God's people as **theirs.** Even Jesus did not keep sheep for Himself. He kept them for His Father. We are **His** people, the sheep of **His** pasture. We answer to Him, as to how we handle the assignments He gives us. Both pastor and congregation alike belong to God. We are **His** people!

My assignment is to be a compassionate evangelist and teacher of the Word of God by spoken word and lifestyle. But rather than blindly trusting my words or those of another minister all of us must bear the responsibility of hearing from God ourselves. Some issues in life have no clear-cut answers. We need not question the clear-cut commandments of Scripture. Justification may be offered for disobedience, it is sinful to disobey His obvious will. Though the Bible may not be clear on every situation, this text declares that His law is written in our minds and in our hearts. Our minds can confirm a decision as right and our hearts can feel right about it. It can "sound" right and "feel" good.

In such a case this Scripture promises, "None of them shall teach his neighbor, and none his brother, saying, 'Know the Lord.'" When it comes to conduct we should not expect discernment to be difficult. **Some people go to others for opinions in order to justify avoiding doing what they already know to be the will of God.**

The will of God is not nearly so difficult to **know** as it is to **do.** It is easy to clamor after rules and regulations rather than what church fathers called "**the communion of the Holy Ghost.**" Jesus promised that the Holy Spirit would lead us into all truth. If we allow others to control us we will ultimately blame them for our failures. God's law, written on the hearts of His children, is interpreted by the Holy Spirit. He leads into truth, just as He promised.

How can we know that God speaks to us today? Since His will is written on our very hearts it is **inside** us in a more personal way than it was in Moses or Abraham. God speaks to our hearts if we will simply listen. Seven times Jesus cried out to the seven churches of Revelation, "He who has an ear let him hear what the Spirit says..."

The reason for this inward voice of God is found in the words, "**for all shall know Me, from the least to the greatest of them.**" This is the basis for the inward leading of the Lord. Without knowledge of God there is no reliable inner witness. The knowledge of God spoken of here has little, if anything, to do with knowing **about** Him. It is a personal relationship with God. The result of knowing Him, of walking with Him, is the revelation of His will and ways to the heart.

Some mistakenly think that their personal discipline merits God's revelation of Himself to them. God never reveals Himself because we adhere to a set of rules. He first reveals Himself to us and then through that relationship enables us to live a life pleasing to Him. The Israelis knew God **before** they received the law. God made a covenant with them (Ex. 19), and then He gave them the law (Ex. 20). They first had to know Him and then they would know His will. This is God's process. Whenever someone suggests following a set of rules in order to know and please God, they are going about it backwards. Fellowship with God produces knowledge of His will.

The word sequence in Jeremiah 31:34 is not incidental. "For all shall know Me, **from the least to the greatest.**" Our natural inclination is just the opposite. We would expect Jeremiah to say,

"From the greatest to the least." God's order so often is the reverse of ours. We pay attention to the so-called "greatest;" God sees no such distinction. If there is greater knowledge of God it is among the "least" rather than the "greater." We grieve the Lord when we do not care for the "least." Jesus said, "I thank You, Father, Lord of heaven and earth, that You have hidden these things from the wise and prudent and have revealed them unto babes. Even so, Father, for so it seemed good in Your sight" (Lk. 10:21). Whether it has to do with the least intellect, influence, or ability, our Lord's method is to move from the least to the greatest.

Some are afraid of the will of God because they are not sure of His love. Once a person knows Him they discover how foolish their fears were. God loves us. The enemy of our souls tempts us to doubt that love.

We get to know God better by spending time with Him. This can be difficult. We long for activity, for noise. Even in prayer we often talk more than we listen. God wants to make Himself known by communicating with us. Prayer is dialogue!

Finally, all we have said rests on the promise, **"For I will be merciful to their unrighteousness, and their sins and their lawless deeds I will remember no more."** We cannot know Him unless our sins are forgiven. It is the pure in heart that shall see God. When our hearts are pure, we know Him and when we know Him we know His will. His will cannot be written on a polluted heart. Purity is never gained by struggle, but by the amazing grace of God.

The promise is for individual hearts, but it is also true for a nation. Our nation needs a revival, a turning back to God. When that happens there will be a new consciousness of God's forgiveness, which produces a new fellowship with God, and issues in a new awareness of His will.

Unfortunately, some politicians begin where God ends. They want to start by establishing a new order to solve all our problems. God starts with moral cleansing, with the forgiveness of sin. Out of that forgiveness flows relationship with God and a knowing of His will both individually and nationally. We are far from God's ideal for us as a people. We have great needs in our land, but if we really want to get to the heart of crime and disease we must get right with God.

If we want to know God's will and way for our lives, first, we must have our hearts cleansed; second, fellowship with our Lord, and then we will hear His voice within saying, "This is the way. Walk in it." When we constantly say, "I only wish I could know His will," we declare our distance from Him. Live within this covenant: forgiveness of sin, fellowship with God, and knowing His will.

Perhaps someone is saying, "That all seems too simple. Surely God wants me to do something more than simply trust Him. Doesn't that make it cheap?" G. Campbell Morgan was once approached by a miner who said that he would give anything to believe that God would forgive sins, but he could not believe sin could be forgiven just for the asking. It seemed too cheap. Dr. Morgan said to him, "You were working in the mine today. How did you get out of the pit?" The miner answered, "The way I usually do. I got into the cage and was pulled to the top." "How much did you pay to come out of the pit?" asked Dr. Morgan. "I didn't pay anything," answered the miner. "Weren't you afraid to trust yourself to that cage?" Dr. Morgan asked. "Was it not too cheap?" The man replied, "Oh, no! It was cheap for me, but it cost the company a lot of money to sink the shaft."[2] God's love cost Him the very life of His own dear Son. For us, however, it is free!

Therefore, brethren, having boldness to enter the Holiest by the blood of Jesus, by a new and living way which He consecrated for us, through the veil, that is, His flesh, and having a High Priest over the house of God, let us draw near with a true heart in full assurance of faith, having our hearts sprinkled from an evil conscience and our bodies washed with pure water. Let us hold fast the confession of our hope without wavering, for He who promised is faithful. And let us consider one another in order to stir up love and good works, not forsaking the assembling of ourselves together, as is the manner of some, but exhorting one another, and so much more as you see the Day approaching.

Hebrews 10:19-25

CHAPTER 22

A Bold Entrance to a New Way

(Study No. 22 in the Book of Hebrews)

Those who embrace the Lord Jesus experience a new direction in life. Being a Christian, however, is certainly more than keeping a set of rules, more than being a disciplinarian. One may live a disciplined life and yet be, not only unchristian, but even anti-Christian. A Christian is to live life as God intended it to be lived, and that means a certain lifestyle is expected from those who name His Name. Thomas Hobbes said: "The king has placed hedges along the road, not to stop the travelers in their journey but to keep them on their way."[1]

Hebrews 10:19-25 has been called this letter's "center of gravity." Here is the light and heat of this epistle. The practical results of the great doctrines concerning the Priesthood of Christ are here stated. We are challenged by this text to "put shoe leather" on our religion.

The readers needed to hear these words for they had become self-centered by allowing hardships to turn their thoughts inward. As they focused on their personal problems it grew increasingly difficult to be concerned about the needs of others. When we dwell incessantly on our own predicament we minimize the needs of others, magnify our own needs, and therefore, lose our joy.

The remedy to this unhappy situation was **to turn to their Lord, to one another,** and **to the world.** Therefore, a three-fold command is given: "**Let us draw near (to God)**" (v. 22), "**let us hold fast the confession of our faith**" (v. 23), and "**let us consider one another**" (v. 24). The first has to do with worship, the second points to evangelism, and the final command concerns fellowship in the Christian family. A triad of Christian graces is given in these verses: "Let us draw near...in full assurance of **faith**," "Let us hold fast the confession of our **hope**," and "Let us...stir up **love** and good works."

The three commands, beginning as they do with the words "let us," have caused some to facetiously call this "God's Salad Bowl" or "Three Heads of Let-us"—good ways to remember this three-fold command.

We are asked to take these three steps because we have access to the "Holy of Holies by the blood of Jesus by a new and living way." Jesus has gone into heaven with His own blood and sprinkled it on the mercy seat. His blood expiated our sins which had prevented our coming into the Presence of God. Washed in that precious blood, we are invited to stand boldly in the Presence of a Holy God. This boldness is not rashness or irreverence, but confidence in the efficacy of His sufficient sacrifice. Access to His Presence is based on the value God attaches to the blood of Jesus. If that blood means to us what it means to God, we have full freedom and liberty to His Presence. No legitimate reason remains for not drawing near the Father.

This "new and living" way is "new" because it had only recently been opened; and "alive" because Christ is the Way, the only Way to the Father (Jn. 14:6).

Living in the Presence of God provides the resources to obey this three-fold directive. The first directive, "**let us draw near,**" suggests an act of worship to be done with a true heart. When we see God, as Isaiah did, "high and lifted up" with seraphim crying, "Holy, holy, holy," we realize why we must approach Him with a sincere and honest heart. There can be no hypocrisy. This privilege was extended to the Old Testament priest once a year, but it is constantly extended to us! Never before was this possible! With absolute confidence in Him we approach with full assurance of faith.

Having our hearts sprinkled from an evil conscience is an allusion to the garments of the Aaronic priests being sprinkled with blood. Thus they were accepted as ministers of the sanctuary. The blood of Jesus not only satisfies Divine justice, it also qualifies us for God's service.

Having "our bodies washed with pure water" reminds one of the laver in the outer court where the priest washed himself before entering the Holy Place. Paul, referring to our cleansing, said, "Therefore, having these promises, beloved, let us cleanse ourselves from all filthiness of the flesh and spirit, perfecting holiness in the fear of God" (2 Cor. 7:1).

The second directive is "**Let us hold fast the confession of our hope.**" A confession is to be given before others, not secretly. The world doesn't mind our "being religious" as long as we keep it to ourselves. Some claim their religion to be a private matter. How could Christianity ever be a private matter? How would your spouse respond if you said, "I don't mind being married to you but I prefer keeping this a private matter. It just might interfere with other important relationships." Refusal to acknowledge Christ denies Him. One might as well try to keep the rising sun secret! When the dark night of sin has given way to the rising of the Sun of Righteousness how can we keep it secret? God has not called us to "force-feed" Christianity to anyone, but when our Lord Jesus breaks chains of sin, puts marriages back together, heals diseased bodies, provides financial needs, how can we keep silent? If our confession makes others nervous, so be it! Jesus is the Answer!

St. Abraham, a man in the sixth century, the night before his scheduled wedding day, went into the desert. For the next 50 years he walled himself up in a monastery cell, leaving only a small opening for food. He gave all his belongings to the poor except a cloak, a goat skin, a bowl, and a map. After 50 years a bishop persuaded him to preach to a neighboring village and many were greatly moved by his ministry. But for 50 years he lived in isolation. God calls us to be salt and light, to penetrate our society. (2)

Nicodemus and Joseph of Arimathea for a time were "secret disciples," but in an open society this is not to be imitated. Paul wrote to Timothy, "Fight the good fight of faith, lay hold on eternal life, to which you were also called and have **confessed the good confession in the presence of many witnesses.** I urge you in the sight of God Who gives life to all things, and before Christ Jesus Who **witnessed the good confession before Pontius Pilate,** that you keep this commandment without spot, blameless until our Lord Jesus Christ's appearing" (1 Tim. 6:12-14). Paul's confession was open and unwavering!

What is the basis for our faithfulness? We are to be faithful, because "He Who promised is faithful." When Jesus called us to follow Him He knew every difficulty we would face along the way. He is never surprised by any hindrance the enemy puts in our path. Knowing all these obstacles, He still promises victory. We cannot congratulate each other for not wavering, for all of us lean heavily on the One Who promised never to leave or forsake us.

The third directive is "**consider one another.**" A "good confession" refers to our witness before the world, while "considering one another" has to do with the Church, the family of believers. "Consider" suggests attentive, continuous care or concern.

We are to "stir up love and good works." Some people stir up everything else but love and good works! This is not an invitation to be busybodies, but an admonition is to be concerned about others within the body of Christ.

Unfortunately, some want to take advantage of the Church. Their attitude is not what they can **do** for a body of believers, but what they can **get out of it.** We should not place our concerns above those of our brothers and sisters.

One way we "consider one another" is by "**not forsaking the assembling of ourselves together.**" **Forsake** means to **abandon** or **let down.** Some of these first-century saints were negligent about meeting with fellow believers. One probable reason was the harassment they received for identifying with other Christians. They were, indeed, harassed for their faith, but when we forsake meeting with our brothers and sisters we often return to destructive lifestyles. One of the craftiest designs of the devil is to get someone to believe their Christian life will not suffer by a lack of commitment to a body of believers.

A tribe of Indians lived many years ago in the state of Mississippi next to a very swift and dangerous river. The current was so strong that anyone who fell into it was in danger of being swept away. One day the tribe was attacked by a hostile group. They had their backs to the river and their only chance of escape was to cross the rushing river. Those who were strong picked up the weak and put them on their shoulders. The little children, the sick, the old and the infirm were carried on the backs of the strongest. They waded out into the river, and to their surprise they discovered that the weight on their shoulders carrying the least and the lowest helped them to make it safely across the river. We need one another. [3] Expending energy on others increases our own strength.

We are, by nature, worshipers. When we forsake worshiping God, we worship self. We simply **must** have a "god." We will worship the true God or some other god. One of the most pitiful cries in the Old Testament comes from the idolater, Micah, in Judges 18:24: "You have taken away the gods that I made...now what more do I have?" Micah knew that some would feel that the loss of a false god was a severe blow; how much more the loss of the true God? David cried out, "My soul longs, yes, even faints for the courts of the Lord; my heart and my flesh cry out for the living God" (Ps. 84:2). May God give us that yearning for Himself!

Malachi 3:16 tells of a dark day in Israel's history when "those who feared the Lord spoke often to one another." Robert Fulgim said, "Most of what I really need to know about how to live, and what to do, and how to be I learned in kindergarten. Wisdom was not at the top of the graduate school mountain but there in the sand box at the nursery school. Think of what a better world it would be if the whole world had cookies and milk around three o'clock every afternoon and then laid down with our blankets for a nap, or if we had a basic policy for our nation and other nations to always put things back where you found them and clean up our own messes. It is still true; no matter how old you are when you go out into the world, it is best to hold hands and stick together."[4]

The writer exhorts about a coming day when we will be glad that we had met together for worship and fellowship. He calls that time "the day approaching," the Day of the Lord, the day when Jesus Christ will return to this earth. When that happens we will be glad we have served Him. Thank God, only "some" of them had been careless about assembling with others. If we need prodding about gathering with our church family, let this passage speak to us. It is a serious matter.

If you are not a part of the family of God but are considering the claims of Christ perhaps the following story will be of help. A chaplain, who was addressing the soldiers in his company, said to them, "There are two possibilities after death—heaven and hell. If you would like to know your destination I will be happy to give you a little test, the results of which will be your answer." They answered in unison, "Okay, give us the test." With pencils and paper the chaplain told them to number off ten spaces. Each question counted ten points and each soldier was to grade himself on a scale from one to ten. Question number one was, "Have you always loved God above all else and not put anything else before Him?" Number two was "Have you ever misused God's Name or made light of Him?" Other questions followed about family, God, and conduct as the chaplain went through the Ten Commandments. When the test was completed, the men tallied up their scores. One thought that he had scored quite well and gave himself a 75. He remembered that 75 was considered passing in school. One of the men asked, "Say, Chaplain, what's a passing score for this test, anyway?" The chaplain answered, "100 points." The men shook their heads. "What's the use of trying? No one could be that perfect. We're all doomed." The chaplain smiled and said, "I've got good news. There was a Man Who walked this earth and took this test and scored 100 points. His Name is Jesus. And He says that the purpose of the test is not to score 100 points but to indicate our need for help. There is mercy and forgiveness for all who receive it. We never score 100 points, but we can substitute His test score for ours. Because of what He has done we are accepted." Jesus Christ has taken the test for you! [5] He is *God's Final Answer!* What incredibly good news!

For if we sin willfully after we have received the knowledge of the truth, there no longer remains a sacrifice for sins, but a certain fearful expectation of judgment, and fiery indignation which will devour the adversaries. Anyone who has rejected Moses' law dies without mercy on the testimony of two or three witnesses. Of how much worse punishment, do you suppose, will he be thought worthy who has trampled the Son of God underfoot, counted the blood of the covenant by which he was sanctified a common thing, and insulted the Spirit of grace? For we know Him who said, "Vengeance is Mine, I will repay," says the Lord. And again, "The LORD will judge His people." It is a fearful thing to fall into the hands of the living God. But recall the former days in which, after you were illuminated, you endured a great struggle with sufferings: partly while you were made a spectacle both by reproaches and tribulations, and partly while you became companions of those who were so treated; for you had compassion on me in my chains, and joyfully accepted the plundering of your goods, knowing that you have a better and an enduring possession for yourselves in heaven. Therefore do not cast away your confidence, which has great reward. For you have need of endurance, so that after you have done the will of God, you may receive the promise: "For yet a little while, And He who is coming will come and will not tarry. Now the just shall live by faith; But if anyone draws back, My soul has no pleasure in him." But we are not of those who draw back to perdition, but of those who believe to the saving of the soul.

Hebrews 10:26-39
(See also Habakkuk 2:1-4; 3:17-19)

CHAPTER 23

Living by Faith
(Study No. 23 from the Book of Hebrews)

B oth this passage and chapter six deal with apostasy. Having begun this Christian walk we dare not turn back. If those who rejected Moses died without mercy, the author reasons, how much more severe must the ultimate state of those be who embrace the Lord Jesus and then deny Him.

The stern warning given here concerns judgment from the hand of God Himself. These Hebrews were to recall their patient endurance of earlier suffering as a result of their faith. They had suffered personally from vicious insults and cruel persecutions, and they also suffered because they identified with friends who were subject to harassment and imprisonment. They had not allowed the confiscation of property to destroy their joy, for they had a greater possession in heaven.

The Lord Jesus, they knew, identified with them in their suffering. The president of Gallaudet University in Washington, D.C., was replaced because the students were unhappy with her. She was deposed for a very unusual reason. She was not deaf, and Gallaudet University serves 21,025 deaf students. The Student Body President and the new Chairman of the Board of Trustees met to talk about the future of the school. When they came out of the meeting, the President of the Student Body turned to the new President of the University and said with tears in his eyes, "There was no interpreter." That was true because the new president, I. King Jordan, is also deaf. These young people needed someone like them to lead their school, someone who shared their struggle. [1]

Since Jesus identifies with us in our suffering, how could these Hebrew Christians cast away their confidence which held such a rich reward of hope? They needed patience in allowing God's will to be done in their situation, however unpleasant it seemed. Until the coming of Christ they were to live by faith. If they drew back through fear the Lord would not be pleased. Rather than defect to their own ruin, they were to maintain their faith until their salvation was completed.

The familiar words quoted here, "the just shall live by faith," were first used by the prophet Habakkuk who ministered during a time of great political upheaval. National collapse was imminent. God did not seem to be answering prayer. He seemed silent. When He spoke to Habakkuk, saying that He was using the Chaldeans, a treacherous heathen power to punish Israel, the prophet could not understand. How could God possibly use such a wicked nation to punish His own people? Habakkuk climbed up into his watchtower, evidently his prayer place, to seek an answer from the Lord. All serious situations must be met by prayer.

God's answer was that Habakkuk should write the vision down clearly. The prophets probably wrote their prophecies and hung them up in the temple area to be read by all the people. "Write the vision and make it plain on tablets, that he may run who reads it," was the command of God. These words have been interpreted in different ways. They may mean that the person who reads the words should then run with the message, or that the words of the vision should be so clear that a person running by need not slacken his pace to read this message—"the just shall live by faith." The second interpretation is the better translation: God wants the message of living by faith to be so clear that a person on the run need not slow down to read and understand it.

A person who lives by faith puts that faith to work in practical ways. This is one reason why Christianity is growing so fast in Korea today. The once dominant Buddhist and Confucian religions made religion mystical, speculative, and remote. The Christian faith came into Korea with a message of involvement, love, and compassion. From the beginning the Christians started feeding the starving, sheltering the homeless, and teaching the illiterate. The people were receptive to that kind of self-giving religion. So the Christian community grew by leaps and bounds as the Korean church became the self-giving body of Christ, living out their faith in practical ways."[2]

This message of faith, so central to Christianity, is not to be shrouded in mystery. It is not a message to be taught in seminars by the spiritual elite. Someone may say, "I want faith so that I may work miracles. Therefore, I must have lessons on faith." Why is it that those in very primitive areas of the world who know so little about what we call faith seem to witness more miracles? The message of faith in God was never meant for a select few. The more academic we become about faith the less it seems to function. Faith must be so clear that a running man can understand the meaning without slowing his pace.

Habakkuk did not call the people to pray away the coming Chaldean invasion. The invasion could not be wished away. God said it was coming. Faith is realistic. It deals with life as it is, with fact, not fancy. It must withstand tests, not rely on simplistic answers.

A group of Methodists were holding a camp meeting in which top-flight preachers from across the country were coming to share. One of the main speakers was forced at the last minute to cancel out. The Bishop said to a young promising pastor, "I want you to fill in and preach in that service after lunch." The young pastor said, "Well, Bishop, how can I do that? I didn't bring any sermons with me. I came strictly to listen and to worship. How could I get up there and deliver a sermon to this large congregation?" The Bishop said, "Son, just trust the Lord. Trust the Lord." The pastor was dumb-founded. In his despair he picked up the Bishop's Bible from a shelf nearby and started thumbing through it to find a text. While thumbing through, he came across a set of notes and decided he would preach from them. So when the time came for the service, the young man preached the sermon he had found in the Bishop's Bible. The response was overwhelming. Everybody congratulated him on the wonderful sermon. It was an exciting moment until the furious Bishop spoke to him. "Young man, what have you done? You preached the sermon I was going to deliver tonight. What am

I going to do now?" With a twinkle in his eye the young man said, "Trust the Lord, Bishop. Just trust the Lord."[3]

We smile at the young preacher's simplistic answer, but in reality, faith does not give simplistic answers to difficult questions. Why does a righteous God permit the rule of wrong? Why does violence and oppression swallow up good? These questions troubled Habakkuk. There really wasn't much difference between the Israelites and the Chaldeans but the Israelites could not understand why the Lord God could use the Chaldeans for judgment. Habakkuk, who stood in the presence of God and voiced these questions, was told he must simply trust God. The answer was not in answers, but in God! "The just shall live by faith."

Paul's faith caused him to say, "And we know that all things work together for good to those who love God, to those who are the called according to His purpose" (Rom. 8:28). This is an answer that satisfies the heart, not the intellect.

How did God's answer affect Habakkuk? Consider his words in Habakkuk 3:17-19 (NIV): "Though the fig tree does not bud and there are no grapes on the vines, though the olive crop fails and the fields produce no food, though there are no sheep in the pen and no cattle in the stalls, yet I will rejoice in the Lord, I will be joyful in God my Savior. The Sovereign Lord is my strength; He makes my feet like the feet of a deer, He enables me to go on the heights."

How did Habakkuk get to this place of gratitude and jubilation, from doubt to confidence? That's important, for if he got there, so can we!

First, **Habakkuk believed that God would provide even though the normal resources were destroyed.** Can we believe that the same God Who provided water out of a rock, quail out of nowhere, oil for a widow, food and water for Elijah can provide for His people without the normal resources? Yes, He is a miracle-working God!

But this conviction is not what brought joy to the heart of the prophet. What produced the confidence and joy that sustained him was finding a new and deeper relationship with his God. He found that God Who seemed to be inactive and insensitive, was intensely interested in His people. Habakkuk learned that fullness of life lay in God Himself and not in what God might do in certain circumstances.

It was not miracles that produced the joy. It was God Himself! His statement, "I will rejoice in the Lord, I will be joyful in God my Savior" literally means "I will jump for joy in the Lord and I will 'spin around' in the God of my salvation."

Do you lack this kind of joy? If we lose our joy we need to consider why it is missing. It could be a symptom of a greater loss, a loss of a close relationship with the Lord.

Habakkuk's joy was "in the Lord," not circumstances. Circumstances did not produce the joy Habakkuk sensed. **Our joy must be in God!**

When negative things happen, when someone disappoints us, when we fail to understand a situation, we need to check out our emotions. Perhaps we need to lift our eyes to a higher plane and get them on the Lord God, where they belong. He is our joy...**and He never changes!**

Habakkuk's starting point was **being honest with God about his doubts.** Instead of talking to others about his doubts, he talked to God. God always responds to the person who honestly confronts Him. Elijah, Jonah, and Job came to God with their doubts, frustrations, and anger. Though they were not correct in their positions, God heard them out. Their answer was ultimately found in a relationship with God.

Finally, **Habakkuk simply waited before the Lord**, probably the most difficult thing for us to do. "Wait upon the Lord" and "Be still and know that I am God" are two of the most difficult verses for some of us to obey. We want a quick, easy fix...30 to 60 seconds time slots allotted to TV commercials will be just fine.

There was no lengthy explanation of the circumstances for Habakkuk. He had to learn that **regardless of what was happening** God still governed. He did not go away from his watchtower saying piously, "Now I understand it all. I think I will write a book on faith. I'll tell people how predictable God is and what they must do to get God to do what they want Him to do." Habakkuk assures us that God is in the midst of the circumstances that surround His children. He is not surprised by your present situation. He is at work in it, and though He may use strange means to bring about His will, He is in control. Let us then rejoice in the Lord; let us joy in the God of our salvation!

Remember you are a child of Royalty no matter what the situation may be. Your confidence and joy is secure. A young African was kidnapped from his home and forced to cross the ocean on a slave ship, a stinking barge of festering humanity. After months of rotten food, disease, the ever-lingering stench of human waste, and the deaths of many about him, the young man arrived in America. The traders pushed the youth onto the slave auction block to be sold. To their surprise, this slave didn't hang his head in shame and humiliation, as most did. He stood rigidly erect, thrust his chest out and lifted his chin high, his eyes fixed straight ahead. The crowd stirred as the proud black man stood on the block. Why was he so different? The slave trader who knew the answer said to the crowd, "This boy is the son of a King in Africa and he can't forget it."[4] No matter what the circumstance we are sons of God, heirs of God, and joint-heirs with Jesus Christ and we can't forget it!

We often hear about faith that changes circumstances. Thank God for such faith; but there is a nobler faith that changes the individual, whether the situation changes or not. Remember we are children of a King. Don't forget it!

Now faith is the substance of things hoped for, the evidence of things not seen.

Hebrews 11:1

CHAPTER 24

Faith Defined

(Study No. 24 in the Book of Hebrews)

Someone wrote *Reader's Digest* about a wedding she attended with her bachelor son. The son appeared unaffected by the ceremony until the bride and groom lighted a single candle, and then blew out their own. He brightened and said, "I've never seen that done before." His mother whispered back, "You know what that means, don't you?" His response: "No more old flames?" We, too, are joined to our Lord and are not meant to go back to the old way. Hebrews, however, was written to some believers who were considering going back to their former ways.

In our text we have the only definition of faith given in the Bible. "Faith is the substance of things hoped for, the evidence of things not seen." "Confident assurance" is a better expression than "substance." "Faith is the confident assurance of things hoped for," or "being sure of the things we hope for." It is "the conviction of the reality we do not see."

We have heard that, "seeing is believing." But seeing is not believing; seeing is seeing and nothing more. Believing is being sure even when you don't see. This same writer says of Moses, "He endured as seeing Him Who is invisible." People of faith see the invisible!

When the Old Testament prophet, Elisha, saw how fearful his servant was as the enemy approached, he cried, "Lord, open his eyes" and his servant saw "the mountain was full of horses and chariots of fire round about." Faith sees what is invisible to natural vision!

For quite some time we awaited the birth of our little grand-daughter. Our faith was working. Had we ever seen this little girl? No. What evidence did we have that she was going to be part of our family? We had the word of the parents-to-be. Months before there was any physical evidence, we believed she was on the way. A few months later the evidence was overwhelming. Our assurance grew as the mother's body gave evidence that a little one was being formed inside. Faith, then, before there was physical evidence, was being built on someone's word. God's Word is the basis of our confidence.

Someday little Sarah Elaine will be asked, "Who is your mother?" and she will say, "Her name is Melissa." How can she prove that Mel is her mother? Of course, she can produce a birth certificate, but such certificates can be forged. She must believe someone's word as the ground for her confidence. That confidence produces faith, faith that grows into unshakable conviction. She will be absolutely sure of her parentage. **Faith is assurance, an assurance that produces confidence, a confidence that gives birth to a conviction.**

Is it any wonder that faith can sing in prison? Jeremiah, Ezekiel, Paul, John, all men of faith, were imprisoned. The prophecies of Jeremiah, Ezekiel, and many of the writings of Paul and John were inspired by the faith of these men while suffering confinement. John Bunyan's great drama was composed in prison. Put people of faith in jail and they will sing like Paul and Silas until they "bring the house down!"

If faith produces such positive results what a terrible loss to be without it! There is a disturbing word in Matthew 13:58 concerning Jesus' return to Nazareth: "He did not do many works there because of their unbelief." But He came back to them just as He keeps coming to us. He never violates our wills, never forces the door of our hearts open. Of course, He may shake the house a bit so that the windows rattle, but He will never put His hand on the doorknob. We alone have the ability to open the door to the Savior. But if we keep shutting Jesus out we will paint ourselves into a corner. Jesus Christ will never "crash our party" but then, we will never have real life without Him!

What a disastrous day when Nazareth shut the door of the city to Christ. There He was, the very Son of God, God manifested in flesh, and they totally missed Him! Earlier they tried to kill Him; now at His second visit they were full of unbelief and apathy. He could not respond to their needs in such an environment.

Neither the city nor its citizens could lay the blame for this tragic day on Jesus. He wanted to minister to them. He was not simply passing through town. His interest was real. He was not studying these people as specimens; His interest was not simply academic. He knew them; knew all about them, for He was raised among them. But He loved them nevertheless. Had they responded to Him in faith rather than in unbelief, they would have found that He was **able, willing, anxious, and seeking** to help them. His purpose that day in Nazareth was not to merely sympathize with them; He came to offer them a power that would change their lives. They said nothing about Jesus being unable to help them, but even after seeing His works and hearing His words they were still filled with unbelief.

The message is clear—God is concerned about our faith. It is the difference in winning and losing, not only for this life, but all eternity as well. Without faith it is impossible to please God. It is the difference between victory and defeat.

It takes faith to get married, and faith to stay married. We must keep trusting and believing in that person. Most couples believe they can have a successful union, but even in marriage "faith without works is dead." Faith is active rather than passive. A person might buy a computer to help in their business and get so fascinated by the computer itself that the business suffers. Faith is not a plaything to be studied and admired; it is to be lived by!

Columbus believed the world was round. Others agreed with him, but it was Columbus who got into the ship and sailed beyond the place which certainly looked like a dropping off point. Some believed a lunar landing was possible, but a few Americans put their lives on the line to prove it.

Faith's message is this—if you believe in Jesus **act like it, live like it!** Some have a faith no better than the devil's. He "believes and trembles." When we really believe God, really put our trust in Him, we **stop trembling!** Faith works! A little boy bought a Superman cape but later brought it back and threw it on the floor crying, "It didn't work! It didn't work!" Faith is not fantasy. It works!

There are always those who criticize others who exercise faith. "Every great oak was once a nut that stood its ground!" Faith stands its ground when the world seems to be crumbling about you.

If you believe that Jesus Christ is all He claimed to be, your life will be changed. Your new life will lead to a new lifestyle, a new character. Do you believe He is all He claimed to be? He claimed to be **present universally.** "Where two or three are gathered in My Name I am there." **He claimed to be the answer to every human need.** He said, "I am the Bread of Life." **He claimed to embody all strength and wisdom.** He said, "I am the Way, the Truth, and the Life." **He claimed absolute timelessness.** "Before Abraham was I am," He said. **He even claimed power over death** when He said, "He that believes in Me shall never die." **He said that He came to liberate the human spirit.** "If the Son shall make you free you shall be free indeed." **He claimed unconditional availability.** "He that comes to Me," He said, "I will in no wise cast out." **And what of His claim to forgive sins?** Jesus kept company with sinners and offered them forgiveness. He still does! Be careful about claims concerning your personal holiness. Remember that the devil was once an archangel. There is no evil that we are incapable of. Potentially we are all drunkards, blasphemers, robbers, adulterers. Thank God for His amazing grace!

When we really believe that Jesus is all He said He was we become people of action. A man crippled for 38 years got up and carried his bedroll away at Jesus' command. Another fellow heard Jesus say, "Stretch your hand out," something the man could not do; yet he did it! When a person believes Jesus he obeys Him. He may be telling you to come to Him, to rise up, to reach out.

Some may be crippled in spirit, reluctant, fearful, to reach out to Him. But if you believe He is all He claimed to be, that He is Who He said He was—the Savior of the World, the Friend of Sinners—act on your faith now.

Many have the opinion that faith is simply a creed, a systematized theology which, if correctly used, can secure things from God. Richard Halverson writes, "Faith is thought of as a means of getting what one wants from God. If one just has enough faith he gets his answer. Faith is a quantitative commodity—one has more or less faith...the more he has—the greater his buying power with God. Such thinking leads to frustration—or worse...guilt. As in the case of those who blame themselves for the death of a loved one. 'If we had just had enough faith, he would have lived.' Or—if we just had enough faith, he would be healed. Thinking this way—how much is enough? Faith ought to be thought of as the means whereby one relates to God—trusts in Him—has confidence in His wisdom, His integrity—His faithfulness—His utter dependability. Faith in the Biblical sense is to believe God no matter what. It is to trust God whether feelings or circumstances encourage or support such confidence or not. In fact, true faith often has to choose to believe God against feelings—against circumstances—against anything that opposes faith. Job had the right idea: 'Though He slay me, yet will I trust Him' (Job 13:15). Paul put it this way: '...let God be true and every man a liar' (Rom. 3:4). Faith holds fast to the fact that 'God works in everything for good to those who love God; who are called according to His purpose'" (Rom. 8:28). [1]

So faith has little to do with selfish desires. Whether you drive an expensive car or ride a bicycle is not heaven's greatest priority! Faith has to do with **relationship.** Faith in a marriage partner makes a house into a home, a union into a unity. Faith in Jesus Christ opens the door to Him and lets Him settle down and be at home in our hearts.

By faith Enoch was taken away so that he did not see death, "and was not found, because God had taken him"; for before he was taken he had this testimony, that he pleased God. But without faith it is impossible to please Him, for he who comes to God must believe that He is, and that He is a rewarder of those who diligently seek Him.

Hebrews 11:5, 6

CHAPTER 25

Requirements for Coming to God

(Study No. 25 from the Book of Hebrews)

What could be more important than being sure of a relation-ship with God? This text gives us assurance and mentions two requirements for coming to Him.

It is not works, but faith that pleases God. This pleasing faith believes first, that **God is,** and second, **that He is a rewarder of those who diligently seek Him.** How is it that believing that God exists and rewards causes us to come to Him?

The Bible never argues for the existence of God nor attempts to prove that He is a rewarder of those who seek Him. The scrip-ture assumes that belief in God is innate in the human heart, that all of us, unless we have been tampered with, naturally believe in the existence of God. The person who denies the existence of God is, in Scripture, almost contemptuously dismissed by the words, "The fool has said in his heart, 'there is no God'" (Ps. 14:1).

A six-year-old boy was assisting his mother with some spring gardening. The mother was absorbed in her work while the little boy explored the miracle of exploding, growing things. All at once the boy picked up a daffodil bud, sat down on the ground and stud-ied it. Then with his two little hands, he tried to force it open into full blossom. The result was a disappointing mess of limp petals and a dead flower. Frustrated, he cried out, "Mommy, why is it that when I try to open the buds, it just falls to pieces and dies? How does God open it into a beautiful flower?" Even before his mother could answer, a broad smile broke across the child's face, and he exclaimed, "Oh! I know! God always works from the inside."[1]

Since the knowledge of God is innate in the human heart, **it the worst form of child abuse to tell a child that there is no God, or to live a godless life in the presence of the child.**

The first requirement in coming to God is to **believe that God is.** As noted, we are not given arguments in scripture relative to God's existence. Theologians study arguments for the existence of God. Among these arguments are the cosmological argument, the anthropological argument, the ontological argument, the Christological argument, and the teleological argument. We may use all these arguments in an attempt to prove to someone that God exists, but the Holy Spirit must still touch that person's heart. Conversion does not spring from man's intelligence, but from God's Spirit! A reasoning man could hear all these arguments and assent to them, but still not believe that God is kindly disposed toward him. The second requirement for coming to God deals with this very issue — **we must believe that He is a rewarder of those who diligently seek Him.** Little children will generally only come to a person they believe in and who, they believe, will do them good. Our Lord requires such confidence. Coming to God has little to do with intellectual conviction; it is expressed in heart obedience. God reveals Himself to those who **diligently seek Him**, not to those who simply become religious. The word "diligently," suggests that our hearts are involved. It means to investigate or crave; so we cannot be casual about it. "Ask, seek, and knock." Effort is implied.

Man is the only creature that God made with a capacity for seeking Him. Given the right situation any person will pray, especially those who claim there is no God. Just as a fish's fins suggest water and a bird's wings suggest air, our capacity for prayer argues for a God Who rewards those who diligently seek Him. Untold thousands testify how God changed their lives when they sought Him in prayer.

Since God is a rewarder of those who seek Him He must be infinitely interested in us, every one of us — in what we do, think, eat, where we live, in all of life. Never think for one moment you must convince God to be interested in you. When Jesus said, "He that comes to Me I will in no wise cast out," He had you in mind!

One whose name will live in infamy was raised by a dominant mother who showed no affection, love, or discipline. His school friends had little to do with him. At thirteen the school psychologist said this young man didn't know what it meant to be loved. Girls teased him; boys beat him up. To escape the abuse he joined the marines, but only found more abuse. He hated it when they called him Ozzie the Rabbit. He got into fights, rebelled, and was finally dishonorably discharged. Without family, friends, or love he was losing his hair, and had already lost all self respect. Eventually he married an immigrant, who bore him two children; but soon, even the marriage, his only source of security, began to crumble. His wife hated him. Having lost all self-worth he crawled to his wife, begging with tears, for some attention. In front of others, she mocked his failure and ridiculed his impotence. His ego lay shattered and he was without human affection. A few days later, November 22, 1963, he went into the garage, took a rifle, drove to Dallas, and put two large holes in the head of our former president, John F. Kennedy. His name was Lee Harvey Oswald. [2]

Who can tell how history may have been changed if someone had taken time to tell Lee Harvey Oswald that he was loved, that God had him in mind when He sent Jesus Christ to die? Perhaps if he had heard that beautiful old story he would not only have believed that **God is,** but **that He is also a rewarder of those who diligently seek Him.** That's what Enoch did...and pleased God. Our faith pleases Him to.

By faith Abraham obeyed when he was called to go out to the place which he would receive as an inheritance. And he went out, not knowing where he was going. By faith he dwelt in the land of promise as in a foreign country, dwelling in tents with Isaac and Jacob, the heirs with him of the same promise; for he waited for the city which has foundations, whose builder and maker is God. By faith Sarah herself also received strength to conceive seed, and she bore a child when she was past the age, because she judged Him faithful who had promised. Therefore from one man, and him as good as dead, were born as many as the stars of the sky in multitude— innumerable as the sand which is by the seashore. These all died in faith, not having received the promises, but having seen them afar off were assured of them, embraced them and confessed that they were strangers and pilgrims on the earth. For those who say such things declare plainly that they seek a homeland. And truly if they had called to mind that country from which they had come out, they would have had opportunity to return. But now they desire a better, that is, a heavenly country. Therefore God is not ashamed to be called their God, for He has prepared a city for them.

Hebrews 11:8-16

For here we have no continuing city, but we seek the one to come.

Hebrews 13:14
(See also Revelation 21:1-27)

CHAPTER 26

Looking for a City

(Study No. 26 in the Book of Hebrews)

Ayoung lady on a cruise ship kept glancing at an attractive young man. He was quite flattered because he could not help but notice her attention. Finally he took courage and asked, "Is there something wrong? It may be my imagination, but I could not help but notice that you have been looking in my direction." She blushed and replied, "Oh, no. It's just that I can't help but notice how much you look like my first husband." The young man looked puzzled and asked, "How many times have you been married?" With a mysterious smile she answered, "Oh, I haven't been married yet."[1] That humorous story illustrates the woman's faith! In Hebrews 11 faith is both defined and demonstrated.

It is obvious from the record of the three men mentioned first in this chapter that this world is less than ideal. Enoch walked with God in a perverted society, but ultimately God caught him up and out of it. Noah was faithful in a corrupt generation whose thoughts were always impure. Abraham, the friend of God, burdened by the corruption of his day, looked for a city which had foundations, whose builder and maker was God. Though he walked on an earthly plain his mind was fixed on the heavenly. Heaven's instructions for him were simply, "Get up and get out." So he left Ur of the Chaldeans not knowing **where** he was going, but knowing full well

why he was going. His obedience to God was as spontaneous in Ur as it was later at Bethel, where it was accounted as righteousness.

Abraham's life was especially associated with two things—a tent and an altar. The tent and the altar represent all that any person really needs in this life. The tent suggests our pilgrimage and the altar our commitment to God. The altar is forever central. If our hearts are obsessed with the tent— possessions, houses, lands, clothes—our lives become distorted. We can focus our minds on material things and forsake the altar, yet all the while continue to go through the motions of worship. Jesus defined a heathen as one who was always concerned about what he were going to eat, drink, or wear. We should never live as though this life is all that matters, for "here we have no continuing city,"

A lady wrote Ann Landers with this complaint: "I'm 44, husband same age (swell guy). We get along OK—no drinking, no gambling, and no skirt chasing. He has a good job and our home is paid for. Our children are healthy and normal. They do well in school and our three older ones (teenagers) have never caused us any trouble. So why am I writing? Because my life is a blah. Something is missing. What is it?"[2] Her complaint is not unusual, but the answer to her dull, drab life is in Jesus Christ. Relationship with Him, not religion, offers the fulfillment she seeks.

Abraham was not so foolish as to look for fulfillment in temporal things. He looked for an eternal city. As we study these verses our purpose is **to discover some of the characteristics of that city** and **to see what difference seeking this city makes in this present life.**

The City of God does not represent an effort by the Creator to salvage what was lost in Eden. God's purposes have always been in this city. All the potential for the city was in the garden. Page one of our Bibles reads, "In the beginning God created the heavens and the earth" (Gen. 1:1). The close of the Book reads, "Now I saw a new heaven and a new earth" (Rev. 21:1). John, in the Spirit, saw this city which Abraham sought. Human history began in a garden and will culminate in a city. All that satisfies the human heart is in that city.

Dwight L. Moody told a story about an optimistic, cheerful lady who was bedridden and lived in a run-down building. She was all alone in a shabby fifth-floor room of this old apartment building which had no elevator. One of her friends brought a wealthy woman to see her. They came to cheer this bedridden shut-in, but found that sometimes things work in reverse. As they entered the building, the wealthy lady was struck by the depressing surroundings. As they mounted the stairs to the second floor it was almost more than she could handle. "Such a dark and filthy place," she said. Her friend responded, "It's better higher up." They climbed the stairs to the third landing. "It's even worse here," she said. Again her friend responded, "It's better higher up." Finally they got to the fifth floor and entered the shut-in's tiny, run-down apartment. As she greeted her guests the shut-in's face was aglow with the love of Christ. The wealthy woman sympathetically said, "Living like this must be difficult for you," but the shut-in smiled knowingly and said, "Yes, but it's better higher up." [3] Indeed! Once we know that, then things seem better down here.

John says that the city comes "down **out of heaven** from God, prepared as a bride adorned for her husband" (Rev. 21:2). This is **the administrative center of the Kingdom of God established on the new earth. It is the ultimate answer to the prayer our Lord taught us, "Your kingdom come. Your will be done on earth as it is in heaven."**

This city is not the result of spiritual evolution. Some have taught that through spiritual evolution mankind will cause the Kingdom of God to be established on earth. Just the reverse seems to be happening. Civilization seems to worsening.

When we find a parking meter with time left on it we may say that we are "parking on another man's nickel." We seem to be doing that today. We are blessed by the residue of more righteous generations that have preceded us. God help us to leave something better for the next generation!

This city comes, not because of man's righteousness, but because its "builder and maker is God." Man spoils all that he touches. Babel was destroyed because it represented man's best effort to establish a name for himself. Nothing built by man endures. The city Abraham sought lasts forever!

This city has twelve gates that open to all points of the compass. God welcomes into that eternal city the redeemed from all nations. What a joy to see the saved streaming into the City of God from north, south, east, and west; from Asia, Africa, North and South America, Europe; from the islands of the seas, and all retaining their national identity! The redeemed will sing a new song to the Lord Jesus, "And You have redeemed us to God by Your Own blood out of every tribe and tongue and people and nation, and have made us kings and priests to our God; and we shall reign on the earth" (Rev. 5:9,10). What joy to see our Lord so honored!

We are so accustomed to war and bloodshed that it is hard to believe that such a day could ever come. Indeed, many scoff and say the Day of the Lord will never come. But it will! A man in New England in 1938 went to an Abercrombie and Fitch store and bought a new barometer. He took it home, proudly placed it in his study window, and consulted it to see what the weather would be that day. You can imagine his disappointment when the barometer called for a hurricane. The very idea of a hurricane there in New England was absurd. In a huff he grabbed the barometer and rushed back to the Abercrombie and Fitch store. When asked what the problem was, he said, "Here I've traveled all the way to this store to buy a barometer and now it's reading hurricane." The clerk apologized and gave him his money back. He got his refund and completed his long journey home, but by the time he arrived his house had been blown away by the hurricane that hit New England in 1938! His disbelief had not prevented the hurricane. [4] No amount of unbelief can prevent the coming of that prophetic Day of the Lord.

"God will wipe away every tear from their eyes." We presently struggle to wash away tears. In the cartoon, *For Better or for Worse*, little Elizabeth, comes to her father who is lying on the couch. "What's the matter, Daddy?" she asks. "I don't know, kiddo. I don't know if I'm bored, or tired, or depressed," Daddy answers. Elizabeth responds, "Everybody feels like that sometimes, Daddy. It's nothing to worry about." "What do you think you are, a doctor?" her dad asks. "No," she said, "But I wrote a 'perstription' for you." Her father reads the note, hugs Elizabeth, and says, "I feel better now." When Mom comes in she asks, "Honey, what does the note from Elizabeth say?" He smiles and hands her the note which reads, "Take two hugs and call me in the morning."[5]

Though we can help others in depression, when we wash away one set of tears, others appear. When God wipes them away they are wiped away forever! Tears will never flow again, for death no longer exists, sorrow ceases, and crying is hushed. Death itself will die! Thanks be to God!

One of the most common universal sounds will never be heard in that city—the sound of crying. Someone said, "Man comes into the world with a cry and goes out with a groan." But in eternity crying will only be heard in hell. Today we hear cries of pain, hunger, suffering, oppression, danger, death. But in that blessed day there will be only hallelujahs from the lips of the redeemed. Some today who smile most convincingly are the ones who often carry the deepest sorrow. Some day all sorrow will cease. Even secret sorrows will be forever gone!

How should the knowledge of this coming city affect our present lives? Our Lord expects His redeemed to live in the light of the future. John said those who were living in the hope of Jesus' coming would purify themselves, just as Christ is pure (1 Jn. 3:3). Whatever we truly believe about the future effects us today.

Dr. Murdo Ewin McDonald, a Scottish Presbyterian, was a prisoner of war in the Second World War. One morning Dr. McDonald was awakened by a friend who had been secretly listening to the BBC. Good news had been received about the Allied invasion of Normandy. The bearer of the good news whispered only three words in Gallic: "They have come." McDonald threw reserve aside, ran back to the barracks and began shouting, "They have come! They have come!" Response was instant and incredible. Weak men shouted as they jumped for joy; rugged men hugged each other and wept with glee. Some stood on tables and shouted while others rolled on the floor in fits of elation. Their German captors, not knowing of the D-Day Invasion, thought them crazy. These jubilant allies were still prisoners within intimidating walls. Nothing had changed outwardly, but inwardly they knew that everything had changed. Victory was yet to be accomplished but they still lived in the joy that the invasion had already occurred. [6] The city Abraham sought is not realized now, but we rejoice in its certainty!

Three truths are mentioned about the coming city: **its Builder and Architect is God, all nationalities are welcome, and there will be no tears.** These facts profoundly affect those who truly believe them. Consider them in the reverse order.

What are the implications of knowing today that **all tears will be wiped away by God Himself?** That means that God is presently touched with the feeling of our infirmities, He sorrows with us, and genuinely cares about our tears. We, too, must be able to weep with those who weep. How can we be aloof from the suffering of others? How can we be judgmental rather than sympathetic?

Someone may say, "I am a private person and I find it too difficult to reach out to others. Let them help themselves as I did." Aren't we glad that Jesus Christ did not assume that attitude? If anyone had a reason to step aside from human need, He did. Watch Him touch a leper, a man whose flesh was rotting away. See Him stop the funeral procession at Nain and restore a son to a sorrowing widow He probably had never seen before. See Him kneel before His disciples, take a basin and a towel, and wash their dusty feet. What a Savior!

We understand that one who says, "I want to be left alone. Give me solitude with my Lord and I'll let someone else deal with people." After years of ministry I sometimes still struggle to reach out to others. This may stem from feelings of inadequacy or fear of rejection, but we who love the Savior must share His love with others, or it will spoil within us and make us bitter and unloving. Since God cares about our sorrows we should care about the sorrows of others.

Second, how should it affect us today to know that **this future city opens to all points of the compass?** People from all ethnic groups will be there, in that "sweet bye and bye." What effect should that have on me in the "now and now?" It means that I can never entertain racial prejudice. Imagine meeting someone in that city who I had avoided in **this** life, not *hated*, simply avoided. We better learn how to associate with other ethnic groups here, for we will be together eternally! May the Holy Spirit examine us in this area. It is sinful to even be prejudiced against prejudiced people!

Third, what difference does it make now that **the coming city is built by God?** No human hands are used in its construction. This speaks of the great grace of God. The human touch has the kiss of death, for we are all sinners by nature.

The famous French author, Balzac, fancied himself as a handwriting expert. He believed he could determine the character of a person by analyzing their script. One day an elderly lady brought him a little boy's homework book and asked the great expert to give an opinion of the child's potential. Balzac very carefully studied the irregular, untidy script and then asked, "Are you the boy's mother?" The woman replied, "No." "Perhaps you are related?" he asked. "Not at all," she said. "Then I will tell you frankly," he answered, "the youth is slovenly, probably stupid. He will never amount to much." "Ha!" said the woman, "It might surprise you to know that this was your notebook when you were a little boy in school."[7] We need no handwriting expert, for the Bible teaches what human nature confirms, that there is a potential for the worst sort of sin in all of us.

Our hopes of seeing our own lives, as well as society changed, can only be realized as we trust God to do it in His own way. He uses people who are in sympathy with Him, and He will use you and me to bless our homes, churches and communities if we do it His way. We should be in constant prayer for our cities, for all who look for a city to come will be concerned about the city in which they presently live.

No Christian can say, "Well, I'm only passing through this old world so it doesn't matter to me what others do. I'll just let the rest of the world go by." If we love Jesus, we will love the ones for whom He died. Every saint should leave the fragrance of a godly life lingering wherever he or she has been.

There is comfort in knowing that God alone will build that city. He is in control of all history. This God, Who someday will rule with all enemies under His feet, controls the present. If we trust Him for that day to come, we can surely trust Him now!

By faith Noah, being divinely warned of things not yet seen, moved with godly fear, prepared an ark for the saving of his household, by which he condemned the world and became heir of the righteous-ness which is according to faith.

Hebrews 11:7

CHAPTER 27

An End-Time Faith

(Study No. 27 in the Book of Hebrews)

Noah's name is one of the most familiar in literature. He manifested an incredible faith in circumstances no other man in history faced. **Our purpose is to look at this unusual man, to consider the times in which he lived,** and, **to see how his faith operated in those dark days.**

First, **consider the man, Noah.** He is often remembered for two things: he built an ark by which the human race was saved...and then he got drunk! We know little about him, and yet he is one of the most exceptional men in history. He was an obedient, faithful worker during the worst of all times.

He must have been a lonely man. Neither his faith nor his message was ever accepted by his hearers. Even after 120 years this "preacher of righteousness" had not one single convert. Enoch, for 50 years Noah's contemporary, probably was in sympathy with him, but was caught away by God long before the flood. After Adam's day it is only said of two men, Enoch and Noah, "walked with God." Methuselah, son of Enoch, another contemporary, died just before the great flood. Lamech, Noah's father, prophesied that his son would bring comfort (Gen. 5:28-32).

Noah is described as **"a just man, perfect in his generation"** who **"walked with God."** Noah's walking with God suggests that he and God were going in the same direction and that he was keeping in step with God, not lagging behind or running ahead. He kept himself free from the rampant immorality of his day, lived a life of holiness, and was sensitive to the Holy Spirit.

He was also a man of determination. In a faithless generation he remained faithful, working tirelessly to build the ark amid 120 years of scoffing. Imagine people listening to the same message for 120 years without really hearing it! The truth of a message can never be judged by the response to it.

Noah was "**moved with godly fear**" as he prepared the ark. This marvelous quality is a scarce commodity today. This fear is not that paralyzing terror that neutralizes effectiveness. It is a genuine respect for Almighty God that prompts true worship and makes sin repugnant rather than attractive. It is that fear of God which "begins wisdom," that awe which comes to the soul of one who truly knows God.

"**Noah found grace in the eyes of the Lord**" (Gen. 6:8). This is the first appearance of the word "grace" in scripture and it clearly indicates that, though Noah was a tireless worker, he was **not** accepted on the basis of his works. A man who had trouble with coyotes on his ranch decided to handle the problem in his own way. He rigged up an ingenious sapling cage trap to catch the coyotes in order to shoot them. On one occasion he decided to do something different. Instead of shooting the coyote, he tied a stick of dynamite to its neck, lit the fuse, and released the coyote. The coyote unobligingly ran under the man's pickup truck and blew it away! [1] It is even more disastrous to try to deal with our sins in our own way. God has a better plan!

"Noah found grace," but his works grew out of his faith. He not only "walked with God," he also worked with God. Someone said that we should not expect God to do through miracle what He expects us to do through muscle!

Second, consider **the times in which Noah lived. "The wickedness of man was great in the earth and every intent of the thoughts of his heart was only evil continually**" (Gen. 6:5). So great was the opposition to this man of faith that not a single person in 120 years responded positively to his preaching. Imagine a corruption so pervasive that the entire civilization had to be destroyed.

When civilization is on the skids the downhill slide seems irreversible.

We in the Church must never fail to see the distinction between righteousness and sinfulness. The antediluvians could not, and the resulting corruption demanded destruction. Paul urges, "Let everyone who names the name of Christ depart from iniquity" (2 Tim. 2:19). A disgruntled church member, unhappy with the imperfection of his church, compared it to Noah's ark and said, "If the flood on the outside were not so bad, you couldn't stand the smell on the inside." But even with all its faults, the Church is still beloved of its Lord. He is not through with us yet!

One fatal characteristic of Noah's day was **the breakdown of the sanctity of marriage and family life.** Hebrews 13:4 says, "Marriage is honorable among all, and the bed undefiled; but fornicators and adulterers God will judge." Bruce W. Thielman, pastor of First Presbyterian Church in Philadelphia, tells about his tenth-grade biology class in which his teacher fed a live white mouse to his pet four-foot boa constrictor. The students gathered around to watch the shiny, emerald-green serpent lying casually in beautiful folds in one corner of the cage. The teacher dropped a five-inch mouse into the cage. Totally unafraid the mouse, running all around the cage, up over the snake, over the folds, and right in front of its face seemed to be having a grand old time. Then, slowly but surely, the serpent began to move. It moved so slowly that the only way you could tell that it was moving was to watch the lines of print on the newspapers at the bottom of the cage disappear beneath its head. The mouse noticed the movement, but was not bothered by it. As the snake moved steadily and stealthily, the mouse became fascinated and then came to attention. Its tail wasn't stirring; it was totally engrossed in this moving, green thing. The mouse even sat up on its hind legs, holding its little paws like human hands. With whiskers still twitching, the mouse sat entranced as the snake came closer. Suddenly there was a blur of green faster than the eye could catch, and the snake coiled itself around its little victim. [2] Sin works that way. Sexual sin, particularly, fascinates, then mesmerizes, and the result is judgment.

Jesus said of Noah's time, "For as in the days before the flood, they were eating and drinking, marrying and giving in marriage, until the day that Noah entered the ark, and did not know until the flood came and took them all away, so also will the coming of the Son of Man be" (Matt. 24:38,39). Jesus was warning that we can become casual about a sinful environment.

The pilot thought that the few hundred pounds of ice on the wings wouldn't make a difference as he took off in the snowstorm from Washington National Airport. But the additional weight did make a difference. In a few moments over 100 people perished when the plane crashed in the Potomac River—lost because of carelessness. We dare not be nonchalant about the destructiveness of sin.

Noah's generation ridiculed the very thought of righteousness and judgment. They indulged in a false security. How could it possibly rain? What was rain? For that matter, what was an ark? But a righteous God must judge evil. His long-suffering must never be mistaken as reluctance to judge sin. God is no sentimentalist Who cannot bear the thought of judgment. Sin will be judged, if not here, then hereafter; but usually both here **and** hereafter.

A farmer was spraying a certain beetle that was threatening his crops. His little girl was upset with her father killing all those helpless little bugs. Her father patiently explained that their family was dependent on the garden and the beetles could literally cause them to starve. "You see," said the father, "I'm not so much opposed to beetles. It's just that I am for our garden."[3] God is opposed to anything that is destructive.

It is tragic to live in a sinful situation and not realize it. The reason Noah saw the exceeding sinfulness of sin was because he was walking with God. If we walk far from God we will be unable to see the danger of sin; and that which God condemns and weeps over we will see as "normal," something that "everybody is doing."

A young fellow out in the crowd decided to have some fun with an evangelist who was preaching about the weight of sin. He interrupted the evangelist by asking, "How much does this guilt of sin weigh? Ten pounds? Twenty pounds? A hundred pounds?" The evangelist thought for a minute and said, "Let me ask you a question. If you laid 200 pounds on a corpse would it feel the weight?" The youth answered, "No. It's dead." The evangelist responded, "That spirit is also dead that feels no load of sin."[4] When we can be in the presence of sin and fail to sense the weight of it, we are in great peril.

Mankind in Noah's day had sunk so low that the "intent of the thoughts of his heart was only evil continually" (Gen. 6:5). With immorality so acceptable, so widespread, today we seem to be fulfilling our Lord's prediction: "As it was in the days of Noah..."

Evidently Noah had help in the construction of the ark. He and his sons could never have built the ark alone. Construction began before his sons were born. Can you imagine his workers hearing Noah's warning for 120 years, and then perishing as the very ark they had helped build was carried away by the flood that drowned them? It is possible to be in sympathy with the Church, to sing its songs, never deny its right to preach, even support it to some extent, but still be left behind on the day when Jesus comes. God help us to never have a form of religion that denies the power of God!

Finally, **what of the operation of Noah's faith during those terrible days?** If we can understand how Noah was sustained we can be victorious in our time. **If Noah could not have endured, God would never have asked him to build the ark.** Jesus would never have summoned Peter to walk on the water if he could not have done so. Whatever your present test, be assured that you can be victorious else God would never have allowed it to happen. You can make it! Without doubting, "Let us hold fast the confession of our faith without wavering, for He Who promised is faithful" (Heb. 10:23). We determine whether Jesus Christ will be Lord of our lives, or if self will rule. There is no middle ground, no compromise, no fellowship between light and darkness. Jesus said, "No man can serve two masters; for either he will hate the one and love the other, or else he will be loyal to the one and despise the other. You cannot serve God and mammon." (Matt. 6:24)

Circumstances are not always encouraging. Noah obeyed God though for the entire 120 years he did not see one drop of rain. He must have been considered the most eccentric man of his day, but he pleased God as he faithfully worked. There may be no quick fix to your problem, but God is still in control! Trust Him! It was of Noah's day that our Lord said, "My Spirit shall not strive with man forever" (Gen. 6:3). A day will come when "the Lord Jesus is revealed from heaven...in flaming fire taking vengeance on those who do not know God, and on those who do not obey the gospel of the Lord Jesus Christ" (2 Thess. 1:7,8). If we think that living for God is difficult, we must remember that we are not only free from future judgment, but we also have the assurance of our Lord's Presence in every life situation.

We live in a day like Noah's. Free rein has been given to man's sensual desires. Standards concerning the home and family are ignored. Noah refused to be intimidated or influenced by his society. **His faith was built solidly on the Word of God.** Convictions must be built on the Word of God and not on the opinions of others. Convictions may prove costly, but do not be surprised. Every one of these men and women mentioned in this faith chapter paid a price for their confession. Though many have given their lives as martyrs, most of us have not resisted unto blood.

Millions of Christians have been inspired by the life and death of Dietrich Bonhoeffer, a German pastor who was killed during World War II. Bonhoeffer spoke out concerning the sins of Adolf Hitler as John the Baptist did of Herod. Friends in the United States and England, knowing the consequences of opposing Hitler, arranged for Bonhoeffer to leave Germany. However, after a few months Bonhoeffer returned to his homeland where he preached even more strongly against what was happening to his people. He aroused great opposition and was forced underground. Later he was imprisoned and martyred. Out of his struggles he wrote a monumental work, *The Cost of Discipleship*. It stands as a judgment on those who want Christ but refuse a cross. [5]

When Noah started building the ark there were only two people alive, he and his wife, who would ride out the storm. But, through his faithfulness, his entire family was saved. God rewards faithfulness! "He is a rewarder of those who diligently seek Him" (Heb. 11:6). Though Noah's contemporaries ignored him, God did not!

A day came when the ark was filled and God shut the door. There was only one door, and it was not left for Noah to close. God Himself did that. The occupants of the ark used the door twice: they entered and they exited. Jesus Christ is the Door, and no one can be saved other than by Him. He is not one of many; He is the ONLY Door! No one knows when this Door to safety will be closed. It may be today. But we do know it is now open for all who enter in. Some of the saddest lines in all of literature were uttered by the

Lord Jesus when He said they "did not know until the flood came and took them all away" (Matt. 24:39).

Hebrews is filled with such warnings. Noah was "divinely warned of things not yet seen." May God grant that all of us will be warned by this passage. No, it is not a "warm blanket," it may not make us comfortable...but it could save our souls!

Psychologist M. Scott Peck in his book, *The People of the Lie*, offers a glimpse of one of his toughest counseling situations with a lady he calls Charlene. At a crucial point in their counseling, Peck asked what the purpose of her life was, from a Christian point of view. "We exist for the glory of God," Charlene said in a flat low monotone as if she were sullenly repeating an alien catechism, learned by rote and extracted at gunpoint. "The purpose of our life," she said, "is to glorify God." "Well?" Peck asked. There was a short silence. For a brief moment Peck said he thought she might cry. "I cannot do it. There is no room for me in that. That would be my death," she said in a quavering voice. Then with a suddenness that frightened the psychologist, her choked-back sobs turned into a roar, "I don't want to live for God. I will not. I want to live for me, for my own sake." Charlene's outburst expresses the deepest and most profound cause of the guilt many of us carry. We want to live for ourselves. He had nothing to say to Charlene. He decided her case was hopeless. [6]

After 120 years of Noah's preaching, an entire generation proved hopeless. Such is not our case. Thank God, for us the Door is still open!

By faith Abraham, when he was tested, offered up Isaac, and he who had received the promises offered up his only begotten son, of whom it was said, "In Isaac your seed shall be called," concluding that God was able to raise him up, even from the dead, from which he also received him in a figurative sense.

Hebrews 11:17-19
(See also Genesis 22:1-19)

CHAPTER 28

A Father's Faith

(Study No. 28 in the Book of Hebrews)

This story concerning Abraham, if considered in isolation from the rest of his life, would be confusing. We must remember that this is one event in a long series of experiences Abraham had with God. If we read Genesis 22 and conclude that God suddenly appeared to Abraham demanding the death of his only son, we would certainly be confused about the character of God. At least six previous intimate experiences with God prepared Abraham for this unusual demand. There can be no doubt that this experience revealed the character of both Abraham and his God more than all the earlier encounters.

Abraham is "the father of the Hebrew nation," but more than the father of one nation exclusively. God's promise to him was "... in you all nations shall be blessed." When God laid His hand on Abraham's shoulder, He had all of us in mind, not just the Jews. In order to bless the world God chose a human instrument. God has always chosen to reach people through people. When God chooses someone to do His will He chooses one in sympathy with Him. A study of the seven encounters Abraham had with God reveals that his heart was in sympathy with the great heart of God. Consider each of these experiences.

First, when God came to Abraham in Ur of the Chaldeans the message from the Lord was simply, "Get up and get out" (Gen. 12:1-

3). The old Chaldean lifestyle was to be left behind and a new one embraced. In this initial encounter with God, Abraham learned that **God is a God of movement, of change, that God is discontented with things as they are, that He always moves ahead, that there is always a new experience.**

Abraham learned in the **second** appearance that **God not only calls from something, but to something** (Gen. 13:14-18). Abraham went from Chaldee to Canaan. All he had when he was camping in Canaan's land was an altar and a tent, everything a person really needs in life. In this instance God promised him land, lots of it. The lesson Abraham learned is one all of us need to know — a person with a tent and an altar centers his life around the altar. If the center is not correct, the circumference will be off kilter. Those who make the land or the tent (their possessions) central will experience a disturbing imbalance in their lives.

Genesis 15:1-6 records God's **third** contact with Abraham. An incredible promise was given to this aged couple. They are to have a son! At this juncture, "Abraham believed God and it was accounted unto him for righteousness." Here he learned **that faith produces patience.** An age that insists on "instant everything," glibly saying "now," to God must learn this same lesson; faith does not demand instant gratification. Daniel Webster, discussing with some of his friends what he considered the most beautiful passage in literature, slowly quoted these exquisite words: "Although the fig tree shall not blossom, neither shall fruit be in the vines; the labor of the olive shall fail, and the fields shall yield no meat; the flock shall be cut off from the fold, and there shall be no herd in the stalls; yet I will rejoice in the Lord, I will joy in the God of my salvation" (Hab. 3:17,18). Faith teaches that when things fail to happen as we think they ought, when our plans are put on hold, we hold even firmer to the promises of God.

In the **fourth** experience Abraham had a strange vision (Gen. 15:12-21) — a "horror and great darkness fell upon him." A prophecy was given that Abraham's children would be 400 years in Egyptian bondage and then come out with great possessions. Abraham learned **he was in fellowship with the God of History.** How can we be fearful knowing that our lives are in the hands of the God Who knows the beginning and the ending and everything in between?

When God came to Abraham the **fifth** time He revealed Himself as El Shaddai, the All-Sufficient One (Gen. 17:1). Though Abraham was now 99 years old the promised child had not been born. Through this encounter he learned that a 99 year-old man and a 90 year-old woman may become parents, obviously not by their natural powers, but because **God is sufficient.** Both the Word and the Spirit reveal God's sufficiency, no matter what the situation. Is this a lesson we need to learn?

In the **sixth** encounter (Gen. 18:16-33) Abraham interceded for Sodom. If we fail to understand the judgment of God we are wise to say, as Abraham did, "Shall not the Judge of all the earth do right?" Abraham learned **that he was in fellowship with a just God.** In an age when some confuse the love of God with sentimentality, this is a lesson desperately needed. God *may* be merciful, but He *must* be just.

These six truths that Abraham learned seemed to be contradicted in the **seventh** experience when he is suddenly commanded, "Take now your son, your only son Isaac, whom you love, and go to the land of Moriah, and offer him there as a burnt offering..." (Gen. 22:1). Human sacrifice was commonplace in Ur of the Chaldeans, but how could Jehovah make such a demand?

During this painful testing time Abraham learned **that God always has a reason for the events in our lives, though He seldom reveals them ahead of time.** Part of the "sweetness" of the "sweet by and by" will be an understanding of those things that happen in the "now and now." Until then, Romans 8:28 remains a statement of faith, not of understanding.

If anyone could have understood to some degree the agony of the Father's heart when He gave His only begotten Son, it would have been Abraham. Abraham was called into the fellowship of God's suffering. Did anyone ever tell you amidst great trials, "I know just how you feel," and you knew there was no way they could possibly understand? Common suffering brings people together like nothing else. Paul prayed, "That I may know Him and the power of His resurrection, and the fellowship of His suffering, being conformed to His death..." (Phil. 3:10). In this final revelation Abraham learned **to fellowship with his Lord in suffering.**

The wife of a young husband died leaving him with a small son. After the funeral they went home to bed. There was nothing else the father could think to do. As they lay in the darkness, numb with sorrow, the little boy broke the stillness with a disturbing question, "Daddy, where is mommy?" The father tried to get the boy to sleep, but the questions kept coming from his sad, confused mind. After a while the father got up and brought the son to his own bed, but the restless child kept probing with heartbreaking questions. Finally the youngster reached out a hand through the darkness, placed it on his father's face, and asked, "Daddy is your face toward me? If your face is toward me, I think I can go to sleep."[1] Our Father's face is toward us. We thank Him for that! There is no fellowship more precious than the fellowship of suffering. God was requiring of Abraham identification with the suffering He would experience 2000 years later.

Fathers should note the obedience of Abraham and children should consider the obedience of Isaac. A father can never be what he should be without obeying God. A father who urges his children to obey should be an example of obedience. A mother was working in the kitchen, preparing a special recipe for supper. Her little boy was running in and out, and ignoring his mother's threats. When he finally knocked the special dish off the table, his mother grabbed a broom and started after him. He crawled under the house so she decided to let her husband take care of him. As soon as the father arrived, she yelled, "Go discipline your son! Do something about your son!" The father crawled under the house, saw two bright eyes peering around a pillar, and heard a soft voice ask, "Dad is she after you too?" Discipline is never easy, but always necessary.

Like the Lord Jesus Himself, Abraham persisted in obedience. Notice the basis of this persistence - his determination to carefully obey God—"The lad and I will go yonder and worship, and we will come back to you" (Gen. 22:5). Hebrews says that Abraham was "concluding" (accounting, KJV) that God was able to raise Isaac up, even from the dead..." (Heb. 11:19). "Concluding" or "accounting" means "arguing within oneself to reach a conclusion." How did Abraham conclude that God would raise Isaac from death? He came to this conviction because he had learned to know God in the six earlier encounters with Him. Those earlier experiences prepared him for this moment. This faith, accounted to him as righteousness, was rational for it was based on the character of Almighty God. It always makes sense to have faith in the All-Sufficient One. Faith is built on a knowledge that flows from a relationship with God.

Without faith in God we will never be our best intellectually. The rich farmer who left God out of his life was not called a sinner by our Lord; he was called a fool. The five virgins who failed in preparing to meet the bridegroom were also fools. Lack of faith not only affects the heart, it affects the head as well. Those who come to know the Savior wonder, "Why didn't I do this earlier? How foolish I have been." Anyone who misses heaven will have all eternity to reflect on their foolishness in not accepting the Lord Jesus and living for Him.

The pain that God would feel over the death of His Son was felt to some degree by Abraham in spite of the assurance that Isaac would be raised from the dead. **Faith never dulls feelings.** Hebrews says of the death of Jesus, "...Who for the joy that was set before Him endured the cross, despising the shame, and has sat down at the right hand of the throne of God" (Heb. 12:2). Though joy awaited, endurance was necessary. If He was to have the joy, He had to travel the way of the cross...so He endured it.

Allow the Holy Spirit to speak clearly on this issue, for here we often fail God, ourselves and others. We seldom long to identify with the Savior in suffering. When we think of surrendering time, money, abilities, or position our flesh resists. When Peter urged Jesus not to go the way of the cross, Jesus replied, "Get behind me, Satan" (Matt. 16:23). It is here that many fail the Lord.

It is fitting for a father to be willing to sacrifice for the Savior. If a father is not willing to lay all on the altar for his Lord, how can he be the kind of father he ought to be? The father who best fulfills his position in the home is never a stranger to sacrifice. He willingly sacrifices for his children. When Mother Teresa received the Nobel Prize a man asked her, "What can we do to help promote world peace?" She replied, "Go home and love your family."

A married couple went to their pastor for counseling. At one point in the counseling session the husband said to the wife, "I've given you everything you've ever asked for—a new home, a new car, all the clothes you can wear..." The list went on. When he had finished the wife sadly said, "That much is true. You have given me everything but one thing—yourself."

Isaac escaped death because a substitute was found; but no one took the Lord Jesus' place. "God so loved that He gave." He gave Himself. What an incredible price He paid for our redemption that we might claim Him as Father.

By faith Isaac blessed Jacob and Esau concerning things to come.
Hebrews 11:20

CHAPTER 29

Isaac, the Passive Patriarch

(Study No. 29 in the Book of Hebrews)

The writer of Hebrews tells how three men of faith—Isaac, Jacob, and Joseph—approached death (Heb. 11:20-22). It is important to **live** a life of faith, but it is imperative that we **die** with faith. As we grow older, we begin to anticipate the end of our earthly life. Faith gives peace as we prepare to face life on the other side of the grave.

Isaac, the son of Abraham, has been called the "the passive patriarch." Consider first, **the man, Isaac;** second, **his deterioration;** and finally, **the ultimate victory of his faith.** His story can help us in our walk with God.

The man, Isaac did not have a biography as impressive or exciting as Abraham's. **He seems passive in his approach to life.** He is not as aggressive, creative, or visionary as his father. Abraham got up and got out of the land of his birth. Isaac was the only patriarch who **never left the borders of the Promised Land.** He seems to be a retiring, gentle individual, one who would go out into the fields in the evening to meditate on the things of God. This does not imply that he was weak or incapable, but that he expressed his faith in a more passive way than his father, or Jacob his son.

He could have been like that person who arouses your concern when he absents himself from Christian fellowship. As long as he is with other Christians he stands, but with unbelievers he wavers. Conflict with the world system is inevitable, and we must face it

259

without becoming entangled. Paul said, "You therefore must endure hardship as a good soldier of Jesus Christ. No one engaged in warfare entangles himself with the affairs of this life, that he may please Him Who enlisted him as a soldier" (2 Tim. 2:3, 4). We must be militant in our stance for God!

The Waldenses were an eleventh century group of Christians that had to hide in the valleys of the Alps because of their Christian testimony. Persecuted and despised, they still shared their simple faith. They had little of this world's goods, yet gave generously to God. As they traveled across the continent, selling precious stones and other wares, they would often go into the homes of nobility. After they had shown their wares, they would gather the household members together and say, "We have one more precious Gem, far more valuable than all of the others, which we would like to share with you. This Gem will open the knowledge of God to your hearts." When the family would ask to purchase this precious Gem, a Waldensian would carefully unwrap a hidden Bible and point the family to Christ. In the face of persecution and at the risk of their own lives, they would share the Word of God. We admire those who, notwithstanding the dangers, become involved in service for their Lord. [1] A passive person shuns a demanding life.

Abraham gave all that he had to his son, Isaac (Gen. 25:5). Sometimes a gift from others is a burden in that it stifles initiative. Second-generation Christianity is no substitute for an up-to-date experience. Indeed, a hand-me-down Christianity can inoculate one against an authentic Christian experience.

Abraham, concerned that his son could marry a Canaanite who might turn him away from his faith, sent his servant, Eliezer, back to his homeland to get a bride for Isaac. Evidently, Isaac had confidence in the judgment of his father's trusted servant. Later, Isaac and Rebekah would be heartbroken over their son, Esau's marriage to two Hittite women.

If Isaac was passive, as we suspect, the old-timer Eliezer, probably did a lot better than Isaac would have done in choosing a bride. When God led Eliezer to Rebekah he bowed his head and asked God if this young lady was really everything she seemed to be. The council of a third party is valuable to those planning to be married. It helps when family and friends approve of a marriage. Eliezer would have been a wise counselor later on when the marriage experienced hard times.

The meeting of Isaac and Rebekah is one of the most romantic in scripture. He was virile and she was beautiful. Isaac wanted a son and Rebekah wanted to be the mother of a special race. But for 20 years they were denied children. The twins that were finally born to them would each in their own way, break their parent's hearts.

So Isaac and Rebekah did not "live happily ever after." The marriage wore thin and by the time the twins, Jacob and Esau, made their appearance Isaac and Rebekah had all the ingredients that produce conflicts. Esau was no match against a scheming mother who doted on his brother, Jacob. Isaac, on the other hand, was drawn to the hunter, Esau.

Isaac was given everything by his father. Eliezer brought him a beautiful wife. Esau, his favorite son, brought him savory venison. It is easy for a man who has so much given to him to become passive. His wife was dominating and scheming, twisting the world into the right shape for her favorite son, Jacob. What an explosive domestic situation! Isaac poured his love on Esau, and Rebekah countered with shrewd manipulations designed to discredit Esau and exalt Jacob. Instead of loving each other more after the children came, Isaac and Rebekah transferred their love to their favorite child. Nobody wins in that kind of investment!

What could have prevented this troublesome situation? For one thing, they needed someone to help them see their problems objectively. I wonder what happened to old Eliezer. How they could have used a trusted, wise, third party! We often go quickly to others for prayer and counsel when we are ill, but we are slow to admit problems in family relationships. Pride should never stand in the way of a successful marriage. One wise minister said bluntly to a young groom, "Now that you've caught the fish, don't throw the bait away." Both husband and wife must work at their relationship.

One of the unique facts about Isaac was **his determination to dig wells** (Gen. 26:18-35). He redug Abraham's wells which the Philistines had filled. When Isaac's servants dug a productive well in the Valley of Gerar the herdsmen of Gerar quarreled with Isaac's herdsmen. Isaac responded, "Let's call this well Esek (contention) and move to another location." When his crew uncovered another well a similar quarrel developed. Isaac said, "We'll call this well Sitnah (opposition) and move on." Finally they dug a well over which no quarrel developed. I have an idea that if Isaac's father, Abraham, had been challenged over the ownership of either one of those wells he would have made his enemies sorry that they had ever raised the question; and if Isaac's son, Jacob, had ever dealt with anyone who questioned his ownership, he would have bargained with them over the well and they would have ended up trading all their cattle for a few gallons of water per month! But Isaac does not seem to be of that nature. If there was going to be contention or opposition over a well he would simply dig another one, and another one, until he could call one Rehoboth, the name of the last well, which means "room for everyone."

How does one explain **Isaac's deterioration**? It is best seen in the account of **the giving of the blessing of birthright.** Isaac wanted to bless Esau, the son who fed him. He loved Esau's venison. It seems that Isaac was governed by appetite. He wanted Esau to hunt a deer, kill it and cook it, and **then** he would give the blessing. Food first...then the blessing!

All this in spite of the fact that God had said the divine blessing would be upon Jacob, not Esau. There was no effort to stop the purpose of God, but **to do it another way!** That temptation is ever with us. We may not argue about the purpose of God, yet strive to accomplish it **our** way! When we think we are helping God out we are **flesh governed!** Isaac touched Jacob and thought he was feeling Esau. Thus he teaches us not to walk by feeling, but by faith! Isaac's spiritual discernment was no better then his physical eyesight. God used Moses, Joshua, and many others in their old age, but there is no record of Isaac being productive in the remaining 43 years after his deception.

A low point in Isaac's degeneration was **when he told Abimelech, King of the Philistines, that Rebekah was his sister** (Gen. 26:6-11). He was afraid the men of Gerar would kill him for his wife, so he lied to save his own skin. Rebekah's respect for her husband must have suffered after such an episode. After an incident like that a woman might decide to take things into her own hands! How could God, she might have reasoned, trust a man like Isaac to carry out His purposes?

Tragically, as a result of Rebekah's scheming, she evidently never got to see Jacob again. No matter how we justify our schemes, God does His will His way! God brings to pass what He says. We spend time "helping God out" as if He were a million miles away, unconcerned about His children, yet He is as close as the breath in our bodies!

Consider **the ultimate victory of Isaac's faith.** First, this is evident in **the blessing he pronounced on Jacob.** He expected the blessing of God upon his offspring. God honored the patriarchs not because they deserved it, but because they had faith!

Isaac manifested faith **when Esau entreated him to change the blessing and he refused.** Hebrews 12:17 records, "For you know that afterward, when he (Esau) wanted to inherit the blessing, he was rejected, for he found no place for repentance, though he sought it diligently with tears." Despite his tears he could not get his father to repent, i.e., to change his mind. "By faith Isaac blessed Jacob and Esau." When God, by His own grace, overrules our foolishness we must say, "Amen" and not insist on our own way. David, when his terrible sin was laid before him by Nathan, cried out to God for forgiveness and cleansing. He offered no alibi, made no accusation against Bathsheba, nor did he claim that circumstances had over-whelmed him. He owned up to his sin and asked for forgiveness. Peter failed miserably after boasting that he would never defect from following the Savior. But bitter weeping led to his restoration. Isaac could not be persuaded by Esau to go against the will of God. Some of the darkest hours of our lives come when we set ourselves against the will of God. Isaac refused to do that.

Though Isaac may have been weak here is proof **that faith in God is victorious over personal weakness.** God repeatedly says, "I am the God of Abraham, Isaac, and Jacob." We have little prob-lem with the God Who is the "God of Abraham," but oh, what grace makes Him "the God of Isaac" or "the God of Jacob"! Isaac, whether passive or active, was loved by God. How encouraging!

The writer refers to Isaac, Jacob, and Joseph as old men about to die (vv. 20-22). Whatever our age we do not know how much longer we have in this present life. We cannot afford to waste a moment! If we are to die in faith we must live in faith...Now!

By faith Jacob, when he was dying, blessed each of the sons of Joseph, and worshiped, leaning on the top of his staff.

Hebrews 11:21
(See also Genesis 32:22-32 and Hosea 12:3-5)

CHAPTER 30

Jacob, Prodigal and Prince

(Study No. 30 in the Book of Hebrews)

One might search long to find a more interesting person than Jacob, son of Isaac, grandson of Abraham. Jehovah, Who had appeared to Abraham seven times, appeared to Jacob five times, but always with a different purpose than when He appeared to Abraham. Each manifestation to Abraham brought him closer to God until he at last was asked to sacrifice his son. The six earlier appearances had so deepened his relationship with God he was now ready to actually offer his son in worship as a sacrifice. With each successive revelation of God, Abraham's faith grew.

The appearances of God to Jacob, however, were corrective in nature. They had to do with his blunders, with getting him back on track. God wants to finish what He begins. Paul puts it this way: "Being confident of this very thing, that He Who has begun a good thing in you will complete it until the day of Jesus Christ" (Phil.1:6).

Jacob ultimately became a changed man, but his transformation was not immediate. Sorrows, heartaches, disappointments plagued him along the way. As we consider Jacob's experiences we may discover ourselves in this "plotting prodigal."

Jacob knew how to use others. He is like the man who walked into the post office, bought a card, then turned to the man next to him and requested, "Sir, would you mind addressing this card for me?" The man, willing to assist a fellow who could not write, gladly helped him out. When he handed the card back, the man asked for another favor. "I hate to bother you again," he continued, "but would you mind writing a short message on the card for me?" The kind gentleman agreed to this second request and wrote out the dictated message. He gave the completed card to the man who looked at it for a moment and then asked one final favor. "I know this is an imposition, but would you do one more thing for me? At the end of the message would you please apologize for the horrible handwriting?"[1] Those who dealt with Jacob probably felt used also!

First, consider **Jacob, the prodigal.** He was not a teenager when he ran away from home after defrauding his brother, Esau, of his birthright and blessing. He was 70 when he fled for his life and 90 when he returned. When it came to cleverness he was more than a match for Esau, but no amount of cleverness would save his skin after tricking his brother twice. Esau asked, "Is he not rightly named Jacob? For he has supplanted (tricked) me these two times. He took away my birthright, and now look, he has taken away my blessing."

If Jacob's **motives** were right, his **methods** were surely wrong. He cannot be blamed for wanting his father's blessing, but he went about it the wrong way. He showed **faith** by believing he was the one to be blessed by his father, but he showed **fear** in "helping God out" by trickery. This curious mixture of faith and fear is seen in his taking advantage of his hungry brother.

Jacob might have endorsed the half-truth, "God helps those who help themselves." There is a sense in which that saying is true, but God does not help those who think they help God by their own cleverness. Someone might reason, "God told me that I should do thus-and-so; now I must take this action to make sure it happens." God doesn't need our craftiness.

This plotting prodigal, Jacob, also proved to be too much for his father-in-law, Laban. Laban is one of the meanest men in the Old Testament. Never turn your back on a person like Laban. He was one who actually could "get blood out of a turnip!" We take no pleasure in Jacob's scheming, but one could feel good about his getting the best of a con-artist like Laban! Jacob's own words to Laban were, "I have been in your house for 20 years; I have served you for 14 years for your two daughters, and six years for your flock, and you have changed my wages 10 times" (Gen. 31:41). Laban could not charge Jacob with dishonesty, for he had never robbed him; he simply outwitted him!

These two schemers parted with what has become known as the Mizpah Benediction: "May the Lord watch between you and me when we are absent one from another" (Gen. 31:49). This is a beautiful expression, but when originally spoken it was an agreement between two schemers who could rip-off their closest friend. "May the Lord watch between you and me..." is a good prayer when dealing with someone like Laban or Jacob! One is not surprised to hear Jacob called a "worm" in Isaiah 41:14!

After 20 years, when Jacob was finally on his way home with his family and possessions, he heard that Esau was coming to meet him with 400 men. His first thought was, "How can I help God save me from this precarious predicament?" He remembered both of his parents had been quick to "assist God" in accomplishing His will; it was a trait he had observed first-hand.

Jacob's first tactic was to divide his company so half of them might escape if Esau attacked the other. Then, to appease Esau, he arranged for successive droves of livestock to be presented as gifts. If Esau were still angry after the first drove was presented, then the second drove would be given to him; if still unhappy, the third would follow. Jacob's mind was working as it had all his days, "Sure, God has promised to bless me and my lineage, but I've simply got to take care of this situation." He thought something was always left undone; there just had to be something for him to do! This is the man who was to meet God face to face that night at Peniel.

That dark night, as he anxiously anticipated the arrival of Esau and his 400 men, Jacob's life was to take a sudden and dramatic turn. He, who had proven himself craftier than his brother Esau, his father Isaac, and his uncle Laban now was paralyzed with fear. The gifts to Esau were confessions that deep down he knew he was wrong. His mind might not agree that he had sinned, but his heart could not deny it.

What a self-reliant believer! He believed it was God's will that he have the birthright. To make sure, he had cheated his hungry brother out of it. He sincerely believed he was to have the patriarchal blessing. Why not use a little subterfuge to make sure? Every error he made was to "help God" out of a "difficult situation." The desire to manipulate people and control events is with us today even in religious circles. It is often cleverly done under the guise of spirituality and with Madison Avenue techniques!

Jacob desperately needed to realize that God could do very well without his cleverness. He needed to accept God's deliverance as a **gift** rather than a victory which "he and God" had collaborated in achieving. Some of the so-called "great works" done by "God and man" in our day have crumbled. God doesn't need our cleverness or inventiveness to accomplish His purposes.

But Jacob was to become **a prince with God.** It happened that night at Peniel when God, appearing as a Man, engaged Jacob in a wrestling match. Jacob came face to face, not only with God, but with his own weakness. Hosea tells how Jacob struggled with the Angel and prevailed, not because he was courageous or confident, but because "he wept, and sought favor from Him" (Hos. 12:3-5). This was more than simply a physical wrestling match, for no one wins a physical contest by prayer and tears. The distinguishing feature of the conflict was the weeping and the supplication, not the physical strength or determination of Jacob. Some think Jacob was so determined to be blessed that he demanded it. While this is true in a sense, if that had been the only attitude he manifested God may have destroyed him instantly. It was through a newly acquired humility and self-surrender that he prevailed. He also prevailed because God permitted him to do so. Submission was a difficult assignment for Jacob as it is for many who fear vulnerability. Some men will drive a hundred miles off course rather than stop and ask directions. Men often have difficulty verbalizing emotions. One little boy was told, "Big boys don't cry." Later he took a bad spill without shedding a tear. "I've learned," he explained, "to cry in my brain." Jacob would have profited by admitting earlier that he needed help.

We can not get God into a corner and secure His help to accomplish our will. **His** will must be done on earth. That must be our desire. Genesis 32:24 says, "A Man wrestled with him." It does not say Jacob wrestled with the Man, although that is true. We must remember that it was **God Who initiated this struggle!** The Angel was not crippled; it was Jacob who suffered the limp! He was never the same after meeting with God that night. No more self-sufficiency! What a blessing that God crippled him!

During the wrestling Jacob said, "I will not let You go unless You bless me." He said these words while weeping and seeking the favor of God. Although he had received a blessing from his father by deceit, this one was sought with tears. At last he was ready to confess his failure. Failure can then be turned into victory—a victory that exalts God, not human flesh. Years later, Jacob referred to this angel as "the Angel Who redeemed me from all evil" (Gen. 48:16).

The scripture says of Jacob, "Just as he crossed over Peniel the sun rose on him, and he limped on his hip" (Gen. 32:31). Did he notice this affliction? A wounded soldier sometimes becomes aware of his injury only when he notices that he is bleeding. He is so absorbed with the conflict that all else, even his own wounds, are unnoticed. It is logical to believe Jacob had been so overtaken by the Presence of God that he failed to notice his wounded thigh. The person who has had an encounter with God is not so quick to point out the difference in his life as others are to notice it. God, Who crippled Jacob because He loved him, can do the same today.

This experience changed Jacob's name to Israel, which means "God will rule," "God-governed," or "God controlled."[2] A "God-governed" man allows God to go before him and turn enemies into friends. Jacob, limping now toward Esau, completely powerless, had cast himself upon the mercy of God. Earlier one might have felt uneasy around Jacob, a man who probably never had a close friend. But now his most dangerous enemy, the brother who had threatened to kill him, fell on his neck, kissed him, and wept with him! It was not the 20 years of absence that changed Esau, but rather, the fact that Jacob had turned everything over to God.

Jacob lived through much sorrow after this life-changing night. No experience with God will produce a life free from stress. He had to bury Rachel, the bride of his youth; he had to grieve over a blood-stained many-colored coat, apparent evidence that Joseph had been killed by an animal. But his sorrow changed to joy when he found his beloved Joseph, alive and well. Joseph, who instituted the first rationing system recorded in history, not only saved Egypt, but Jacob's family as well.

From this night on Jacob blessed others. When this aged grandfather was asked to bless Joseph's children, Manasseh and Ephraim, he crossed his hands, placing his right hand on Ephraim's head and his left on Manasseh's. Joseph protested that Manasseh, the eldest, was to receive the blessing, but Jacob let him know that he knew what he was doing. The scripture calls him Israel, "God-governed, God controlled," as he blesses the boys. He not only knew what he was doing, he also "worshiped, leaning on the top of his staff." A transformed person worships God and refuses to rely on his own strength.

Some of us, like Jacob, struggle independently, trying to make it on our own. We work long and hard at doing it our own way. If we insist on that pattern, and if God loves us as much as He loved Jacob, we will run headlong into a crisis. As in Jacob's situation, God will lay His hand upon our weakness and we will "limp" ever after. God comes in mercy to lay His hand on us. Instead of managing our own lives, we must submit to Him. Though He cripples the crippling can turn a prodigal into a prince!

Jacob's experience surely teaches us that God always has the last word! He has demonstrated this by sending His Son—*God's Final Answer!*

*By faith Joseph, when he was dying, made mention of the depar-
ture of the children of Israel, and gave instructions concerning his
bones.*

Hebrews 11:22
(See also Genesis 37-50)

CHAPTER 31

Joseph, the Man Whose Faith Was Tested

(Study No. 31 in the Book of Hebrews)

This chapter shows that faith in God touches all of life, accomplishing incredible victories for some, while sustaining others in apparent defeats. These heroes of faith were called to diverse tasks, and therefore, manifested different qualities of faith. "Abel represented **redemption** through faith; Enoch exemplified the **walk** of faith; Noah demonstrated the **confession** of faith. Abraham manifested the **obedience** of faith; Isaac, the **meekness** of faith; Jacob, the **training** of faith; and Joseph, the **triumph** of faith."[1]

All of us exercise a different type of faith. God has an exclusive plan for every life. Those who give faith "formulas" promising desired and predictable results need to seriously study this chapter. It teaches that faith in God sustains in **any** life experience, not simply those which have a "fortunate" conclusion. This chapter shows faith operating in a variety of circumstances.

A study of the relationship between faith and death in chapter eleven would make an interesting review. Isaac, Jacob, and Joseph manifested faith during their final days. The words, "Jacob, when he was dying," and "Joseph, when he was dying" indicate that a living faith suffices in death, a death which glorifies God. Though he could have chosen many other interesting facts about Joseph, the writer of Hebrews refers only to Joseph's faith. Above all the exemplary qualities in his life, it was his faith that pleased God.

Genesis begins with the words, "In the beginning God" and ends with, "a coffin in Egypt," a dismal scenario caused by sin. The bones in that coffin were Joseph's.

The final fourteen chapters of Genesis record his story. Joseph, Daniel, and Mordecai, three Jewish men went into foreign countries and rose to positions of great prominence. Joseph and Daniel lived such exemplary lives that their characters seem flawless. Joseph is perhaps more like Christ than any other Bible character.

In verse 22 we see first, **his instructions when he was about to die;** second, **the faith that prompted his instructions;** and finally, **how his instructions harmonized with his entire life.**

His dying instructions were "You shall carry up my bones from here" (Gen. 50:25). His bones were to be taken out of Egypt to Canaan. **What a strange request!** Why did Joseph think the Israelis would leave Egypt and return to a land that had not been kind to them? Did Canaan create pleasant memories in Joseph's mind? One would think that everything that happened to him there—the death of his mother when he was only a boy, the hatred of his brothers, and being sold into slavery—would have made Canaan distasteful. His brothers' last memory of Canaan was being driven out by famine. His request had to spring from faith rather than logic.

The request concerning his bones was not only strange, **it seemed ridiculous.** They were living in favorable and comfortable circumstances in Egypt. The irrigated plains were ideal for their flocks. Later descendants would be in slavery; but how could Joseph know? He had a faith that looked beyond the present, a faith that told him that his people would go back to Canaan. Joseph believed **they were the people of God.** His bones were to acknowledge that they were people of destiny, that they were meant to possess the Land of Promise.

Joseph also knew by faith that **he would not be alive when they marched out of Egypt.** If someone inquired a few years after Joseph's death about the great prime minister who saved the then-known world from starvation, people would ask, "Who was that?" People forget. God never forgets! Joseph's bones, carried into the Promised Land, testified to continuity, to his belonging to the purposes of God. This was an inspirational, symbolic act for all Israel. When Christians come out of "Egypt" we are to let the world know that we are God's people. No one should have to **guess** about that.

Second, consider **the faith that prompted his instructions.** When people are urged not to look at the circumstances the reference is always to negative circumstances. Joseph knew that the Israelites were enjoying positive circumstances, but he predicted the present conditions would not last. This dying man predicted the storm long before it broke! Would some today chide him for not being more positive? "He made mention of the departure of the children of Israel." By faith, he looked into the future, where no human eye could see, and saw the divine purpose. When we face death eternal things matter while temporal things lose their significance. What really matters in all circumstances is a relationship with God. These men of faith all died without having received the promise; but they died in hope rather than despair. We all have unfulfilled dreams, but God has called us to faith in Him whatever the situation.

How could a boy of 17 be carried away captive into a hostile, idolatrous society, out of contact with any other believer in God, with no Scripture to read, amid all sorts of temptations, and still be true to his Lord? He was falsely accused and thrown into prison for 13 years, but none of this disturbed his faith in God.

During trials we have the choice of responding like Jacob or like Joseph. Jacob said, "All these things are against me" (Gen. 42:36), while Joseph's response was, "You meant evil against me; but God meant it for good" (Gen. 50:20). Do we deal with difficulties by the "Jacob approach" or the "Joseph approach?" If Joseph had picked up his father's attitude, life would have been filled with perpetual complaint! God cannot use a whiner. Joseph not only fed a devastated world, he also saved the Hebrew people.

Joseph's request concerning his bones seemed strange, even ridiculous, but **it harmonized with his entire life.** Consider **the incident with Potiphar's wife.** Potiphar trusted Joseph implicitly, but day by day, Potiphar's wife tried to seduce this handsome young man. Joseph not only persistently refused her advances, he tried to avoid her. His two-fold motive for maintaining his morality was keeping his master's trust and knowing that such a sin would be principally against God.

He could have rationalized, "Who could ever know? My position would be more secure. If I don't submit I could lose everything. We are both consenting adults. God made me with these desires; why not satisfy them? After all, everyone sows some wild oats."

Joseph's temptation came unexpectedly and persistently. It is always necessary to take a strong stance against temptation immediately. Saying "no" immediately makes succeeding temptations easier to resist. Saying "no" when one is alone is evidence of strong character. Joseph fled from Potiphar's wife perhaps fearful of his ability to continue to withstand. If we think we could never handle temptation as Joseph did remember that there is a time to stand and a time to flee, but victory is available in either case. Joseph knew that God was there and that sin is always an offense to Him.

Though Joseph was pure in his lifestyle, loyal to his master, and virtuous in his character, **he was charged with attempted rape and thrown into prison.** Mrs. Potiphar could not have known she was helping to prepare this young man for a glorious future.

God gave Joseph favor in prison and "whatever they did there, it was his doings" (Gen. 39:22). Imagine being in prison and carrying the keys! God's blessing was upon Joseph in prison just as it had been in Potiphar's house. God's **way** is the best way, God's **time** is the best time, and God's **grace** is sufficient. With God **down** is sometimes the way **up!**

A person of lesser convictions might have despaired up at this turn of events. Joseph had seen God work in adversity as well as in benediction. Charles Spurgeon once preached in Surrey Music Garden in London where some 20,000 people crowded to hear him. Some foolish person in jest cried, "Fire!" and several in the frightened crowd were trampled to death. Spurgeon was so broken that his mind tottered for days. He thought he would never preach again, but God used that terrible situation to deeply work in Spurgeon's own life. [2] Joseph evidently believed Romans 8:28 long before it was written!

His fellow inmates soon learned that Joseph could help them. When the baker and the butler asked him to interpret their dreams he responded, "Do not interpretations belong to God?" He acknowledged God as the Giver of spiritual gifts. Each time Joseph used a spiritual gift the results were significant. If using our gifts fails to bless others we should be concerned.

Though Joseph's true interpretations should have secured his release from prison **he was forgotten for two full years!** When one is forgotten the temptation to despair is strong. This was a new temptation for Joseph. As a child, he had never been forgotten by his father. As a teen-ager, he was never forgotten by his brothers. Mrs. Potiphar surely never forgot him. Now for two years he was forgotten by men and, seemingly, by God. Such a trial often leads to hopelessness.

When he at last was remembered by the butler and brought **before Pharaoh** he then had to respond to the temptation of a high position. The most difficult temptations may not come in times of severe need. Some handle themselves well during times of stress only to fail in times of prosperity.

Joseph's answer to Pharaoh concerning his dream was the same he had given to the prisoners, "It is not in me; God will give Pharaoh an answer of peace." He refused to draw attention to himself. What a blessing when the gifts and fruit of the Spirit are present in the same vessel. The gifts of God should be accompanied by strong character.

The dreams Joseph interpreted in prison had private application, but the one he interpreted for Pharaoh had national and international consequences. Can you imagine domestic or foreign policy being based on the interpretation of someone's dream? The Word of God and the Spirit of God are unquestionable Guides, but God can also speak to us through dreams.

Joseph's meeting with his brothers who had sold him into slavery is one of the most dramatic moments in the entire Bible. At last he could get revenge. We might expect him to say, "Look at me! You harbored murder in your hearts against me and sold me into slavery. I told you that you would bow down before me some day. Now, down on your knees! You can see that through my diligence and intelligence I have secured a high office here in Egypt. Prepare to pay for your injustice."

Who could have blamed him for such a response? But notice his words: "Do not be grieved or angry with yourselves because

you sold me here; for God sent me before you to preserve life...
So now it was not you who sent me here, but God" (Gen. 45:5, 8).
Not an ounce of bitterness or resentment had festered in him over
the years. How we respond to life's situations is **as** important, if not
more, than the situations themselves.

Joseph's benevolent attitude did not mean that he ignored his
brothers' sins. "But as for you," he said, "you meant evil against
me; but God meant it for good" (Gen. 50:20). We are not to simply
"put up with" aggravating situations; we must see God working
in them for our good. God had not sent Joseph to Egypt simply to
work for Potiphar or Pharaoh, but for the salvation of the people of
God. What a difference when we acknowledge the "big picture."

God was working all things together for good in Joseph's life.
So Joseph could say, "Years from now when you are leaving this
land take my body with you. God will lead us out just as He led us
into Egypt. The greatest things are yet to come!"

The commentary on Joseph's request and his faith is given in
Exodus 13:18, 19: "So God led the people around by way of the
wilderness of the Red Sea. And the children of Israel went up in
orderly ranks out of the land of Egypt. And Moses took the bones
of Joseph with him, for he (Joseph) had placed the children of Israel
under solemn oath, saying, "God will surely visit you, and you shall
carry up my bones from here with you."

A striking truth in this story is that none of us have to be "one of
the crowd." We can stand tall and live for God without compromise
whatever others may do. And this we will do if we share Joseph's
testimony, "I fear God" (Gen. 42:18).

By faith Moses, when he was born, was hidden three months by his parents, because they saw he was a beautiful child; and they were not afraid of the king's command. By faith Moses, when he became of age, refused to be called the son of Pharaoh's daughter, choosing rather to suffer the affliction with the people of God than to enjoy the passing pleasures of sin, esteeming the reproach of Christ greater riches than the treasures of Egypt; for he looked to the reward. By faith he forsook Egypt, not fearing the wrath of the king; for he endured as seeing Him who is invisible. By faith he kept the Passover and the sprinkling of the blood, lest he who destroyed the firstborn should touch them. By faith they passed through the Red Sea as by dry land; whereas the Egyptians, attempting to do so, were drowned.

Hebrews 11:23-29

CHAPTER 32

Moses' Legacy of Faith
(Study No. 32 in the Book of Hebrews)

What a joy to see the faith of parents and grandparents repro-
duced in their offspring. The faith of Moses' parents was
duplicated in Moses himself. Verse 23 refers not to Moses' faith, but
to the faith of his parents. The story in Exodus 2:1-6 only records
that baby Moses cried.

Moses' parents, Amram and Jochebed, were part of the multitude of Hebrews who were enslaved during the years following
Joseph's death. Another Pharaoh, one "who did not know Joseph"
(Ex. 1:8), had ordered that all new-born male Hebrew children be
slain. When Moses was three months old and could no longer be
hidden, his mother Jochebed fashioned a basket from bulrushes,
waterproofed it, and placed its precious cargo in the reeds along the
Nile River. Miriam, Moses' older sister, was sent to observe.

This action revealed **the faith of Moses' parents.** The previous three illustrations of faith in Isaac, Jacob and Joseph have to do
with death; this example has to do with birth. Faith in God encom-
passes all of life!

What comfort to know such faith can be born in the hearts of
two obscure slaves! This husband and wife, working in harmony,
were yoked together by a mutual love and a beautiful child. Here is
an act of **love** born out of a **faith** that inspired **hope.** The parents did
not know what would happen when they placed their baby on the

Nile; but when they laid him on that river of death they laid him on the heart of God, trusting their child would be spared.

Their faith created boldness. "They were not afraid of the king's command," but were persuaded of a Power higher than Pharaoh's. They heard the king, but they also heard God! Faith drives fear from the heart. We submit to government until we are asked to compromise the will of God. The Egyptian king violated the law of God which forbids murder. In such cases we must disobey government, "For God has not given us a spirit of fear, but of power, love, and of self-control" (2 Tim. 1:7 TCNT).

Though faith created boldness it **did not make them irrational.** Jochebed waterproofed the basket, put it where Pharaoh's daughter was apt to notice it, and sent Miriam to observe. Miriam heard Pharaoh's daughter request her maidens to bring the ark; she watched as the princess opened it and heard the little boy's cry as he looked up into the strange Egyptian face. Miriam, seeing the expression on the Egyptian girl's face, chose that precise moment to ask, "Shall I go and call a nurse for you from among the Hebrew women?"

Thus Moses was restored to his mother who taught him about Abraham, Isaac, Jacob, and Joseph. Thus he would know that he was one of God's chosen. Why would he otherwise have defended a mistreated Israeli slave or have been disturbed at seeing two of his Israeli brothers fighting among themselves? As a parent should, she taught him the legacy of faith.

Faith is rational. Faith and foolishness are incompatible. Though faith rises above the rational, it is not irrational. Faith believes in God, but also appeals to reason. Hiding Moses for three months broke Egyptian law. There is a time to openly confront ungodly laws; but there is also a time for action like that of Amram and Jochebed. Faith need not be reckless, presumptuous, or needlessly expose to danger. For instance, though we believe that God heals the sick we nevertheless, submit our faith to the higher law of love. Love never insists that another person suffer or die because of our claim to faith. "And now abide faith, hope, love, these three; but the **greatest** of these is love" (I Cor. 13:13). Though our hearts may be full of faith our heads need not be empty of reason. When Cromwell said, "Trust in God, and keep your powder dry," he meant that faith and works are complementary.

Faith operates within the will of God. Baby Moses was "pleasing to God" (Acts 7:20). Something about the child suggested he was special in the sight of God. God willed that the little boy not die, but God also works with human instruments, especially those in sympathy with His purposes. Amram, Jochebed, and Miriam consciously worked within the will of God. When Pharaoh's daughter opened her heart to the cry of a helpless baby, she also opened the palace door, never realizing she was being used to accomplish God's will. Stephen says in his great sermon, "Pharaoh's daughter took him away and brought him up as her own son. And Moses was learned in all the wisdom of the Egyptians, and was mighty in words and deeds" (Acts 7:21, 22). The faith of Moses' parents was based solidly upon God and His will, not simply upon some grandiose self-conceived plan for the deliverance of the Israelites. In all this we see the sovereignty of God.

After showing young Moses' faith to be rooted in that of Amram and Jochebed, the writer then turns to **the faith of Moses "when he became of age"** (v. 23). Moses spent forty years in Egypt, forty years in the wilderness as a shepherd, and forty years leading the children of Israel through the wilderness.

Notice the six actions that grew out of his faith (vv. 24-28). "By faith he refused to be called the son of Pharaoh's daughter" (v. 24). Instead, he chose "to suffer affliction with the people of God than to enjoy the passing pleasures of sin" (v. 25). By faith he esteemed "the reproach of Christ greater riches than the treasures of Egypt" (v. 26). "By faith he forsook Egypt, not fearing the wrath of the king" (v. 27). By faith "he endured as seeing Him Who is invisible" (v. 27). "By faith he kept (or instituted) the Passover" (v. 28).

Consider the first three in reverse order. "**By faith he esteemed...**" Esteem means "to account" or "to consider." He balanced things in his mind and came to a decision after weighing the evidence. Being in Egypt for forty years he observed the overwhelming treasures of that nation from his princely position. Evidence abounds today of Egypt's enormous wealth in Moses' day. The two thoughts he considered were the **treasures of Egypt** and **the affliction of God's people,** called here "the affliction of Christ." Which would we have chosen—a lot with a bunch of pitiful slaves or the greatest treasures of the world? If we are glad we do not have to make that choice we miss the meaning of this text. We all must choose **who** or **what** we will identify with. Some might reason, "Why not remain in Egypt, become the next Pharaoh, take the treasures, and improve the lives of the slaves?" But God was not interested in "improvement." He had deliverance in mind!

In identifying with the slaves Moses saw more than poverty; he felt "the affliction of Christ." "Christ" means "Messiah." We are reminded of Jesus' words, "For if you believed Moses, you would believe Me; for he wrote about Me" (Jn. 5:46). Moses anticipated the Messiah. His suffering for these poor slaves was not based solely on pity or on a common ethnic origin. It was linked to the hope of God's promised Messiah. Thus, he made the only reasonable choice. We do not know if Moses struggled with this decision, but God commended his act of faith. God grant us the same wisdom.

On the basis of his accounting, or esteeming, **he made his choice to suffer affliction rather than enjoy the temporary pleasures of sin.** He contrasted the promised Messiah with the temporary pleasures of sin and made a deliberate choice. Some deny that there are pleasures in sin. The Bible does not say that; it acknowledges the pleasures in sin. Dr. A.J. Gordon's song, "My Jesus, I love Thee," is well known. I looked through 20 different hymnals which have the words, "My Jesus, I love Thee, I know Thou art mine; for Thee all the follies of sin I resign." Dr. Gordon did not write his song like that. He wrote, "For Thee all the **pleasures** of sin I resign." Whoever tampered with the old hymn evidently thought Mr. Gordon could never have meant to sing about "the pleasures of sin." The question is not whether or not sin is pleasurable, for it is. The question has to do with its short-term pleasure. Moses decided that the pleasures of sin are only for "a season," and are followed by misery. He thought this through; he balanced it out. His thinking may have taken a while, but his choice did not. Daniel enjoyed a high government position and Joseph stayed in the palace, but Moses renounced the "good life." God had a different plan for him, as He does for us.

These first-century Jewish believers faced a similar decision, just as we do. They would be accounted as dead by family and friends if they continued to follow Jesus as Messiah. They had to choose. The cost of following Jesus Christ is high, but the cost of **not** following Him is greater! Correct choices are not made by gritting our teeth and clinching our fists in firm resolve, but by faith. When we say, "O Lord, I will follow You but please do not ask me to bear a cross," we are doubtful about the strength of our faith. He never requires more than faith can produce!

"By faith...he refused to be called the son of Pharaoh's daughter." Think of all the possibilities available to Moses! Yet he clearly saw, through faith, the fading, fleeting, transient glory of Egypt. Faith moves us to renounce the world, flesh, and the devil. Moses had to choose to be an Israelite or an Egyptian, but he couldn't be both! Neither can we remain neutral about Jesus Christ.

Moses must have felt indebted to his Egyptian mother. How could she possibly understand? Would he not seem insensitive, unappreciative? Had she not rescued him from death and opened up great opportunities? It was no easy choice! Josephus, the Jewish historian, claims that Pharaoh had only this one daughter and that she had no children. This destined Moses for the throne and intensifies the words, "he refused." The world will never understand such reasoning, for it is based on faith in God. The philosophy of the world is opposed to God's Word. If Moses made the correct choice so may we.

"By faith he forsook Egypt, not fearing the wrath of the king." When Moses came upon an Egyptian brutally beating a Hebrew slave he responded. Such violence must have been common, but Moses could not allow it to go unchallenged. Thinking he was unobserved, he killed the Egyptian. Later, when trying to settle a fight between two Hebrew slaves, he was challenged, "Who made you a prince and judge over us? Do you intend to kill me as you killed the Egyptian?" As Moses fled to Midian he knew there was no turning back. There comes a time when a break must be made with the world and a full commitment made to God. Jesus' disciples "forsook all and followed Him" (Lk. 5:11). We are called to do the same.

Moses was in the desert for 40 years. It is no accident that many notable men of God were shepherds who spent time alone with God in nature until He was ready to use them. God has a preparation time for those He calls.

By faith **"he endured as seeing Him Who is invisible."** One can imagine some smiling at the words, "seeing Him Who is invisible." How can one see anything that's invisible? God made Himself personally known to Moses at the burning bush. "And the Angel of the Lord appeared to him in a flame of fire from the midst of a bush. So he looked, and behold, the bush was burning with fire, but the bush was not consumed. Then Moses said, 'I will now turn aside and see this great sight, why the bush does not burn.' So when the Lord saw that he turned aside to look, God called to him from the midst of the bush and said, 'Moses, Moses!' And he said, 'Here I am.' Then He said, 'Do not draw near this place. Take your sandals off your feet, for the place where you stand is holy ground'" (Ex. 3:2-5). Here God manifested His compassion, declared His sovereignty, and called Moses to deliver His people. Moses, who failed at delivering **one** Hebrew slave, now returned to deliver **them all!** A personal encounter with I AM changed his life. Forty years of tending sheep prepared him to shepherd a nation. God can use all our experiences!

Finally, "**by faith he kept (or instituted) the Passover.**" Can you imagine a greater act of faith than that expressed during the Passover night in Egypt? Afterward the Passover annually reminded them that they were a redeemed, ransomed, and released people. When the death angel passed over Egypt their redemption was not based on any personal virtue or righteousness. The angel of death simply looked for the blood of the sacrificed lamb. Homes without the applied blood were visited by death. Only the blood of the lamb was sufficient. A Holy God demands atonement for sin. The blood must be applied. It was not enough merely to choose, or slay a lamb; the blood had to be applied. Even Jesus' death is not enough. We must also appropriate His cleansing blood as our atonement.

When the angel of death passed over Egypt racial or national identity was not enough. Faith had to be exercised in applying the blood to **every** door post. It was not **one** way of escape; it was the **only** way—*God's Final Answer!*

> *What can wash away my sin?*
> *Nothing but the blood of Jesus;*
> *What can make me whole again?*
> *Nothing but the blood of Jesus.*

Nothing can for sin atone,
Nothing but the blood of Jesus;
Naught of good that I have done,
Nothing but the blood of Jesus.

Oh! Precious is the flow
That makes me white as snow;
No other fount I know;
Nothing but the blood of Jesus.
(Robert Lowery)

By faith they passed through the Red Sea as by dry land; whereas the Egyptians, attempting to do so, drowned. By faith the walls of Jericho fell down after they were encircled for seven days.

Hebrews 11:29, 30

CHAPTER 33

Victory, Going Out and Coming In

(Study No. 33 in the Book of Hebrews)

These verses sum up Israel's **exodus from Egyptian bondage** and **their entrance into the land of promise.** "By faith they passed through the Red Sea" and "by faith the walls of Jericho fell down." Consider these two faith events.

As a treatise on faith these verses come as a surprise. Did not even our Lord call them "a faithless and perverse generation" (Lk. 9:41)? Yet here they are included in the same roster with Noah, Abraham, Joseph, and others of such stature. We read repeatedly of their failures. The writer of this letter knew of these failures, and yet he writes of two instances of faith in the life of the nation. We need to be slow in criticizing what we judge to be faithlessness.

The writer looked over the 40 years of a people struggling to become a nation and fastened upon two events— the Exodus out of Egypt, and the entry into the Land of Promise with the capture of Jericho.

Remember they had been in Egypt for about 400 years and in slavery for about a century. Their revelation of God had been passed down from earlier generations. When Moses returned to deliver them after an absence of 40 years few people would have remembered him. Nevertheless, when he returned, the elders bowed and worshiped (Ex. 4:31).

The Children of Israel, even when they were slaves in Egypt, still realized that they had a special relationship with God and maintained their identity as a people. When circumstances seem to overwhelm us we must maintain our identity with the Lord and with other believers.

After the people were saved from the death angel by the blood of a sacrificed lamb, they fled the wrath of Pharaoh and came to the Red Sea. Terrible distress filled Egyptian homes that night. Their grieving soon gave way to anger and Pharaoh's war chariots and cavalry went in hot pursuit of the escaped slaves. With the approaching Egyptian forces behind them and shut in by mountains on both sides, the Israelites' situation was desperate. Resistance would mean indiscriminate massacre.

They cried out to God, not in faith but in despair, and turned on Moses, blaming him for their predicament. The same people who had worshiped God for sending Moses to deliver them, now sarcastically asked, "Did you bring us out here in the desert because there were no graves in Egypt?" Egypt was known for its tombs. Their sarcasm said, "We told you so." How cutting and cruel clever words can be! Some who are expert at cutting with words would never consider physical abuse. A sarcastic critic may be admired, but he will never be loved. If our words are filled with sarcasm, if we are experts in finding faults, no one will be close enough to care for us when we need comfort.

The fleeing slaves were in a situation where man could do nothing; God must do everything. Their faith was tested. God had tested them by asking that they slay a lamb. No reason was given; it was simply a command of God. The danger was thinking it unnecessary to obey. Intellect had to submit to faith. Crossing the Red Sea meant freedom; but how was that passage possible? They had to place all their confidence in God.

This crisis gave rise to their faith. Without Pharaoh pursuing them and no mountains on either side they might have laughed at God's command to go forward (Ex. 14:15). We lack knowledge of what God can do in our lives until we are shut up in an impossible situation. **How** God would accomplish the solution to their problem was indefinite, but it was certain that He **would** do it.

As the Israelites stood in fear facing the sea, the guiding cloud which went before them now went to the rear and an amazing thing happened. The cloud became light to the Israelites and darkness to the Egyptians! While the darkness prevented the Egyptians from attacking, the light provided the opportunity for escape.

Light to the believer is often darkness to the world. Even the attributes of God have this double perspective. When the sinner thinks of the justice of God, he trembles; but when the believer considers God's justice he remembers that God is "faithful and just to forgive us our sins and to cleanse us from all unrighteousness." A sinner shrinks from the omnipotence of God, but the believer is drawn to his all-powerful God. When the unbeliever dwells on the eternity of God he is fearful, but the believer rejoices that he will be forever with the Lord. The same is true of habit; a good habit is marvelous, but a sinful one is a curse. To a believer the Word of God "is a light to my feet and a lamp to my path," but to the unbelieving the Word is full of difficulties and contradictions. It blesses the person of light but judges those in darkness. "The message of the cross is foolishness to those who are perishing, but to us who are being saved it is the power of God" (1 Cor. 1:18). The same waters in Noah's day that drowned unbelievers floated the ark! Light to the Israelites was darkness to the Egyptians. It is still true.

Any of us can be confronted with a life situation from which there seems to be no deliverance. Moses said, "Stand still and see the deliverance of God." God responded, "March forward." God has a word in your present pressure. Let faith rather than panic rule the hour.

Next the writer mentions the **capture of Jericho** as a victory which required great faith. Their strategy seemed illogical, but again faith challenged reason. They went around the city once each day for six days as priests blew their trumpets. On the seventh day after silently circling the city seven times, they shouted! Can you see anything rational about such a program? They seemed to be exposing themselves to an attack from Jericho. What power is there in the sound of a trumpet or marching feet to make a city wall fall down? The inhabitants of the city had heard how God delivered His people by opening the sea, so they had shut up their city in fear.

Neither the devil nor the world system fears an intimidated Church. The devil tolerates a certain amount of good as long as it misses the principle goal of setting people free by the power of the living God! When the enemy sees a militant, marching Church he gets nervous.

The march around Jericho claimed it as God's property. If Jericho, the first and strongest city in Canaan, fell to the people of God, the message would be out—these people could take the entire land. But as surely as they did not cross the Red Sea by their own ability, they did not take this city by their own strength. The weapons of their warfare were not carnal.

Many world cities today are "shut up" like Jericho; shut up by humanism, materialism, drugs and the breakdown of family life. Though in the midst of beautiful palm groves, Jericho was a hotbed of Canaanite pollution. As surely as Jericho was conquered we must believe that the spiritually polluted cities of our world can be claimed by Christ.

Our cities can be subject to the Lordship of Jesus Christ. Some try to establish His Lordship through political means. If the world uses that method, they reason, why shouldn't the Church? If we elect godly people won't righteousness reign? But notice God's method—a group of former slaves with a certain presence about them silently circling an impregnable city and carrying an odd looking box! Who would have been threatened by such an army?

Jerry Kramer tells about his days with the Green Bay Packers, the most dominant team in the NFL under Coach Vince Lombardi. The Packers felt a player wasn't worth anything unless he came out of poverty. Poverty made them hungry; privilege made them weak. Whatever our past has been, God can use us. "The message of the cross is foolishness to those who are perishing, but to us who are being saved it is the power of God" (1 Cor. 1:18). "God has chosen the foolish things of the world to put to shame the wise, and God has chosen the weak things of the world to put to shame the things which are mighty" (1 Cor. 1:27).

If the area where you live is polluted by crime, by gang activity, by the breakdown of family life, as you go about that neighborhood claim it for Christ! Though the devil may remind us that the walls are still there, we know that the seventh day is yet to come. God's victory is sure!

Those who hide behind the "walls of Jericho" will be left defenseless. Loss of wealth, job, popularity, health, or a loved one can suddenly shatter our defenses. The inhabitants of Jericho, rather than fighting against Israel, found that they were fighting against God. The Israelites did not tear the walls down. God did! The battle is the Lord's! Without faith in God there is no victory, but with faith fixed in Him there can be no defeat.

By faith the harlot Rahab did not perish with those who did not believe, when she had received the spies with peace.

Hebrews 11:31
(See Joshua 2:1-21; 6:22-25; and James 2:25)

CHAPTER 34

Faith and the Scarlet Cord

(Study No. 34 in the Book of Hebrews)

To this point Hebrews 11 has dealt with Jews, notable patriarchs. Now we are asked to consider a Gentile woman, a harlot, as an example of faith. One of the fascinating things about the capture of Jericho is that a harlot helped facilitate its defeat.

Rahab lived in a house built over the gap between the two massive city walls surrounding the city. From her window she could look out over the outer wall. Rahab was not only a harlot, a foreigner, and a member of a race considered accursed, but she also became a woman of faith. Though Abraham was an idol worshiper, Jacob a deceiver, Moses a murderer, all were esteemed men. But here a Gentile woman, a harlot, is introduced as a model of faith! If you think that God cannot use a person with such a background, read this story and be amazed by God's grace!

Let's consider **the woman Rahab, her faith,** and **the results of her faith.** First, as for **the woman herself**, she is a Gentile Amoritess, an ethnic group God said He would destroy. And she is a prostitute. The Hebrew word also means "innkeeper," but the Greek word in Hebrews 11:31 and James 2:25 makes her profession clear. The Holy Spirit does not gloss over this fact. One is reminded of the Syro-Phoenician woman who came to our Lord for the healing of her daughter. She was outside the covenant of blessing, yet

Jesus delivered her child and commended her great faith. God looks for faith, not perfection.

In our society the word "harlot" provokes a corrupt and malignant image. It is difficult for us to understand that Rahab was not only accepted in her society, but may have been an integral part of its worship system. Immoral acts were carried on as part of their religion. Her profession was not only tolerated, it was encouraged. She may have been a priestess, rather than a "sinner," in her culture. Of course, family life would suffer, public spirit would lessen, and disease would be rampant as a result of such perversion; but this religion would continue and would threaten the very existence of the Hebrews as a people after they entered the land.

So Rahab would not be convicted over such a lifestyle since Canaanite religion was centered on sexuality. When Don Richardson presented the story of Judas to a certain primitive tribe they considered Judas to be the hero of the crucifixion story. He seemed clever to them! Even those who have little regard for the Christian faith still owe a great deal to the noble convictions which our society has received from the Word of God.

Those who think one religion is as good as another need to realize what Jesus Christ has done for womanhood. Some religions sacrifice young ladies and children to their gods while others degrade women by "sacred" prostitution. We should be thankful for the Christian faith which elevates women and affords them the same worth and respect given to men.

God does not have a double standard for the sexes. If those hypocrites who dragged the woman taken in adultery to Jesus had been consistent they would have also brought the man. God does not condemn sin by gender! Jesus said to the self-righteous priests, "Assuredly, I say to you that...harlots enter the kingdom of God before you" (Matt. 21:31). Women in many parts of the world are held in the vice of degrading commercialized prostitution. Jesus Christ came to free them.

Rahab had some good qualities. She was concerned about her family and faith in God was beginning to form in her heart. But measuring her good points against her bad ones is pointless, for no one is ever saved on that basis. All are saved by grace.

Rahab's faith appears in her words to the two young spies who had slipped into Jericho. "I know that the Lord has given you the land, that the terror of you has fallen on us, and that all the inhabitants of the land are faint-hearted because of you. For we have heard how the Lord dried up the water of the Red Sea for you when you came out of Egypt, and what you did to the two kings of the Amorites who were on the other side of the Jordan, Sihon and Og, whom you utterly destroyed. And as soon as we heard these things, our hearts melted; neither did there remain any more courage in anyone because of you, **for the Lord your God, He is God in heaven and on earth beneath**" (Josh. 2:9-11).

What caused this marvelous declaration of faith—"He is God in heaven and on earth beneath?" Her faith was founded on reports about the approaching Hebrews. After she and her countrymen heard about the miraculous crossing of the Red Sea dread spread throughout the land, and Rahab decided to take a certain course of action. Knowing the city's days were numbered she asked for mercy and requested that her family be spared. Her faith in Jericho's destruction may have even been stronger than that of the Hebrews who were coming against the city.

Her faith produced obedience. Though everyone in Jericho was terrified she decided to act, to cast her lot with the Hebrews. Rahab showed her faith by helping the Hebrew spies. Had she not done this, she would certainly have perished. James writes, "Likewise, was not Rahab the harlot also justified by works when she received the messengers and sent them out another way?" (Ja. 2:25) Faith is never neutral. It moves in obedience. "Faith without works is dead" (Ja. 2:20). In all the faith heroes of Hebrews 11—Abel, Enoch, Noah, Abraham, Sarah, Isaac, Jacob, Joseph—faith produced works...and it still does!

Consider **the consequences of her faith.** By hanging a scarlet cord from her window Rahab identified with the people of God, saving both herself and her family. This scarlet cord typifies the blood of Jesus Christ which cleanses from all sin and brings us into the common family of faith. Faith always calls us to relationship, not isolation. A new believer who moments before had little concern for his own salvation, after conversion often suddenly senses a burden for his family and friends. Faith has an expansive principle about it. Salvation strikes at selfishness and makes us want to see others receive this marvelous experience. Let's claim our households for His glory!

Like Noah, safety for Rahab meant being inside rather than outside. For Jericho there was no escape. One day the city enjoyed wealth, ease, and comfort; the next day, destruction. God will not sit still forever and watch indifferently as the poison of sin ruins the world. God punishes sin. In Rahab we see the mercy of God for the redeemed during judgment times. We are safe **inside,** covered by the blood of Christ. Nothing in Rahab commended her or her family to the grace of God. Her salvation, and ours, is totally unmerited!

God's grace opened the door for Rahab and her family to became a part of the people of Israel (Josh. 6:25). Of course, she had to be taught the ways of the Lord. This may explain why she lived for a while "outside the camp of Israel" (Josh. 6:23), to learn the difference between sin and righteousness. Amazing grace! Here is a former prostitute named with one other woman, Sarah, in Hebrews' "Hall of Faith." God is not concerned with **how** lives are wasted, but with the fact that they **are** wasted.

Afterwards Rahab lived in the land of Canaan and married Salmon, of the tribe of Judah. Their son Boaz married Ruth. King David came from Rahab's family and ultimately, the Lord Jesus. Her name, wonders of wonders, is listed by Matthew in the legal genealogy of Jesus! She is named there with four other women— Tamar, Ruth, Bathsheba, and Mary. Tamar sinned with her father-in-law, and Bathsheba committed adultery with David. The only woman who shines with beauty in the list, other than our Lord's mother, is Ruth, and she was a Gentile from Moab. In fact, all four Old Testament women were non-Jews; but God used all of them! Peter said, "In truth I perceive that God shows no partiality" (Acts 10:34). But it was 1500 years before an apostle of Jesus Christ could reluctantly come to this conclusion!

If we are tempted to be prejudiced or to censor others, we should remember Rahab. God can take a vile sinner, unworthy of His grace in any respect, and turn that person into a mighty testimony of His grace. What Rahab **had been** no longer matters; what she **became** is infinitely important.

William P. Barker tells about a machinist with the Ford Motor Company who "borrowed" various parts and tools from the company without returning them. This practice was not condoned but, being more or less accepted by management, nothing was done about it. The machinist, however, became a devout believer and was baptized. He took his baptism seriously. The next morning he arrived at work loaded down with all the stolen tools and parts he had taken from the company during the years. He explained the situation to his foreman, added that he'd never really meant to steal them, and asked to be forgiven. The foreman was so astonished by his action that he cabled Mr. Ford, who was visiting a European plant, and explained the entire event. Immediately Ford cabled back: "Dam up the Detroit River and baptize the entire city!"[1] Authentic faith in Christ still changes people today!

Why was Jericho destroyed? Canaanite culture was polluted and wicked. But that only touches the circumference, not the center, of the cause. The actual ground for their judgment was **unbelief**. The citizens of Jericho heard everything that Rahab had heard, yet refused to believe. Unbelief is the cause of judgment. When we stand before God there will be no balancing of good and bad deeds on some celestial scale. The one consideration will be whether or not we have exercised faith in Jesus Christ, *God's Final Answer*, for faith in His blood cleanses from all sin.

And what more shall I say? For the time would fail me to tell of Gideon and Barak and Samson and Jephthah, also of David and Samuel and the prophets: who through faith subdued kingdoms, worked righteousness, obtained promises, stopped the mouths of lions, quenched the violence of fire, escaped the edge of the sword, out of weakness were made strong, became valiant in battle, turned to flight the armies of the aliens. Women received their dead raised to life again. Others were tortured, not accepting deliverance, that they might obtain a better resurrection. Still others had trial of mockings and scourgings, yes, and of chains and imprisonment. They were stoned, they were sawn in two, were tempted, were slain with the sword. They wandered about in sheepskins and goatskins, being destitute, afflicted, tormented—of whom the world was not worthy. They wandered in deserts and mountains, in dens and caves of the earth. And all these, having obtained a good report through faith, did not receive the promise, God having provided something better for us, that they should not be made perfect apart from us.

Hebrews 11:32-40

CHAPTER 35

Faith that Overcomes

(Study No. 35 in the Book of Hebrews)

What rich illustrations of faith! Let's consider **these people of faith, reflect on what they experienced as a result of their faith,** and **study the end results of their faith.** First, **the people themselves** include five judges, one king, and the prophets. The Hebrew prophets have been called "the most distinguished group of men the world has ever known." Judges were pre-monarchy rulers raised up by God during some of the darkest days of Israeli history. Of this time it is written, "In those days there was no king in Israel, but every man did that which was right in his own eyes"(Judges 17:6; 18:1; 19:25). It is a wonder the Israelites survived as a people during the time of the five judges: Gideon, Barak, Samson, Jephthah, and Samuel.

Gideon illustrates **victorious faith over fear and lack of confidence.** When God called him to bring deliverance to the Israelites, they were living in fear due to Midianite oppression. Gideon was hiding when an angel appeared to commission him to lead the people against their tormentors. His excuse has been repeated thousands of times since that day, "My clan is the weakest in Manasseh, and I am the least in my father's house" (Judges 6:15).

The angel does not say to Gideon, "Your evaluation is not true. Your clan is not as weak as you think and you are certainly not the weakest in your family." Nor did he say, "Yes, you are correct. Your clan is indeed weak and you, yourself, are the weakest in all your family." The angel responded as he would to us. It is of no consequence to God whether we think we are weak or strong, for in the eyes of God none of us are sufficient within ourselves. God would be the Source of victory, not Gideon! We are not to question God's assignment. He Who calls also equips!

Barak was asked by the prophetess, Deborah, to revolt against Jabin, king of Canaan, and his captain, Sisera. Barak conditioned his acceptance of the assignment upon whether or not Deborah would accompany him in the fight. Because he refused to go without Deborah, the Lord delivered Sisera into the hand of a woman. Much of Barak's honor was denied him. But despite his fear of standing alone he went on in faith to victory against the Canaanites.

Some have an unreasonable fear of standing alone. We can be brave with others, but "fade into the woodwork" when asked to battle alone for the Lord. One reason the enemy promotes such fear is to prevent the kind of faith that refuses to compromise with the world system. God keep us from bowing to the world, flesh, or devil! One with God is a majority; but God, alone, is also a majority! When we, by faith, stand alone, we are never alone!

Samson had a strong body but seems to have had a weak mind! We are amazed at his gullibility. His relationship with Delilah was disastrous. No man in Scripture "shoots himself in the foot" so often and reloads so quickly! His biography moves us to pity. He kills a lion with his bare hands, slaughters 1000 Philistines with the jawbone of an ass, catches 300 foxes, ties their tails together and burns the Philistine's grain fields. Like an overgrown schoolboy he steals the great iron gates of Gaza and carries them away. Fighting was his forte. But he seems to have had an idle brain in an active body. But in spite of all this, he was moved by faith. Though blinded by his enemies and grinding in the mill like an animal, he courageously stood in his last moments for the God of Israel.

Perhaps you consider your life a failure. You may feel you are grinding in the devil's grain mill and that a productive, positive life is out of the question. Whether you are like Jacob, with an unconsecrated mind, or Samson, with an uncommitted body, God has not given up on you! While there is life, there is opportunity to turn your self—mind, heart, and will—over to God. He can take you just as you are and make you into what you need to be!

Jephthah probably never smiled. His life was a tragedy. Born out of wedlock, his "legitimate" brothers drove him away. Jephthah and his gang, described as "worthless" in Judges 11:3, raided the countryside. This illegitimate child, who became a strong leader, was eventually asked by those who had exiled him to return home to save them from certain destruction.

Our past can cause us to feel **there is no way we can ever amount to anything.** The devil uses this argument effectively. Thousands are paralyzed by fear of their past, wondering what people think about them. Pride makes us assume that others are always thinking or talking about us. Those who have the mind of Christ are not to be harassed by the past. Judgment passed on the basis of our "pedigree" is not worthy of our worry! Faith helps us rise above such fear and worry.

Of the five judges mentioned here, **Samuel** is the most outstanding. He has been called "the only Hebrew of his time" because he rose above tribal identity and preserved the unity of the people. Thus He was to the Israelites what Abraham Lincoln was to the United States. You can be sure that in the constitution Samuel wrote for Israel (1 Sam. 10:25) there was nothing about the divine rights of kings! He was a king-maker, anointing Saul and then David, and for a long while was the power behind the throne of Israel. If he started the "School of the Prophets," as many believe, he also inaugurated religious education in Israel.

Yet Samuel **knew great disappointments.** At one of his lowest points God consoled him by saying, "They have not rejected you, but they have rejected Me" (1 Sam. 8:7). He suffered terribly over Saul's failure. Faith is no guarantee against disappointments. Sometimes the bottom drops out of our world. Family and friends may reject us. At those times faith in God lifts the spirit. Personal peace must never be established by current events! Peace is found in Jesus Christ, and faith in Him makes the difference.

King David, the only king in this list, is the most famous of Israel's kings. Consider his accomplishments: he was a poet, singer, musician, warrior, statesman, administrator, and a man at home in the field or in the palace. David loved his friends and forgave his enemies. Yet he was also an adulterer, a murderer, and a hypocrite. The Bible does not hide the sordid story of his sin with Bathsheba and the murder of her husband, Uriah. His moral failure could have tainted his past and ruined his future.

It is possible to have a history of good works and yet have a "fly in the ointment," a dark page that reminds us of our guilt. **Faith in God cleanses the heart from guilt over the past.** God gives a new start! He forgets! Absolutely! Since God forgives how foolish for us to continue in guilt. We must forgive ourselves!

The Hebrew prophets, probably the most renowned group of men who ever lived, laid the foundation for the freedom we enjoy as a democracy. These great men spoke of the love and holiness of God and the rights and responsibilities of the individual. They ministered at great cost. Yet Jesus spoke of Jerusalem as "the one who kills the prophets and stones those who are sent to her!"(Lk. 13:34) What a price they paid to declare God's will and character.

What is it that sustains you when you are subject to ridicule and persecution for doing the will of God? Peter said, "Beloved, do not think it strange concerning the fiery trial which is to try you, as though some strange thing happened to you; but rejoice to the extent that you partake of Christ's sufferings, that when His glory is revealed, you may also be glad with exceeding joy"(1 Pet. 4:12,13). So we have not been singled out to suffer by an unkind God. It is a common experience. But our faith tells us that suffering is temporary; a better day is coming!

These faith heroes had **both negative and positive experiences.** They **subdued kingdoms.** We are promised victory over three kingdoms—the world, the flesh, and the devil. The world system cannot be allowed to press us into its mold. Our own flesh cannot dictate its will to us and the devil is no match for the Power which dwells within!

They **worked righteousness.** Through faith, the holiness of God within us works its way into visibility. Our own righteousness, which is as filthy rags, is replaced by Jesus' righteousness, an active good will that honors Him.

They **obtained promises.** "For all the promises of God in Him are Yes, and in Him Amen, to the glory of God through us" (2 Cor. 1:20). God's promises are sure! We never need to shake God's promises in His face, like spoiled children reminding a parent of a promise. A child saying to a parent, "But you promised..." is expressing doubt, not faith.

They **stopped the mouths of lions.** Daniel, a praying man, refused to compromise in his stand for God. God can muzzle lions for those with Daniel-like faith!

They **quenched the violence of fire.** Those who stand tall for their Lord, through faith quench the fiery darts of the enemy. We are in little danger of being thrown **into** the fire, as the three Hebrew children; but when the fire is thrown **at us** it is quenched by faith! They **escaped the edge of the sword.** The devil wants to "kill, steal, and destroy." In some countries where there is threat of life for Christian testimony many still have this same testimony.

They **were made strong.** Unbelief gives birth to weakness, but the faith that comes by hearing the Word of God produces strength.

They **became valiant in battle.** How easy in spiritual warfare to become fearful. Faith makes the difference. Courage does not come by gritting our teeth and determining, despite everything, to hang on. It's a product of faith.

They **turned to flight the armies of aliens.** Our actual enemies are not flesh and blood but "principalities, powers...rulers of darkness of this age...spiritual hosts of wickedness in the heavenly places" (Eph. 6:12). These enemies are put to flight by faith in the Lord Jesus. They have convincing reason to recognize Him as the Champion!

Women received their dead raised to life again. Jesus is still able to physically raise the dead. But just as surely as He brought Lazarus back to Mary and Martha, He is also able to restore family relationships that have died.

Notice the **negative experiences** in which faith was manifested.

Others were tortured. Some were delivered from torture by their faith, while others were tortured **because** of their faith. Still others **were mocked (ridiculed), scourged, put in chains, imprisoned, stoned and sawn asunder.** Isaiah is said to have been put inside a hollow log and sawn in two. **They were tempted** to deny the Lord God in the face of such terrible cost. **Some were slain with the sword** while others **wandered about in sheepskins and**

goatskins, destitute, afflicted, tormented, lived in deserts, mountains, dens, and caves. What an enormous price to pay for their faith; but it was their faith that produced the courage to pay such a price.

What were the results of their faith? First, **they received a good testimony.** Whether they lived or died their faith produced a good testimony. Faith's first priority is not to make **us** look good; it gives good reason for others to believe the gospel.

Second, **the world was not worthy of them.** The world that persecuted them was undeserving of them. What blindness that they were the world's true wealth, yet were unrecognized as such!

Finally, **"all these...did not receive the promise, God having provided something better for us, that they should not be made perfect apart from us."** They will find what they sought, but not without us. These dear saints all died not having received this promise which was the very basis of their faith. The promise was made to Abraham who "looked for the city which has foundations, whose builder and maker is God." They looked for a city, which comes "down out of heaven from God, prepared as a bride adorned for her husband." None have reached that coming city, nor will they without us, for they will be made perfect (completed) with us!

With earlier saints our hearts anticipate that day when we shall reign in that beautiful city God! Until then we rest our faith in Jesus Christ, *God's Final Answer!*

Therefore we also, since we are surrounded by so great a cloud of witnesses, let us lay aside every weight, and the sin which so easily ensnares us, and let us run with endurance the race that is set before us, looking unto Jesus, the author and finisher of our faith, who for the joy that was set before Him endured the cross, despising the shame, and has sat down at the right hand of the throne of God. For consider Him who endured such hostility from sinners against Himself, lest you become weary and discouraged in your souls. You have not yet resisted to bloodshed, striving against sin.

Hebrews 12:1-4

CHAPTER 36

Running to Win

(Study No. 36 in the Book of Hebrews)

⚜

The Book of Hebrews is filled with warnings. It speaks force-fully and consistently about the peril of turning away from faith in Christ. Examples of triumphant faith are given in chapter 11 to show that through invincible faith life can be lived to the fullest.

To encourage a consistent walk the writer comments on the "great a cloud of witnesses," a reference to those named in chapter 11. The picture is of an arena in which these champions of faith are seated, watching our performance and cheering us on to victory. With their race already won by faith, they now not only witness our race, but, by their example, also witness **to** us. They remind us that losing the race is indefensible, for they ran under conditions much less favorable than ours.

We are inspired by their faith and performance, but we need more than inspiration; we need the information given in this text to successfully complete our own race. **Five things promise victory.** We are to **lay aside every weight, lay aside the sin which so easily ensnares us, run with endurance the race that is set before us, look unto Jesus,** and **consider Him.** Like a coach, the writer tells those engaged in this athletic event to practice these five directives. Assurance is given that, having done them, we cannot lose. This information comes from the One Who ran the race before us, Who always knows the condition of the contest and track, how those conditions vary as the race progresses, and every move our opponents will make. With this intelligence there is no reason to lose!

First, we are to "**lay aside every weight.**" Runners in a race do not wear football gear. Brooks Bryan's song, *There Won't Be No Pockets In My White Linen Robe*, tells of two men out hiking who were nearly surrounded by a terrible forest fire. The only way out was across a rope bridge which was carefully marked as to the weight it could bear. One man laid aside every weight and even emptied his pockets to comply with the limit. His friend, thinking a little more weight could hardly matter, lost his life. True..."there won't be no pockets in our white linen robes." Many of us carry too much "baggage."

The Holy Spirit speaks to us about the weights that hinder. The problem with identifying weights is that what is a weight to me may not be one to you. Some who delight in pointing out their neighbor's weights fail to notice their own. Indeed, one weight is trying to discover what your brother's weights are! If we were on board a sinking ship we would be amazed at the things that could be abandoned! Things often considered assets are weights. The Holy Spirit can identify the weights in our lives.

Second, we are to **lay aside "the sin which so easily ensnares us."** These five words, "which so easily ensnares (besets) us," speaks of a sin "which so readily entangles" us (Wey.). This sin is **unbelief.** Many are known by what they **do not** believe. Our Lord Jesus encountered such in the Sadducees. These first century rationalists refused to believe anything they could not explain. For them there could be no miracle, resurrection, or spirit. Such sad souls are evangelistic in spreading their unbelief. Faithless souls seem happiest when they are destroying the faith of others. Never allow anyone to tamper with your faith in Jesus Christ. A heart devoid of faith is "an evil heart of unbelief." A heart stripped of faith in Christ is not fair and unbiased for there is no such thing as a neutral heart.

Third, we are to "**run with endurance the race that is set before us.**" The Christian race is neither a stroll nor a hundred yard dash. In this generation we are strangers to patience and endurance. We want what we want NOW! Some believe that if they simply have faith they will never be troubled or inconvenienced, while others in hostile societies express their faith by endurance under threat of death. While many are being martyred for their faith it seems foolish to measure faith by how we feel or what we have.

A young pastor had been very sick as a baby and remained frail and delicate all his days. His maladies were so severe he could not adequately serve his growing congregation. Instead he wrote letters filled with hope and good cheer. Though his body was frail, his spirit soared. Since the harsh hymns of his day were a disappointment to him, someone challenged him to compose. He wrote over 600 hymns—mostly hymns of praise. When his health completely broke in 1748 he left one of the most remarkable collections of hymns the world has ever known. "Joy to the World; the Lord is Come" is one of Isaac Watts' best known compositions.[1] His story seems to be proof that most of the work done in the world is done by those who don't feel good!

The faith of many Christians in third world countries is seen in their patient endurance. They often ride buses overloaded with human and animal cargo, ride on stinking boats that would send many of us to the rail, and walk carrying unbelievable loads. In those countries you scarcely see a car with only one rider, while in America our most pressing concern is parking space!

"Looking unto Jesus" is the fourth command. We cannot look in two directions at once. While riding my bicycle as a boy I looked over my shoulder and crashed into a telephone pole. While riding a spirited horse through a Virginia meadow I glanced over my shoulder only to look back and see a tree branch clearing the ears of my galloping horse. Believe me, we can never look two ways at once. "Looking unto Jesus" is more than a mere suggestion!

Blondin, an outstanding tightrope walker, made famous walks across Niagara Falls on a slender rope. He finally revealed the secret of his success. As he made his way over the falls, he kept his eyes fixed on a large silver star at the far end. The star guided him to the other side. [2] If we look to criticize how our brother is running his race, we will take our eyes off the Lord Jesus. Close races can be lost when the lead runner looks back, even for an instance, to see where the other runners are.

Other runners in this race are not our opponents. Our opponent is not even in the race. His tactic is to distract our attention from Christ and cause us to lose the race. When a basketball player shoots a free throw opposing fans try frantically to distract him. His mind must be riveted only on the basket. Our race is not being run on friendly ground; we are "playing away from home." Our eyes, therefore, must be fastened on Christ, not on conditions about us.

We are not commanded here to pray, but simply to look, as the snake-bitten Israelites looked at the brass serpent. Looking suffices because we look at Jesus, the Author and Finisher of our faith. Other translations say "the Forerunner and Finisher of our faith" (Con.), "the Pioneer and Perfecter of our faith" (Mon.), "The Source and Goal of our faith" (Phi.), "Jesus, on Whom faith depends from start to finish" (NEB)! Strength comes simply by looking at Him!

What inspired our Lord to finish His race? It was the joy that awaited Him. An encouraging song says, "Hold on, my child, joy comes in the morning." Some cannot joy in present circumstances. But, as Tony Compolo puts it in his famous sermon, "It's Friday, but Sunday's coming!" Jesus knew what lay ahead. Look again at the last chapter of the Book! Victory comes when the trumpet blows!

Some may object at the price to pay! Again, look at Jesus. He "despised the shame," or "thought nothing of it." (Was "heedless of the shame," [TCNT].) He made light of the disgrace of the cross. Shame is only for a moment and any shame borne in Jesus' Name will be transformed into honor. Most of what we consider reproach is only an affront to pride, and has nothing to do with the stigma of the cross. Jesus told the women of Jerusalem to weep for themselves, not for Him.

Though some sermons give graphic details of the physical suffering of Christ on the cross, the Bible does not. He "scorned its shame" (Nor.). Had He thought this present life was all there was, the story might have been different; but He knew of a joyous triumph! Now, He "has sat down at the right hand of the throne of God." From that position He has everything to offer! And He promises that all overcomers will be allowed to sit with Him in His throne, even as He has overcome and is seated with His Father in His throne (Rev. 3:21).

Finally, we are admonished to "**consider Him** Who endured such hostility from sinners against Himself lest you become weary and discouraged in your souls." We are to compare our sufferings with His! The servant is not greater than his Lord. If He suffered the intense agony of the whipping post and the cross, we can stand for Him in any situation. We have not "resisted to bloodshed."

The writer does not mean to "consider others" in the sense of comparing our discomfort with theirs. When we compare our sufferings with our Lord's all complaining stops. As a Baby there was no room for Him in the inn. He came unto His own people and they rejected Him. He was derided, mocked, treated with contempt, called a winebibber and a glutton, and treated as a common criminal. His enemies claimed He was demon possessed and condemned Him to die between two thieves. Not once did He retaliate. Instead, He prayed for their forgiveness. In the midst of our trivial "trials" let us "consider Him."

The Christian race may be compared to a relay race, with a baton being passed on to the next runner. Others have completed their leg of the race, and now they witness our run. Someday all who have run the race will be rewarded. Winners cannot receive the "gold metal" until all are on the victory platform. "Only in company with us should they reach perfection" (Heb. 11:40, NEB). Then, together we will all surely lay our rewards at the feet of the "Author and Finisher of our faith," *God's Final Answer.*

And you have forgotten the exhortation which speaks to you as to sons: "My son, do not despise the chastening of the LORD, nor be discouraged when you are rebuked by Him; for whom the LORD loves He chastens, and scourges every son whom He receives." If you endure chastening, God deals with you as with sons; for what son is there whom the father does not chasten? But if you are without chastening, of which all have become partakers, then you are illegitimate and not sons. Furthermore, we have had human fathers who corrected us, and we paid them respect. Shall we not much more readily be in subjection to the Father of spirits and live? For they indeed for a few days chastened us as seemed best to them, but He for our profit, that we may be partakers of His holiness. Now no chastening seems to be joyful for the present, but painful; nevertheless, afterward it yields the peaceable fruit of righteousness to those who have been trained by it. Therefore strengthen the hands which hang down, and the feeble knees, and make straight paths for your feet, so that what is lame may not be dislocated, but rather be healed. Pursue peace with all people, and holiness, without which no one will see the Lord: looking carefully lest anyone fall short of the grace of God; lest any root of bitterness springing up cause trouble, and by this many become defiled; lest there be any fornicator or profane person like Esau, who for one morsel of food sold his birthright. For you know that afterward, when he wanted to inherit the blessing, he was rejected, for he found no place for repentance, though he sought it diligently with tears.

Hebrews 12:5-17

CHAPTER 37

The Loving Discipline
of the Lord

(Study No. 37 in the Book of Hebrews)

W hen I was a child one of our neighbors was accustomed to sitting on his front porch and reading the newspaper to his family. When he came to a word that he could not pronounce he would say, "Hard word. Skip it." It is easy to feel that way about the present text—"Hard passage. Skip it."

None of us like discipline or chastisement, but the writer insists it is good for us. This text shows us **the value of the loving discipline of our Lord** and tells us **how we should respond to it.**

First, **the value of such discipline**. We are told not to despise the chastening of the Lord. This same word is used in Ephesians 6:4 exhorting fathers to bring up their children in the "nurture (chastening) and admonition of the Lord." It also appears in the passage, "All scripture is given by inspiration of God, and is profitable for... instruction (chastening) in righteousness."

Chastening is not a tragic, but a good thing. Still, since none of us like it, we must be told **not to despise the chastening of the Lord.** Suffering is difficult for us, for we naturally rebel against anything uncomfortable, even if it is for our profit.

There is a two-fold danger in chastening. First, we may **"despise"** it, i.e., consider it lightly or undervalue it. Second, we may **be discouraged by it.** Neither response is correct. We will consider chastening necessary and accept it as part of life, or become discouraged by it and despair.

We may despair if we mistakenly believe that chastisement is coming from God for some previously confessed and forgiven sin. We are not punished for sins cleansed by the blood of Jesus. Chastening and punishment are two different things. All suffering is not chastening! When we suffer because of our carelessness we must not confuse this with God's discipline! But when we suffer because we are living a life pleasing to God, those chastisements are meant to conform us to the image of His Son.

Chastisement is evidence that God loves His children. Verse five, quoted from Proverbs 3:11, teaches that even our natural fathers chasten us out of love. Lack of chastening indicates that we are illegitimate, unloved sons. One of my teen-age sons was concerned about one of his friends: "He says that his father does not love him." When I asked why, he said, "He says his father does not love him because his father lets him do everything he wants to." Even children know that there is a difference between real love and license. Father God, Who has plenty of experience "raising children," knows what is best. Chastisement offers validity to our claim of sonship. Not only does God's chastisement verify our relationship with Him, it proves that God has not abandoned us, that He still is our loving Father!

Our natural fathers have a goal in mind when they chastise us. They are saying, "I want you to know how to behave. This is how we conduct ourselves in this family. For your own good I want you to be formed in a certain way." Even though they are motivated by love, they still can make mistakes. Parental chastisement is not always equitable and sometimes the wrong child is disciplined. But God does not make such mistakes! He properly perfects us by those things which we endure. Even Jesus "learned obedience by the things which He suffered" (Heb. 5:8). Godly character can be produced through the adversities of life. God's goal is to make us "partakers of His holiness." Life is not haphazard for the believer. God has something in mind for us when we go through unsettling, uncomfortable circumstances. His design is to make us more like Jesus. Though imperfect earthly fathers fail in their goals, when

God is finished with His loving chastening, the product will be faultless!

Just as we respect our natural fathers because they love enough to discipline, we should learn to respect, or worship, our Heavenly Father. Yielding to Him means that we will "live." Otherwise, we simply exist and never know life in its fullest potential.

The writer does not deny that **chastisement is temporarily painful** (v. 11). Some shepherds have an unusual way of preventing straying sheep from becoming easy prey for predators. As an act of love, they break the front legs of the sheep and carry it until it is able to walk again. By that time the sheep is so accustomed to the shepherd's loving care that it never strays away. We may have heard our parents say before disciplining us, "This hurts me more than it does you." Though we may have doubted them, those words are true in heaven as well as on earth. It is also true, as the writer attests, that older children, in both natural and spiritual households, are sometimes chastened more severely than the younger. Light creates responsibility.

Hopefully, this chastisement **produces the peaceable fruit of righteousness if we allow ourselves to be trained by it.** Chastisement, if allowed, teaches us how to live correctly. Although suffering can produce character like no other experience can, its effect depends on our response. Every catastrophe, every disillusionment, every affliction can bring "death" to self. God grant we will never waste such occasions!

What response shall we make to chastisement? These Hebrews, who saw their brethren discouraged because they were going through great stress, were first **to strengthen the discouraged.** Everyone, at times, needs the encouragement of others. Moses needed Aaron and Hur on either side to hold his hands up so the battle might be won. Even our Lord pleaded with His disciples in Gethsemane to watch with Him an hour as He prayed. God is pleased when we make it a policy to be encouraging, rather than judgmental.

Not only do we strengthen others, we are also to **straighten out their paths** so they may walk without stumbling. Here is a call to forget self and look to the welfare of others. In World War II a mental institution in Northern England was emptied of its patients when the inmates ventured into the neighborhood to risk their lives for others during the air raids. Their concern for others became therapeutic. [1]

It's our responsibility is to leave straight, clear paths for others to follow. This is especially true for spiritual leaders, "so that the man who goes lame may not stumble out of the path" (v. 13, Knox). We have a responsibility toward others. Chastening brings healing and makes us more compassionate. Loss of a loved one through death enables us to comfort others in a similar situation. Divorcees know how to minister to others going through that same problem. Others going through difficult days are blessed if we have left straight, clear paths for them.

As we go through chastening, we also **pursue peace with all others.** It is so easy during chastening to be irritable toward others. Instead of becoming mean and difficult to live with we are to "follow peace," i.e., *chase it.* Effort is involved; far more than saying, "I don't plan to give anybody any trouble." Jesus did not say, "Blessed are the troublemakers!" His benediction is on peacemakers. Christians must settle their differences in a loving and peaceable manner, considering other's rights above their own. John wrote: "If we walk in the light as He is in the light, we have fellowship with one another, and the blood of Jesus Christ His Son cleanses us from all sin" (I Jn. 1:7). Notice that cleansing from sin comes as we not only walk with Jesus in the light, but also walk in fellowship with one another.

 We should not be surprised that the writer puts the pursuit of peace and holiness in the same verse—**holiness also, without which no man can see the Lord.** Wholesome fellowship with other believers makes possible the pursuit of holiness. Holiness cannot be sought in isolation. When we are right with God we have fellowship with one another; and when we are right with one another we have fellowship with God. So peace with others and holiness before God are inseparable. "Without holiness no man can see the Lord." If it is impossible to make peace with someone, God understands, but we have no choice in "following holiness." The call is not one to full-blown perfection, but to "follow" holiness, a continuing walk.

Failure to pursue peace and holiness **falls short of the grace of God.** What a terrible thing to "forfeit the grace of God" (NEB). The idea is to straggle behind, to drift instead of march. The word depicts a laggard who falls behind and is lost. Not all who start the journey finish it. What a tragedy to fall short!

If we lag behind we can **become bitter, cause trouble, and become defiled.** It is natural to be tempted to become bitter towards those who mistreat us. Mistreatment makes it easy to forget the pursuit of peace and become bitter in spirit. Bitterness is an ugly thing. Evidently, because it is so deep underground, it is the only sin described in the Bible as having roots! But it "springs up" at the least provocation. Like a fatal poison bitterness destroys everything it touches. It makes us whiners. If we hold unforgiveness in our hearts we inevitably become bitter. We cannot afford to hold a grudge against anyone...ever! Bitterness defiles and produces troublemakers. Life situations, allowed by God to mellow and sweeten us, can embitter us and cause others to avoid us. The root of bitterness, though deep, can be removed. Jesus can replace it with sweetness!

Esau illustrates the tragedy of bitterness. He was a profane (godless, irreverent) man who only lived for the moment, and never considered the consequences of his actions. If a person like Esau is hungry, nothing matters but his appetite. If he wants sexual gratification, he satisfies his craving immorally, outside of marriage. Unfortunately, there is a devastating "Esau spirit" in all of us. If it is given its way tears can be shed years afterwards, but to no avail. Verse 17 describes Esau's remorse, years after selling his birthright. He wept bitterly, hoping that the birthright could be restored; but what he had done, he had done. Even the power of prayer cannot "undo" history. Someone prayed as they left a church service, "O God, I pray that we have received all You intended for us to have from this meeting today." It was too late for such a prayer. Either they had received or they had not. God Himself would not change the results of their response to that service.

It is normal to pray that unpleasant situations be changed. But if our present condition is God's design for us at this time, we ought to get mileage out of it. **"If trouble moves in make it pay rent!"**

For you have not come to the mountain that may be touched and that burned with fire, and to blackness and darkness and tempest, and the sound of a trumpet and the voice of words, so that those who heard it begged that the word should not be spoken to them anymore. (For they could not endure what was commanded: "And if so much as a beast touches the mountain, it shall be stoned or shot with an arrow." And so terrifying was the sight that Moses said, "I am exceedingly afraid and trembling.") But you have come to Mount Zion and to the city of the living God, the heavenly Jerusalem, to an innumerable company of angels, to the general assembly and church of the firstborn who are registered in heaven, to God the Judge of all, to the spirits of just men made perfect, to Jesus the Mediator of the new covenant, and to the blood of sprinkling that speaks better things than that of Abel.

Hebrews 12:18-24

CHAPTER 38

What's the Church Coming To?

(Study No. 38 in the Book of Hebrews)

We have all heard the question, "What's this world coming to?" The Biblical answer is obvious. But our question is, "What's the **Church** coming to?" Our text tells what we **have not come to** and what we **are coming to**. Let's consider where the people of God have come from and dare not return, and then see where they are going. The writer contrasts the old and the new covenants by the dramatic analogy of two mountains: Sinai, a fearful scene at the giving of the law, and Zion, the mountain of grace. The awesome display at the giving of the law is compared to the beauty at the inauguration of the new covenant.

See **what the Church is not coming to.** We are not coming to **that threatening mount of flame, thunder, shaking and upheaval.** Gloom, darkness, and a raging storm, a scene that struck terror to the hearts of the people, surrounded the mountain when Moses received the law. Fierce lightning, rumbling thunder, and the sound of the trumpet came in ever-increasing intensity. The "voice of words" was terrifying to their ears, the speech so awesome that the people said to Moses, "You speak to us, and we will hear; but let not God speak with us, lest we die" (Ex. 20:19). Terror-stricken at the sovereign display of God's majesty, they realized that He was unapproachable. Because they heard God speak they were afraid they would die. The people trembled as God's majesty was revealed to touch, sight, and sound. So holy was His Presence, so remote from man that even the beasts that touched the mountain were to be slain. Moses, himself, must have been as frightened at this overwhelming display as he had been at the burning bush where he "trembled and dared not look" (Acts 7:32).

We are not reading about what God's nature **once was.** He is still the same. Unless we are fully aware of His holiness we cannot genuinely worship. Though His nature never changes, our approach to Him has. We do not come to an awful display of power and holiness at Mount Sinai.

What **is the Church coming to**, if not to Mount Sinai? We "**have come to Mount Zion and the city of the living God.**" Mount Sinai is in the desert, but Mount Zion is in Jerusalem. Zion suggests grace while Sinai speaks of the law. Man must come to Mount Sinai before he approaches Mount Zion. Sinai reveals our sin; Zion delivers from it. Jehovah is both God of Sinai and God of Zion.

To the Jews Mount Zion was the earthly dwelling place of God, "the city which the Lord had chosen out of all the tribes of Israel, to put His name there" (1 Ki. 14:21). So Zion applies to Jerusalem, the Holy City where the temple stood, and where God particularly manifested His Presence. Today the Church, the Body of Christ, is the dwelling place of God. Zion most likely means "a sign post, a marker showing the way." It stands for the presence of God, the people of God, His reign over them and for them.

What are **the advantages of Mount Zion**? First, **we are surrounded by innumerable angels.** Angels were present at the giving of the law (Heb. 2:2). Stephen said Israel "received the law by the direction of angels" (Acts 7:53). But the word of the new covenant was spoken by the Lord Himself (Heb. 2:3)! The angels of God are "all ministering spirits sent forth to minister for those who will inherit salvation" (Heb. 1:14). They have one characteristic in common with us—both angels and humans were created to worship God. In worship, the angels of God merge their praise with the redeemed. However, when we bless His Name for redemption they must be speechless, for they have never experienced such grace. Johnson Oatman, Jr. wrote:

Then the angels stand and listen,
For they cannot join that song,
Like the sound of many waters,
By that happy, blood-washed throng;
For they sing about great trials,
Battles fought and vic'tries won,
And they praise their great Redeemer,
Who hath said to them, "Well done."

Holy, holy, is what the angels sing,
And I expect to help them
Make the courts of heaven ring;
But when I sing redemption's story,
They will fold their wings,
For angels never felt the joys
That our salvation brings. [1]

"Angels desire to look into" the gospel (1 Pet. 1:12). What a wonder to that sinless host to see rebellious, sinful beings cleansed by the blood of Jesus, worshiping Him for His amazing grace!

We have come also **"to the general assembly of the church of the firstborn."** "General assembly" is taken from the Greek word "paneguris." "Pan" means "all" and "agora" "a gathering of the people in honor of a god, or for some public festal assembly, such as the Olympic games."[2] One is reminded of Isaiah 51:11: "Therefore the redeemed of the Lord shall return, and come with singing unto Zion; and everlasting joy shall be upon their head: they shall obtain gladness and joy; and sorrow and mourning shall flee away" (KJV). We do not approach Mount Zion with fear; we come as joyful worshipers, not to a place of terror, but celebration, where God, now approachable, dwells with His people.

The Church is called **"the church of the firstborn."** The Old Testament teaches that the blessing of the first-born was restricted to just one in each household. In the Christian family **all** are "heirs of God and joint heirs with Christ" (Rom. 8:17). We are **all elder sons** with God's blessing!

Furthermore, we are **"registered in heaven."** Jesus urged, "Rejoice because your names are written in heaven" (Lk. 10:2).

And John wrote, "Only those who are written in the Lamb's Book of Life" will enter that Holy City, New Jerusalem. God grant that we can answer "yes" to the question asked by the old hymn:

"Is my name written there
On the page white and fair?
In the book of Thy kingdom,
Is my name written there?" (3)

The focus now shifts to **judgment**. The Judge and God of All is the Judge of both the living and the dead. The dead are described as "the spirits of just men made perfect." They have preceded us into the presence of God, "the Father of spirits." "Just men made perfect" are saints now completed or "perfected." We must remember that they are "just," not innocent men. We are not saved because we are innocent, but because we are justified by faith in the finished work of Calvary.

The redeemed who have gone before, as well as those of us who remain, are an integral part of the Church. Our Lord sees the Church as one people, whether on earth or in His presence. So the Church consists of more than those presently alive on planet Earth. All saints, past and present, constitute that one body.

So, what's the Church coming to? How splendid that we are coming to Mount Zion; how magnificent we are coming to an innumerable company of angels; how incredible we are coming to the festal gathering of the firstborn children of God whose names are written in heaven's records. But all this pales when we consider that we are coming **to Jesus the Mediator of the new covenant!** Through Him we have bold access to all other benedictions. What a contrast with the fearful way of Sinai!

Since Jesus is Mediator of the new covenant and stands between the repentant sinner and a holy God, we are able to approach God without being utterly destroyed. The writer calls our Lord by His angel-given Name—Jesus. Thank God, "He will save His people from their sins" (Matt. 1:21).

How does the Lord Jesus accomplish this great salvation? Our approach to God is assured by **"the blood of sprinkling."** His precious blood is more than a replacement of the old system; it is superior to the supplanted. Do you wonder how you can escape the curse of sin? The Israelites wanted freedom from Egyptian slavery, but it only came by their doorposts being sprinkled by the blood of a sacrificial lamb. When the death angel saw the blood, the first-born of every household was spared. Their salvation depended on the blood. The blood of the Lamb of God is our way of escape!

Some wonder how to overcome sinful habits that keep recurring. Under the old covenant the High Priest entered the Holy of Holies once each year to sprinkle the atoning blood of an animal for the sins of the people. This ritual had to be repeated, for man is a habitual sinner. Today we do not come once a year; instead we have permanent and continual access to our Father through Christ's sprinkled blood, which is perfect in every way. He cleanses moment by moment.

If His sprinkled blood **speaks,** what does it say? It speaks of forgiveness, freedom, and access to God. It speaks of peace, rest, and freedom from fear. It speaks of "better things than that of Abel." Abel's was the blood of martyrdom while Jesus' blood was that of sacrifice and atonement. The blood of Abel cried out and accused; the blood of Christ pleads for mercy and pardon. Abel's blood spoke of wrath, but Jesus' speaks of reconciling love. The blood of Abel cried out for vengeance, but the blood shed by Jesus speaks of acceptance, forgiveness, and spiritual power. "[4] Thank God for the precious blood!

"Would you be free from the burden of sin?
There's power in the blood,
Power in the blood;
Would you o'er evil a victory win?
There's wonderful power in the blood." [5]

God has provided the only sufficient Sacrifice. No one can return to the old system and be saved. We have passed from material symbols to spiritual facts. The terror and majesty of the former day has given way to the tenderness and mercy of the new day! There is no other way! Jesus is *God's Final Answer.*

The old covenant was given on Sinai, an earthly mountain, surrounded by gloom and raging storm; the new covenant was given on Mount Zion, with brilliant light and crested with the city of God. Angels, ministering in the winds and fire, gave the old covenant, while a festive band of assembled angels attended the new covenant. The Israelites cowered about the mountain when the old was given, but the Church of the firstborn, living in the new covenant, enters without dread into the Holy of Holies. When the old covenant was given the Lord God, shrouded in fire and darkness, was unapproachable. But the new covenant gives bold access to the Father. Moses, himself, terrified at the giving of the first covenant, provided no mediation for the people, but Jesus became the Mediator between God and man at the giving of the new. The sprinkled blood of the old covenant could not take away guilt nor permanently cleanse, but the sprinkled blood of Jesus offers constant cleansing and atonement. The sounds from Sinai struck fear in the hearts of the people, but the speaking blood of the Lamb of God whispers peace from Zion.

How should we respond to such unchanging grace? With that innumerable host of angels we sing:

> *"All hail the power of Jesus Name;*
> *Let angels prostrate fall.*
> *Bring forth the royal diadem*
> *And crown Him Lord of All!"* [6]

❧

See that you do not refuse Him who speaks. For if they did not escape who refused Him who spoke on earth, much more shall we not escape if we turn away from Him who speaks from heaven, whose voice then shook the earth; but now He has promised, saying, "Yet once more I shake not only the earth, but also heaven." Now this, "Yet once more," indicates the removal of those things that are made, that the things which cannot be shaken may remain. Therefore, since we are receiving a kingdom which cannot be shaken, let us have grace, by which we may serve God acceptably with reverence and godly fear. For our God is a consuming fire.

Hebrews 12:25-29
(See Also Haggai 2:1-9)

Rev 6:12-17
Rev 16:17-19

CHAPTER 39

After the Shaking

(Study No. 39 in the Book of Hebrews)

The writer of Hebrews, interpreting words from the prophet Haggai, teaches that God's method of dealing with mankind is that of shaking. He causes those things which **can** be destroyed **to be** destroyed. Haggai refers to the shaking of the earth at the giving of the law, and to the future shaking of the earth at the coming of Christ.

The Hebrews who received this letter were filled with fear because they were experiencing a severe "shaking." But now they were being reminded that this is God's consistent method. He shakes things so that those things which can be shaken will be removed and those things which cannot be shaken will remain.

The same thought is expressed by Paul, "For He must reign till He has put all enemies under His feet" (1 Cor. 15:25). Paul is **not** saying Jesus must wait for some future day to reign. No! He reigns until all enemies will be underfoot! He is reigning **now**! He is in control **now**! He is shaking now.

Let us consider first, **the fact that things are being shaken today;** second, **why this shaking is taking place;** third, **things which are not being shaken.**

One thing being shaken today is **political systems** around the world. Systems that have been in place for a long time are being challenged and changed. Democratic forms of government have sprung up in unlikely places. Leaders today have also learned that their personal lives do matter to those they serve.

When God gave the Ten Commandments an earthquake shook Sinai. God was not, as Ted Koppel said, giving us the "ten suggestions." Civilizations have built on this code of ethics. Those commandments, though outlawed today from public classrooms and not taken seriously by the public at large, are now being insisted upon in the political arena where they have previously been ignored.

Religious empires are being shaken to their very foundations. Perhaps we have seen the greatest shaking of religion since the Reformation. The failure of certain television ministries has been a shaking experience to many. The shaking continues and aftershocks are apt to occur, simply because there is too much of the world and the flesh in some modern religious efforts. Satan is pleased, but the bottom line is that **it is God Who is shaking things!** The counterfeit, built on human efforts, must be shaken so the eternal may stand. We must not put our trust in the spectacular, or in human instruments. Faith must rest in God Himself and in no other.

Economic systems are also shaking. We know not to trust in uncertain riches, and yet we kill ourselves piling up assets. Our Lord did not call the successful farmer a sinner, though he certainly was one; He called him a fool! He was obsessed with riches. We'll thank God that we refused to trust in anything as fragile as money when material things begin to shake.

We have seen another shaking which is of historical proportions. We have, in great measure, **divested ourselves of historical moral codes.** Like Israel, in the time of the Judges, we do that which is right in our own eyes. We legalized abortion, saying that it is nobody's business how we conduct our private lives. We are experiencing a horrible disease called AIDS. This dread disease is now a part of all society, regardless of lifestyles. Some reap where they have sown; others reap where they have not sown. Millions of little children are being afflicted with this terrible malady.

God sets down certain rules in His Book concerning the way we should live. He did that, not as a dictator, who wants to limit our freedom, but because He opposes anything that will kill, steal, or destroy. Since God has set down certain rules for us to follow, there must be not only certain inalienable rights, but also certain inalienable responsibilities.

Why is God shaking us today? God's declared purpose is separation...the wheat from the chaff, the goats from the sheep. He exposes the true and the false, the permanent and the temporary, through shaking. Since God is responsible for the shaking, we can have peace in it. He is in control! We need not worry about the shaking if we are anchored to Christ!

What is unshakable? One truth which does not shake is **the Fatherhood of God.** He is our Father by creation, and He is our Father by virtue of the death and resurrection of His Son, our Lord Jesus. We are received into God's family as sons and daughters by faith in His Son. As Creator and Redeemer He is preparing an unshakable Kingdom for His family!

The Object of our faith, Jesus Christ will never shake! Whether we live or die our confidence is in Him! He never wavers! Jesus is *God's Final Answer* to the stress and shaking in today's world. How foolish to trust any other! Nothing can take the place of the One Who said, "I will never leave you or forsake you." As Stanley Jones said, "We have an unchanging Person and an unshakable Kingdom!"

Let brotherly love continue. Do not forget to entertain strangers, for by so doing some have unwittingly entertained angels. Remember the prisoners as if chained with them—those who are mistreated—since you yourselves are in the body also. Marriage is honorable among all, and the bed undefiled; but fornicators and adulterers God will judge. Let your conduct be without covetousness; be content with such things as you have. For He Himself has said, "I will never leave you nor forsake you." So we may boldly say: "The LORD is my helper; I will not fear. What can man do to me?" Remember those who rule over you, who have spoken the word of God to you, whose faith follow, considering the outcome of their conduct. Jesus Christ is the same yesterday, today, and forever.

Hebrews 13:1-8

CHAPTER 40

The Basis of Human Relationships

(Study No. 40 in the Book of Hebrews)

"**S**trength for today, and bright hope for tomorrow," one of the lines from *Great Is Thy Faithfulness,* teaches that the Christian faith not only includes the hope of heaven, but also deals with our daily walk. Christians are allowed to keep their heads in the clouds as long as their feet are planted on earth. This very practical text defines behavior toward those in the family of God, including our spouses, and gives the basis for these relationships. We will **reflect on the commands of this passage** and to **see how our Lord makes them possible.**

The chapter begins with **behavior toward others.** Believers are to **let brotherly love continue.** Love is naturally at work in the Christian community, and will continue if "allowed" to do so. Love among Christians should happen normally. We do not love **as if** we were brothers, but because we **are** brothers. In the Christian family we are not free to choose whom we will love; even enemies are not exempt from our love.

Although Christians are to love their enemies, there is nevertheless, a unique love which exists among believers. The New Testament best describes this relationship in family terminology. Those who are experiencing persecution, as these Hebrews were, desperately need to be loved. Love heals. If you hurt yourself as a child it was better to run to mother for love than to the doctor for treatment. Mother's can "kiss away" more pain than doctors can ever cure!

Love draws hurting people into the Church when sermons and singing cannot. Jesus said, "By this all will know that you are My disciples, if you love one another" (Jn. 13:34). The command, "let brotherly love continue," suggests that their love may have been weakening. Love needs nourishment. Someone has said if everybody had only 15 minutes to live, every phone booth in the world would be occupied!

"Do not forget to entertain strangers" is the second command. If we can not love each other we are not apt to love strangers. In that day persecution forced many Christians to flee for their lives. Jesus said, "When they persecute you in this city, flee to another" (Matt. 10:23). Peter exhorted, "Be hospitable to one another without grumbling" (1 Pet. 4:9). Church leaders especially were to be "hospitable" (1 Tim. 3:2; Ti. 1:8). Inns were scarce, filthy, expensive, and usually disreputable. The Hebrews word "harlot" is sometimes translated "inn-keeper."

The Old Testament tells of angels appearing incognito and being entertained as human beings (Gen. 18:1ff; Jud. 13:3ff). What if we turned away someone only to later discover that we had turned away the Lord Himself? Jesus said some would ask, "When did we see You a stranger and take you in?" and He would answer, "Inasmuch as you did it to one of the least of these My brethren, you did it to Me" (Matt. 25:38, 40). It was especially important that these early saints be hospitable.

Consider how far we have departed from the Lord's command that we be hospitable. When the early Church invited someone to a dinner it was for fellowship; today we must be careful that we only have dinners as fund raisers! What a Christian example was left by Corrie ten Boom who, at the risk of her life, sheltered many Jews condemned to death by Hitler.

Third, we are told to **remember mistreated prisoners.** These first-century saints had friends who, because of their faith, were imprisoned. They were to identify with these sufferers. When Saul of Tarsus was smitten on the Damascus road he cried, "Who are you, Lord?" and the response was, "I am Jesus, Whom you are persecuting" (Acts 9:5). Our Lord identifies with His mistreated brothers and sisters. Saul learned that to mistreat a saint is to mistreat the Savior. As "part of the body" we "weep with those who weep" (Rom. 12:15).

Many are being persecuted today for their testimony. We are to hurt with them as though we were personally being exploited. The imprisonment of Peter brought the Church to its knees (Acts 12:1-5) and his release precipitated unusual Church growth. Those suffering today because of their faith need more than sympathy; they need on-going empathizing prayer.

Notice the grace of the writer. He makes no strong accusation, but simply says, "**Let** brotherly love continue...**do not forget** to entertain strangers... and **remember** the prisoners." How gently the Holy Spirit can correct if we are sensitive!

From prisoners, strangers, and brothers and sisters the writer becomes more personal by mentioning **the bonds of marriage.** When God created the physical universe He said "it was good." But not until God created Adam and Eve did He say it was "very good." The establishing of the family preceded that of the Church or human government.

The Christian family and marriage is not only an example to the pagan world, it also illustrates the unique relationship of the Church with the Lord Jesus. Early Christians lived in a society that involved immorality in their worship. Others taught that marriage was unholy and unclean. The Scripture allows a person to remain single, but avoidance of marriage on religious grounds is heresy. The Bible does not teach celibacy, or singleness, as spiritually superior or inferior. If we fault marriage we fault the Creator, for He ordained it. Those who demean marriage and parenthood deny the teaching of Scripture.

One need not have a high IQ to understand why God has confined sexual fulfillment to marriage. The commandments of God are not given to frustrate, but to protect. Rather than breaking God's laws, we break ourselves on His laws. We were not made for fornication, adultery, or homosexuality. This command concerning marriage was given in a permissive society where fornication was common. The Church dare not compromise on the Biblical standard regarding family life.

A minister performed the marriage ceremony for a lovely young man and woman who dreamed of continuing the family farm. Shortly after their third child was born, the wife developed an incurable disease. Everything the young farmer owned slipped away for hospital and medical needs.

On their tenth anniversary the minister was invited to share a simple meal. There was no pie, no cake, no homemade rolls, but the minister remembers, "We had cold buttermilk chilled in a jug in the cold waters of the spring. But it was a feast because love had set the table." The minister went on to say, "I could not help but weep as I saw that young man moving around the table waiting on his wife and three children. The tenderness of that young farmer with his sick wife caught my heart."

As the pastor got up to go, the young man said: "Just a minute, Pastor. Before you go you must see her anniversary present." He went to the dresser and produced a thin flat package containing a string of pearls. The minister assumed they were imitations. How could this farm boy afford the real thing? "Shut your eyes," the young farmer said as he stood behind her to fasten them. She burst into tears, crying, "They are real! They are not mine. They can't be."

Then the young husband told a wonderful story. "You know before we were married you said pearls were the prettiest jewelry in the world. You thought they were prettier than any other jewelry except your wedding band. Before we were married, I asked the Lord to help me put this string of pearls around your neck. You never knew about the box that I started dropping money into, nickel by nickel and dime by dime. I was fond of tobacco but I gave it up. That was good for me anyhow. I was fond of cold Cokes but for thirteen years, three before we were married and the ten after, I haven't spent a nickel on cokes. All that went into the box. These pearls are paid for and they are yours."

"Joe," she asked, "what made you do it? What made you do it?" He fell down on his knees and, putting his face in his wife's lap, cried like a baby. As the minister quietly left the home, he heard that loving husband bubbling through tears, "I did it because I love you." The minister added, "I have often wondered how long that man stayed on his knees weeping in the lap of that woman who had less than a year to live." A love far beyond that was manifested at the cross. The Savior says, "I did it because I love you."[1]

Notice the command in verse seven. "**Remember those who rule over you, who have spoken the word of God to you, whose faith follow, considering the outcome of their conduct.**" We are to follow those who teach us because of the positive effect their teaching has had on their own lives. If we were drowning it would be unimportant if the rescuer were a Christian. If our house were burning down we would not check the creedal statement of the firemen. But if one teaches the Word of God it won't be heard unless it has made a positive impact on his/her own life. Creed must affect conduct. If the truth has not worked in our own lives, others are not bound to receive it from us. This demands that we must, over a period of time, observe the lifestyles of those who teach us. It is not a good practice to get our teaching from those of unproven reputation. This is one of the weaknesses of getting our teaching through the electronic media. The Scripture and experience itself teach us that nothing can take the place of the local Church.

We can understand why verses seven and eight concerning leaders and Christ complement each other. Believers follow those who are consistent in the faith, those who exemplify the One Who is the same yesterday, today, and forever.

How does our Lord make it possible to follow these commandments concerning brothers, strangers, prisoners, spouses, and teachers? **Our relationship with others is founded in Jesus Christ. The unchanging Christ is our Source.** We can keep His precepts "For He Himself has said, 'I will never leave you or forsake you.' So we may boldly say, 'The Lord is my Helper; I will not fear. What can man do to me?'" Commandments, impossible to keep through human effort, are followed because He "is my Helper."

Obedience to these commands means that **we do not need to covet.** Our first parents, Adam and Eve, fell because they lusted after that which was forbidden. We live in a very materialistic society. We should "**be content with such things as you have.**" A state trooper is said to have found a Yuppie by the roadside next to a demolished car, crying, "O my BMW! I've lost my BMW!" The trooper said, "Never mind your BMW. You've lost your left arm." The Yuppie looked down and cried, "O my Rolex! I've lost my

Rolex!"[2] I was grieved as I watched a Hollywood star on a TV news segment showing a reporter through one of her closets with dresses costing $4000.00 or more.

The command concerning contentment (v. 5) refers to our attitude. It does not mean a passive acceptance of whatever comes our way. The Lord knows what we need and has promised to supply our needs. Our contentment is based on the unchanging character of the Lord Jesus. He is always the same and always with us.

Charles L. Allen was a young pastor of a little church back in the mountains. He spent a lot of time with and learned a lot from an old man in the community. The old man would tell his young pastor how life used to be, how little the people had, and yet how happy they had been. One day, he said, the mailman left a mail order catalog at someone's house. The people looked at it, first curious, then longingly. Soon every home in the community had a catalog. As they turned the pages of the catalog, they forgot the beauty of the mountains around them. They thought, instead, of the many things they did not possess. [3] Contentment was gone.

Spiritually, verses four and five link together. Those discontented in marriage are often discontented also with material things. Discontentment stems from lack of fulfillment in Christ. Start with Him and "all those other things will be added unto you." If we do not begin with Him our searching never ends. If life is not governed by Christ it will be governed by things. Jesus said, "Therefore do not worry, saying, 'What shall we eat?' or 'What shall we drink?' or 'What shall we wear?' For all these things the Gentiles (heathen) seek. Your heavenly Father knows that you need all these things" (Matt. 6:31, 32).

Bishop Charles Golden visited a mission school in India where the students sang an old spiritual for him. Because he was Black, as a courtesy they sang, *I Got Shoes*. As they sang the Bishop's eyes fell on their bare feet. He remembered that his own people, when barefooted, had composed that song, a song of hope and trust, for they knew that shoes were laid up in heaven for them. [4]

Covetousness indicates discontent and implies a lack of trust in God and His promises. "He will never leave us or forsake us." The word "leave" is preceded by a double negative which makes it a positive statement—"I will never, never leave you." Three negatives before the word "forsake" makes the promise a triple assurance. Wuest translates verse five, "Let your manner of life be without love of money, being satisfied with your present circumstances. For He Himself has said, and the statement is on record, **"I will not, I will not cease to sustain and uphold you. I will not, I will not, I will not let you down."**

When a Christian response is commanded of us toward brethren, strangers, prisoners, spouses, and spiritual leaders, we can, realizing our weakness, still say with the Apostle Paul, "I can do all things **through Christ** Who strengthens me"(Phil. 4:13)

Jesus Christ is the same yesterday, today, and forever.

Hebrews 13:8

CHAPTER 41

Anchored to the Unchanging One

(Study No. 41 in the Book of Hebrews)

Y ou can be sure that nothing in this world is sure! All earthly things are subject to change, a fact that provokes sighs of sorrow and shouts of joy. Change prevents monotony, yet it can also be a deadly enemy. Someone said the last seven words of the Church are, "We've never done it that way before" or "We tried it once; it didn't work." Some are threatened by change.

Leadership Magazine tells of a man parked at the curb waiting for his wife. He noticed a young lady in her late twenties in the next car dabbing her eyes with a tissue. He wondered what her problem was. Suddenly a man of about thirty came out of a barber shop and approached her car. He was holding a little three-year-old boy whose hair was cut as short as it possibly could be. The young lady grabbed the child and, crying profusely, she began kissing him. Then she turned and said something to the man. He disagreed with whatever she was saying and it looked as if they were now in quite an argument. He shook his head as she talked. Finally the man, red-faced, went back into the barber shop, reached under the barber's chair, picked up a lock of blond hair, and took it out to his wife.

The man who was watching said that if he had gone to the mother and asked, "Do you want your little boy to remain a child forever?" she would have answered, "Of course not! But I have lost my baby."[1]

We want change, but since change can be painful, it is often resisted. When we are threatened and fearful of change we are apt to quote, "Jesus Christ the same yesterday, and today, and forever." Although Jesus Christ is permanently the same, He is infinitely variable in the ways He deals with his people.

Hebrews 6:19 says, "This hope we have as an anchor of the soul, both sure and steadfast, and which enters the Presence behind the veil." Our anchor is cast, not out where rocks and waves threaten, but within the veil, the very Presence of God! This speaks of permanence, not stagnation; freshness, not decay.

Henry Francis Lyte wrote his last hymn, *Abide with Me*, two months before he died. The last verse of that precious old hymn expresses our common cry for permanence:

> *"Swift to its close ebbs out life's little day!*
> *Earth's joy grow dim; its glories pass away,*
> *Change and decay in all around I see,*
> *O Thou, Who changest not, abide with me!"* [2]

Mr. Lyte could write that song because he believed that Jesus Christ **was** the same yesterday, today, and forever. Perhaps he overstates the case when he uses the words "change" and "decay" as though they were synonymous; but he, nevertheless, as he came near his departure, was crying out for permanence. That which he sought is clearly discerned in Jesus, our Lord.

Let us consider Jesus Christ **yesterday**, Jesus Christ **today**, and Jesus Christ **forever**. Jesus Christ **yesterday** introduces considerations beyond the power of our intellect. John wrote, "In the beginning was the Word, and the Word was with God; and the Word was God" (Jn. 1:1). To enter into those eons of the past is too much for minds that forget anniversaries! A man in Memphis opened his car trunk and discovered a dusty package. He had bought a Christmas gift for his wife but had forgotten to give it to her. Sheepishly, he took the package home. When she saw it she burst into tears of joy and said, "O dear, I was so afraid that you had forgotten our wedding anniversary!"[3]

There was never a time when Christ was not, and there will never be a time when He will not be. He is eternal. Though He willingly came into this world to be our Redeemer and died at an identifiable point in history, He was and is, "The Lamb of God slain from the foundation of the world." Jesus Christ, yesterday!

The Christ of yesterday came into this world with history already written about Him...not in some evolutionary slime pit or jungle mud...but written in the eternal bosom of God the Father! Yesterday's Jesus appears in the gospel narratives working out His amazing love for fallen humanity. He never once compromised with sin. He never subscribed to the theory that claims, "We just can't help ourselves," or that sin must be tolerated. We sometimes speak of "necessary evils." We do not get that language from our dear Lord! For Him, if a thing is necessary it is never evil, and if it is evil it is never necessary.

There are no "hopeless cases" in the sight of our Lord. Many bound by drugs or sexual habits feel trapped. Jesus Christ gives the power to say, "No." We hear that it is, "OK to say no." It is not only "OK," it is **right** to say "No;" and He gives us power to say it.

A friend said to William Stidger, who had suffered an emotional breakdown, "When was the last time you singled out an acquaintance who has been gracious to you and expressed appreciation?" The question bothered him, so he wrote that very evening to a High School teacher who had been particularly helpful to him. He had not thought of her for years, but he recalled she had taken interest in him and had helped him discover a love for poetry, which he did not know he had. Three days later he received a letter written in the tremulous handwriting of a long-retired teacher. She wrote, "My eyes are blinded by tears as I write. You are the first student in my entire career who has ever written me a letter to express thanks. I will keep it as long as I live." With her response, he thought of others, and soon he had written letter after letter. As he was expressing gratitude he recovered from his illness. [4] Express your praise to God for all those "yesterdays" and you'll find that beautiful and liberating things happen to grateful people!

What of Jesus Christ **today?** Though we cannot physically see Him now, He said, "A little while and you will see Me" (John 16:16). This could include not only His Second Coming, but the coming of the Holy Spirit Who would cause Christ to be seen as never before. "It is expedient for you that I go away," He said. If He did not go away the Spirit could not come. But now the Spirit is here, and He came to make Christ real. We can have closer fellowship with Jesus Christ than with each other. No man has ever seen God, but neither do we really **see** each other. We only see outer shells when we look at others. Our fellowship with Jesus can be closer than that with our dearest earthly friend.

Karl Barth, the famous theologian, was on a streetcar one day in Basil, Switzerland. A tourist climbed on the car and sat down next to Barth. The two men began chatting. "Are you new to the city?" Barth inquired. "Yes," said the tourist. "Is there anything you would particularly like to see in this city?" asked Barth. "Yes," he answered, "I'd like to meet the famous theologian, Karl Barth. Do you know him?" Barth replied, "Yes, as a matter of fact, I do. I give him a shave every morning." The delighted tourist got off the streetcar and said to himself, "Today I met Karl Barth's personal barber!"[5] Christians with whom we fellowship are temples of the Holy Spirit, people in whom Christ dwells. How often we sit next to other believers, eat with them, sing with them, and yet fail to recognize the Presence of Christ in them.

Without His Presence we are never fulfilled. There is an enormous amount of unhappiness today. One survey reports that every day in the United States 70 people commit suicide and another 1000 attempt it. That means that every year 365,000 people are unhappy enough to try to snuff out their lives! In an average lifetime 15,000,000 people will attempt to end their lives. The suicide rate has increased nearly 300 percent among young people 15 to 24 in the last 20 years.[6] Jesus came to give life in the here and now, as well as hereafter!

A student told the dean at his university that he had not been able to finish his master's thesis on time because he was not feeling well. The dean replied, "Young man, I think it's time you realize most of the work done in this world is done by people who aren't feeling well." Fulfillment does not come by feeling good, but by walking with Jesus, the One Who said, "Come unto Me, all you who labor and are heavy laden and I will give you rest."

Someone recently wrote, "When I am under stress, I don't need God; I need Valium. When I am in pain, I don't need God; I need a good physician. When I am in need, I don't need God; I need to get on welfare. When I am bored, I don't need God; I need to be entertained by television."[7] What a dead-end street! We all need the living Christ! Thank God, there's an empty tomb at Jerusalem and Christ is alive, well, and ruling today!

At the death of Nikita Kruschev a humorous story circulated in political circles. The Communist party was uncomfortable with the idea of burying his body on Soviet soil. They first called the president of the U.S. and asked if the U.S. would take the corpse. When they were refused, the Russian leaders tried Golda Meir, the Prime Minister of Israel. Golda agreed but added, "I must warn you this country has the world's highest resurrection rate."[8] Jesus Christ, Who stripped off those death clothes on that first Easter morning, is not only alive today, He seeks fellowship with us.

He is also the same **forever.** "Forever" means "to the ages." Years come and go but He remains constant. True, "today is the first day of the rest of your life," but it is also true that today could be your last on planet earth.

Life with Jesus Christ is never monotonous. He constantly excites the soul! Married couples sometimes find that the fire needs rekindling in their romance. As a couple sat together in the porch swing she asked, "George, do you think my eyes are beautiful?" George answered, "Yep." In a few moments, "George, do you think my hair is attractive?" Again George answered, "Yep." In a while, "George, would you say that I have a gorgeous figure?" Once again George answered, "Yep." "Oh, George," she said, "You say the nicest things."[9] George sounds rather hum-drum, but Jesus is never monotonous. He makes our hearts sing!

All too many identify with Peppermint Patty in the *Peanuts* cartoon when she said in her school report, "This is my report on daytime and nighttime. Daytime is so you can see where you are going. Nighttime is so you can lie in bed and worry." When we face our tomorrows with confidence in Jesus Christ, Lord of our tomorrows, we need not "lie in bed and worry," for *God's Final Answer* is the same **yesterday and today and forever!**

Do not be carried about with various and strange doctrines. For it is good that the heart be established by grace, not with foods which have not profited those who have been occupied with them. We have an altar from which those who serve the tabernacle have no right to eat. For the bodies of those animals, whose blood is brought into the sanctuary by the high priest for sin, are burned outside the camp. Therefore Jesus also, that He might sanctify the people with His own blood, suffered outside the gate. Therefore let us go forth to Him, outside the camp, bearing His reproach. For here we have no continuing city, but we seek the one to come. Therefore by Him let us continually offer the sacrifice of praise to God, that is, the fruit of our lips, giving thanks to His name. But do not forget to do good and to share, for with such sacrifices God is well pleased. Obey those who rule over you, and be submissive, for they watch out for your souls, as those who must give account. Let them do so with joy and not with grief, for that would be unprofitable for you. Pray for us; for we are confident that we have a good conscience, in all things desiring to live honorably. But I especially urge you to do this, that I may be restored to you the sooner.

Hebrews 13:9-19

CHAPTER 42

Three Gifts on the Altar

(Study No. 42 in the Book of Hebrews)

One of the vital concerns of the author of Hebrews was to stabilize his readers in their Christian walk. He urged them not to be carried about with "various and strange" doctrines, such as trying to please God with certain dietary rules. These strange rules, he said, were not to be imposed on God's people.

The unbelieving Jews thought these Christians foolish to forsake the temple and the elaborate Hebrew worship system. They could hardly imagine a religion without impressive external paraphernalia. On the other hand, the Romans, seeing that the Christians had no visible gods, might conclude that they were dangerous atheists. The writer affirms that they, in fact, did have an altar; but that those who "serve the tabernacle," those under the old covenant, had no right to eat from that altar. In other words, those who were still holding to the Hebrew religion could not be established by the grace of God.

Under the Old Testament economy the bodies of sacrificed animals were taken outside the camp for burning and their blood was offered in the sanctuary. In like manner, Jesus was offered outside the city of Jerusalem. Since He suffered reproach by dying outside the city gate, we should be willing to "go forth to Him, outside the camp, bearing His reproach." Whatever reproach we bear should be borne gladly, for since we have no continuing city, reproach is only temporary. We are "not here for long; we'll soon be leaving." We presently live in the light of that city to come!

We have an altar. Altars are associated with Old Testament characters. For instance, when Abraham reached the Promised Land he built an altar. He built another altar when he offered his son, thus identifying with his God in suffering. Isaac and Gideon built altars. Samuel built an altar and called it Ebenezer, "the Lord has helped us" (1 Sam. 7:12). After the plague that resulted from his sin was lifted, David built an altar at the threshing floor of Araunah the Jebusite. Whether the occasion was sorrow, joy, defeat, or victory, altars were built.

Altars were erected in times of crises. When a crisis arises in our own experience we should take it to the Lord. When we have a new baby, a new job, a raise in wages, we have an opportunity to "build an altar." Unless we do that these times of joy will grow sour. Likewise, when sorrow comes we should bring that to the Lord. If we brood over it or nurse it, it may destroy us. Jesus gives meaning to sorrow, turns it into joy, bringing good out of it.

In the old economy when a crisis came, God revealed Himself. We have an altar, only one, and it has provided us with the ultimate revelation of God. We do not go from one altar to another. The woman at the well asked Jesus about worshiping at Jerusalem or Mount Gerizim. He responded, "God is spirit, and those who worship Him must worship in spirit and truth" (Jn. 4:24). Our altar is not limited as to location, for it centers in the cross of Christ.

Days filled with glory and radiant with victory are times for an altar, as are days shrouded in darkness. Even a day when we slip and fall is an altar time. No matter what experience we have in life this principle applies, whether joyous or sorrowful, victorious or painful, we have an altar that has been raised for us—the cross of Christ! It gives meaning to all of life and offers direction in every crisis hour.

Old Testament altars meant at least three things—worship, sacrifice, and change. In **worship** we submit to God even though we may not fully understand His will. Worship suggests that we not only **need** God, but **want** Him more than anything else. In joy or sorrow, defeat or victory, hunger for God remains.

The altar also means **sacrifice**. Though we submit to God, want God, and need God, the altar indicates that there is distance between God and man that can only be spanned by sacrifice. The cross, our ultimate altar, bridges that distance.

Change is also suggested by the altar. Old Testament patriarchs built altars when they reached a crisis in their experience. From that point on life was meant to be different. Millions testify how their lives were changed as they bowed before the cross.

Notice how the Old Testament saints built their altars. These were God's instructions: first, **they were to build the altar of earth;** second, if they made it of stone **they were not to use hewn stone;** third, **they were not to include steps.** (Ex. 20:24-26).

An altar made of dirt spoke of simplicity. God moves among the commonplace, the ordinary, the natural, the unsophisticated, the normal. God is not impressed with "things." We must not be obsessed with wearing the "right" clothes, going to the "right" places, and being seen with the "right" people. Revelation 3:16 teaches us that such pride makes Jesus ill! Others who share the Lord's sensitivity may even experience some of that nausea. An altar made of earth teaches us to "Keep it simple." If others find you difficult to understand, you may not be "deep," only confused!

Second, **the altar was not to be hewn stone.** God warned, "If you use your tool on it, you have profaned it" (Ex. 20:25). Leave the stones as they are! We don't come to God by our own efforts or the works of our hands. God was not teaching that nature is sacred and not to be defiled. This earth is already defiled, and will not be freed from the curse until **He** frees it! This command against the use of tools has to do with idolatry, with carving objects into the stones, objects which would promote idol worship. We must come to God as the song says, "Just as I am without one plea."

Third, **there were to be no steps to the altar** so "that your nakedness may not be exposed on it" (Ex. 20: 26). For reasons of decency steps were forbidden. Creating our own methods of approaching God only reveals our nakedness. Such feeble efforts magnify our weakness. We can approach God only in His way!

The shame of Adam and Eve after their sin is the first indication of hope in the story. What tragedy when sin produces no shame. Such is true to a significant degree in our present society.

The Jews offered sacrifices for sins upon the altar. The writer mentions **three sacrifices which we continue to offer**, not to obtain forgiveness, but because we are already forgiven.

"The sacrifice of praise, that is, the fruit of our lips, giving thanks to His Name" is properly mentioned first. We are commanded to perpetually praise Him. None of us appreciate a person who must constantly be assured of his greatness. God is not like that vain person who must always be complimented. Though He requires praise it is not simply for His benefit. He knows that as we worship Him we become more like Him.

My wife and I showed a friend the sights along the Blue Ridge Parkway in Virginia, one of the most beautiful drives in the United Stares. His eyes grew large as he asked, "How much money could I make if I owned all the coal under that mountain?" He had missed the meaning of those moments in the mountains. Something within him was distorted. An Iowa farmer who visited "Old Faithful," the geyser in Yellowstone National Park, when asked what he thought said, "It would make a good place to scald hogs." We smile at this unnatural response, but it is just as bizarre to stand in the Presence of God without worshiping. When we know God the normal response is worship.

We must be careful in judging whether or not others are true worshipers by comparing their methods of worship with ours. Some may equate quietness with deadness, while others may regard noise as irreverence. "Make a joyful noise unto the Lord" and "Be still and know that I am God" are taken from the same Bible. The attitude of the heart makes the difference. Techniques of worship may vary, but all are commanded to worship. We do not diminish or add to God by our worship. He commands it, not because He would suffer without it, but because we receive as we worship. As we worship God imparts Himself to us. We gather for worship, to present tithes and offerings, just as He commanded the Hebrews to offer lambs, rams, and doves. Indeed, all of life when lived with the proper attitude is worship, and in worship God communicates Himself to us, causing us to become more like Him.

We also offer **the sacrifice of works** to our Lord. Verse 16 reminds us "to do good and to share, for with such sacrifices God is well pleased." Good works cannot purchase salvation, for that has been accomplished by Jesus at the cross. Good works are the results of salvation and always accompany faith in Christ.

The sacrifice of our wills (vv. 17-19) is also offered. **Obedience to those who rule over us** is an act of our wills. **Submission** is required. Three reasons are given for obedience and submissiveness to spiritual leaders. First, **they watch out for our souls.** True leaders in the Church genuinely care for people. Their concern is not for real estate, money, or ceremonies, but people. A good pastor-shepherd does not identify with any class or clique; he loves people without regard to their station in life.

Some dear people of God are easily taken advantage of today. Sheep are often scattered, fleeced, and wounded by hireling shepherds who seek their own welfare. In Ezekiel 34:1-10 we read of shepherds that do not feed the flock, strengthen the flock, heal the sheep, bind them up, restore them, or seek the lost. "Watching for souls" is compassionately caring for God's flock and protecting them. Often this requires suffering, sacrifice, patience, and sleeplessness on the part of the shepherd.

Spiritual leaders must give account for their work to God! And He is never deceived! We smile over the story of a pastor's assistant who said as he came running and out of breath to the pastor, "I just saw the Lord in the sanctuary. What shall I do?" The pastor replied, "Look busy, man, look busy!" It is certainly true that leadership must give an account to the Lord God!

The third reason to be obedient and submissive to leaders is that **they should be allowed joy in their work.** If they cannot do their work with joy, and must work with grief ("groaning"), it "would be unprofitable for you." It blesses the Church when leadership functions in an atmosphere of joy. Believers can make the work of their shepherd either a burden or a joy. An honest pastor is never distressed by the legitimate needs of the flock. Indeed, he is distressed if omitted from the hurts of the people. But the writer places a responsibility on believers to make the work of those who serve them pleasant.

Unreasonable demands are often made of leadership. A good pastor, in the eyes of some, must be a good mixer, but must never show favoritism. He must fill the collection plates, but never talk about money. He must be a good preacher, teacher, administrator, contractor, singer, personnel manager, and be popular with both the young and the old. He must be out-going, but at the same time humble. He must be young enough, but not too young; old enough, but not too old. He must have children, but not too many or too few. He must be intellectual, yet simple. He must not be too lively or too dull. He must not dress too conservatively or too stylish. It is doubtful that any pastor can please everybody. One pastor said that he pleased everyone—half when he came to the church and the other half when he left!

How can churches help pastors work in an atmosphere of joy? How can my eyes best please my body? By seeing as they should. How can my ears best please my body? By hearing as they should. So we bless the Church as we function as we should—in harmony. So church leaders are blessed when the body becomes a force **with which** they work, rather than a field **in which** they work.

It is never healthy when a church must spend most of its efforts or assets to simply sustain itself. When our bodies work correctly we can take our hands off our pulses and throw our thermometers away! The healthiest church does not need constant introspection. If a church spends its time and energy in worship, fellowship, and evangelism it will remain healthy.

The final command in sacrificing our wills is to **pray for leaders.** Even the apostles needed prayer. Much of the success of their ministry depended on the prayer support of those they served. At the same time, leaders must **live honorably** and with **a good conscience.**

The writer of Hebrews **longed to have fellowship with the Church** and believed that the prayers of the people could determine whether or not he would see them again. Prayer changes things... and people too!

May God find acceptable the **sacrifices of our worship, our works, and our wills.**

Now may the God of peace who brought up our Lord Jesus from the dead, the great Shepherd of the sheep, through the blood of the everlasting covenant, make you complete in every good work to do His will, working in you what is well pleasing in His sight, through Jesus Christ, to whom be glory forever and ever. Amen. And I appeal to you, brethren, bear with the word of exhortation, for I have written you in few words. Know that our brother Timothy has been set free, with whom I shall see you if he comes shortly. Greet all those who rule over you, and all the saints. Those from Italy greet you. Grace be with you all. Amen.

Hebrews 13:20-25

CHAPTER 43

The Hebrew Benediction
(Study No. 43 in the Book of Hebrews)

The writer concludes his letter with a beautiful benediction in which he states his deepest desire for his readers. It is not only a beautiful prayer; it is also an excellent example of how we should pray for others. We will consider **the God to Whom he prays, the prayer itself, the basis upon which his requests are made,** and **the praises he raises to God.** First, notice **how he defines God: the God of Peace** and **the God of Power.** This beautiful expression, "**God of Peace,**" is often used by Paul. Jehovah-Shalom is the Old Testament equivalent.

The compound name for God, Jehovah-Shalom, was revealed to Gideon when he was called to deliver the Israelites from Midianite oppression (Jud. 6:11-24). Three distinct errors are seen in his reasoning as he tries to excuse himself from God's call. First, he thought God could not be with the people if they were experiencing affliction. Second, he maintained that God's presence always meant deliverance. And third, he believed a person's weaknesses made it unlikely for him to be used by God.

These errors are still with us today. "How could God be with me if all these things are happening to me?" is a question often asked. A second error is, "If God were here I would be delivered." Asking, "How could God possibly use someone like me?" can actually immobilize a person. When Gideon recognized the God of Peace, these apprehensions left him. His answers were not in "answers" but in God Himself!

God not only allows and tolerates unfavorable circumstances, He uses them! A king owned a large, beautiful, pure diamond, but one day it accidentally sustained a deep scratch. He called in the finest diamond cutters, but none could repair it. None of them really wanted to try for they feared incurring the wrath of the king if they failed. Finally a gifted jeweler came forward and promised to make the king's diamond even more precious. With artistry and skill he engraved a rose bud on the diamond using the scratch as the stem of the rose so that the diamond's value was greater then before. [1] God uses the scars in our lives to create a beautiful pattern if we allow Him to do so.

When in adverse circumstances, when deliverance is delayed, when faced with our own weaknesses, the answer is not in what God may or may not be doing, nor in whether we are immediately delivered; nor does it have anything to do with our limitations. The Answer is in the God of Peace rather than in circumstances over which we have little or no control.

Peace is not meant to be a condition which comes and goes, but a Person Who constantly abides! Dave Garroway, a former host of the TODAY show, attained wealth, fame, and respect. When someone once asked him his understanding of Christmas he replied: "I've noticed that when people are asked what they want for Christmas, nine times out of ten they say they want something material. That used to be amusing to me, but it's not amusing to me any longer. I happen to be one of those people who can afford anything he wants, but I find that what I really want, I can't buy at all. I want peace of mind; peace of soul; the kind of peace you have when you really don't want anything."[2] Such peace is impossible without the God of Peace. Second, the writer makes his prayer to the God "Who brought up our Lord Jesus from the dead." He is addressing **the God of Power** with Whom all things are possible (Matt. 19:26). Though there is no limit to His power, He will do nothing contrary to His nature. He always acts without coercion and in freedom. God has power over His power. His energy and freedom are inexhaustible. This immeasurable power enabled Jesus Christ to die. "I have power to lay it (My life) down," Jesus said (Jn. 10:18).

What power it must have taken for Christ to remain on the cross, and what power it took to bring Him out of the grave!

No complication is too complex nor any predicament too challenging for Him. If the tomb could not hold its Prey on Easter morning how can we doubt the power of God? He is able!

The prayer is twofold; first, **that they may be completely equipped to do God's will in every good work**, and second, **that they may have God's will worked in themselves.** These two requests should be sought together; neither stands alone.

We are often urged to pray the first without regard to the second. For example, a request we often hear is, "Please pray for my ministry." Our work for God is important, but it is a great tragedy when the work of the Kingdom is done by those who have not had God's will worked within themselves. All that we do may be discredited if God's will does not rule our personal lives.

How can some be so passionate about their work and so unconcerned about their character? Joseph Stalin killed twenty million people, yet showed no sign of guilt. On his deathbed he asked his wife to read him some short stories by Jack London and peacefully went to sleep. [3] God save us from a seared conscience!

We are not ready to proclaim Kingdom truth or do Kingdom work until the King Himself reigns within our hearts. What we **do** must flow from what we **are**. A farmer had two mules, one was named Willing and the other was named Able. Willing was willing but was not able. Able was able but not willing. The farmer didn't get much done! What we are and what we do complement each other.

The basis upon which he makes his request is also twofold: **the blood of Christ** and **the Person of Christ.** Just as he prayed about what they did as well as who they were, he now prays on the basis of **what Jesus did** and **Who Jesus was.**

All that Jesus did would have been to no advantage except for Who He was. He had to offer Himself as a blameless Sacrifice. Had He failed in any respect before going to Golgotha, His death would never have purchased our redemption. His life was sinless, thus His sacrificial death efficacious.

E. Stanley Jones tells us that human sacrifices were offered on the Island of Formosa hundreds of years ago. A kindly emperor by the name of Goho changed all that. According to his law only animals were to be sacrificed. But when a terrible drought caused the crops to fail the people clamored for a human sacrifice. "Very well," said Goho, "tomorrow morning at dawn go into the forest and find your victim for sacrifice. He will be tied to a tree and wearing a red robe. Strike him for he is your sacrifice."

Early in the morning the men arose, took their clubs, and went into the forest. As Goho predicted, there was the promised red-robed sacrifice tied to a tree. They rushed forward and clubbed the sacrifice to death, but when they pulled back the robe uncovering the face, they were horrified to see that it was Goho, their own beloved emperor. In his death Goho did what his law could not; he changed the hearts minds of his people forever. Never again were human sacrifices offered. On Formosa the red robe became the symbol of a changed life. Dingy robes were discarded and red ones worn as if to say, "I am Goho's person." They became known as persons of the robe. [4] There must never be conflict between what we are and what we do.

Finally, observe **the praise he raises!** "And may the glory be given to Him for ever and ever. So be it!" (v. 21, N.T.B.E.) How fitting to end prayer with worship! His praise does not wait for God's response to his prayer, for true praise is not based simply on answers, but on God Himself. Worship acknowledges the worthiness of God (Rev. 4:11). He is the "Audience" when we are alone and as well as when gather for worship. Praise is not simply tied to what God does at the moment. It is centered and circumferenced in Him!

God must never be perceived as a "Celestial Bellhop" Who, when tipped adequately, performs appropriately. God delights in answering prayer, but "The Lord takes pleasure **in His people**" and is enthroned **in their praises**" (Ps. 149:4; 22:3).

If our worship is only based upon what God does for us, it will vary in motivation and depth, or it may disappear entirely in difficult days. If we worship Him simply because He heals us, rather than because He is the Healer, we might cease worshiping during prolonged sickness. Angels continually worship God, not because He has forgiven them or healed them, but because He is worthy.

We can worship alone, but it is imperative that we come together as God's worshiping people. Thomas Aquinas said, "No possession is joyous without a companion" and added, "Notwithstanding the beasts and flowers one could be lonely in a garden." Genuine joy longs to be shared. Corporate praise not only expresses our enjoyment of God; it completes it.

In our gatherings today much emphasis is placed upon the sermon. Things done before the sermon are sometimes referred to as "the preliminaries," reminding one of the undercard of the main event in boxing. If we think of the sermon as the "main event" we may judge everything before it as trivial. Ideally, true worship involves the sermon and all that precedes and follows it, indeed worship should permeate all of life. Since God created us for His pleasure we should fulfill the purpose for which we were made.

A young soldier overseas who wanted to contact his girlfriend decided to send her a telegram. He gave the telegraph operator this message to send: "I love you. I love you. I love you. John." The operator said, "Son, for the same amount of money you can send one more word." The soldier amended the message to read: "I love you. I love you. I love you. Cordially, John."[5] Close relationships, especially with the Lord Jesus are much more than "cordial."

Someone reasoned, "God must know that I love Him. After all, I go to church, sing the songs, give in the offering, and listen to the sermon." **But activity can never substitute for adoration!** Although we live in a busy time when attention spans are abbreviated, our heart, soul, mind, and strength should be disciplined to worship the Living God (Mk. 12:30).

True worship terrorizes the devil, especially when it is given in the midst of adversity. An old legend tells that a master died leaving his servant a bag full of blessings along with a message explaining that the bag would always be full as long as the servant remembered four magic words. The servant immediately began using the blessings, and soon the bag was almost empty. The servant, try as he may, could not remember the four words. Finally he went to a wise man to ask his advice on the matter. The wise man guessed the four magic words were, I WISH I HAD. "I wish I had this. I wish I had that."

The servant tried using the words, "I wish I had this. I wish I had that. I wish I had something else," but the bag was not replenished. Now in his desperation he approached another person for his advice. He suggested the four magic words might be GIVE ME SOME MORE." No matter how much he said, "Give me some more. Give me some more. Give me some more," the bag was now almost totally empty. In despair he sat down, lonely and dejected, took a piece of bread out of his pack, and began to eat it. A hungry child off the street approached him and asked for the bread. The child was in terrible need. The servant gave the child his bread, but before the child ate, he folded his little hands and said a blessing: "I thank Thee, Lord." Suddenly the servant's eyes lighted up and dancing around the street he cried, "That's it. That's it. The four magic words: I THANK THEE, LORD." Soon his bag was filled with blessings. [6]

Some glorious day when *God's Final Answer* is clearly revealed our prayers will be swallowed up in worship! May our praise continue until that day! Amen.

Discussion Questions

Chapter 1
1. Name some possible authors of the Book of Hebrews.
2. What danger prompted the author to write this letter?
3. List the five exhortations mentioned in this chapter.
4. What is significant about the way Hebrews begins?
5. Does the fact that God "has in these last days spoken to us by His Son" suggest that earlier revelations are irrelevant or unreliable?
6. How are we to understand the words "these last days"?
7. What do we mean by "inherent splendor" and "exhibited splendor"?
8. Christ is "the express image of God's person" and man was made "in the image of God." Is there a difference? If so, what is it?
9. How do we generally differentiate between "logos" and "rhema"?
10. Christ "sat down at the right hand of the Majesty on high." Explain.

Chapter 2
1. What is man's general response in Scripture when an angel appears?
2. Give four illustrations from Scripture of angels as "ministering spirits."

3. Discuss the significance of disagreement between Athanasius and Arius.
4. Someone said, "God was about ready to pour out His wrath on the human race and Jesus said, 'No, Father, let Me go and take their place.'" Discuss.
5. Is it possible to "love righteousness" and not "hate lawlessness"?
6. If Jesus was "anointed with the oil of gladness" how is it that He could also be called "a Man of Sorrows and acquainted with grief"?
7. Is there any contradiction between "In the beginning **God** created the heavens and the earth" (Genesis 1:1) and that **Christ** "in the beginning laid the foundation of the earth, and the heavens are the work of Your hands"? Explain.
8. Since the angels "shouted for joy" (Job 38:7) at the creation, how must they have felt when the creation was cursed? What seems to determine how they feel?

Chapter 3

1. What seems to be the greater danger for believers—drifting away from the Lord or suddenly abandoning their faith?
2. What do you understand the word "salvation" to mean?
3. What understanding do you have of Phil. 2:12, 13?
4. What significance do you see for us today in the statement that the gifts of the Spirit were manifested "according to His (God's) own will"?
5. Can a person consistently be motivated by fear to be faithful to the Lord?
6. Which is, in your opinion, the greater danger today—denying the faith or neglecting it?
7. Name five of the seven dangers listed in this chapter.

Chapter 4

1. What is the difference between "transgression" and "disobedience"?
2. Explain "the greater the light the greater the responsibility."
3. Define "sign," "wonder," and "miracle."
4. Will the human race ever reclaim what it lost by Adam's failure? Explain.

5. What is the significance of the writer's statement—"...but now we do not see all things put under Him. But we see Jesus..."?
6. Why can we claim that we see the gospel in Hebrews 2:9?
7. Compare the punctuation in Hebrews 2:9 in the KJV with that in the NKJV. How do they differ? Which seems more harmonious with the rest of Scripture?

Chapter 5

1. How does Hebrews 2:10 harmonize with Revelation 4:11?
2. What enormous difference was there in God's bringing about creation and His involvement in our redemption?
3. What does the writer mean by saying that Christ was "made perfect through suffering"?
4. How is Christ's identification with us pointed out in Hebrews 2:11?
5. Do you have a relative that you are not particularly proud of? Does Jesus have a "right" to be "ashamed to call us brethren"? How should we, then, feel about others?
6. What does the word "destroy" (Hebrews 2:14) mean?
7. How can Jesus Christ be both "merciful *and* faithful"? What is the seeming contradiction here?
8. What does the writer suggest by saying that Jesus will "declare Your (God's) Name to My brethren"?
9. Explain the fact that Christ both "speaks" and "sings" (Heb. 2:12)

Chapter 6

1. What is one indication that God is speaking to your heart?
2. Explain the relation between the voice of God and personal responsibility.
3. What does the word "today" in the text suggest to you?
4. If we fail to respond to God's voice what happens to our spiritual hearing?
5. When God calls us to Himself is He simply trying to recover what He has lost, or does He have something else in mind?

Chapter 7

1. Tell in your own words why Hebrews 3:13 is so disturbing?
2. If a person is not born "hardened" how does he/she get that way?
3. What is the root of hardness?
4. If we all *know* to do right why do we not do it?
5. If I am not as pliable as I once was what can I do about it?

Chapter 8

1. Why is it dangerous to make decisions on the basis of circumstances?
2. What, if any, relation is there between "God's rest" and fatigue?
3. Explain how faith and fear are not contradictory when they have to do with our relationship with God.
4. Consider the statement in this chapter about Calvinists and Arminianists and tell what your opinion is about getting into debates on these positions.
5. Who is the example of what happens to those who turn away from God?
6. Memorize Morgan's statement regarding Moses, Joshua, and Jesus.

Chapter 9

1. Commit Hebrews 4:12, 13 to memory
2. Write a brief paragraph about the correct and incorrect use of the Word of God in the temptation in the wilderness.
3. Give a critique of "This Sword in My Hand." (pp. 48, 49)
4. Name five characteristics of the Word of God?

Chapter 10

1. Why might first-century Romans have thought that Christians were atheists?
2. What is the difference in "priesthood" and "priestcraft"?
3. What are the five truths in this text about our High Priest, Jesus Christ, and how His priesthood should affect us?
4. What three responses should we make as a result of these truths concerning Christ's priesthood?

5. What happened to the Old Testament priest who entered into the Holy of Holies with sin in his life?
6. Is God's throne a throne of judgment or grace...or both?
7. What three requirements do we have in the midst of needs?

Chapter 11

1. Name three factors about Jesus' priesthood.
2. Why could an angel not qualify as our representative?
3. What is the difference in "wayward" and "ignorant" in this passage?
4. What lesson does the writer teach us by exalting the Lord Jesus rather then attacking the Hebrew priests who had failed?
5. Name the six qualifications for priesthood that the writer mentions.
6. What does the expression "the days of His flesh" mean?
7. How is the "order of Melchizedek" superior to the Levitical priesthood?
8. Define "prayer" and "supplication." How do they differ?
9. Explain: Christ "learned obedience by the things that He suffered."
10. What seems to make us "dull of hearing"?

Chapter 12

1. What disadvantage was it to these first century Hebrews that they did not have the New Testament as we have it today?
2. Give three reasons for "spiritual anorexia."
3. What are the two things we must do to cure "spiritual anorexia"?
4. Define these six elementary truths: Repentance, faith toward God, baptisms, laying on of hands, resurrection of the dead and eternal judgment.
5. If we "leave behind" these truths does that mean that we abandon them?
6. Why do you suppose that the writer calls these truths "elementary"?
7. What is the writer considering when he says, "If God permits"?

Chapter 13

1. Name the five characteristics of believers in Heb. 6:4, 5.
2. Why is the possibility canceled for an apostate to be forgiven?
3. Name the three positive assurances in verses 10, 18, 19 and 20.
4. We have a hope that is based on "two immutable things." What are they?
5. Define "forerunner".

Chapter 14

1. If we know the Most High God as an "all-sufficient" God what two consequences will come of that knowledge?
2. The reason our Priest, the Lord Jesus, needs no successor is that His priesthood is based on what?
3. Explain how Christ could be "separate from sinners" and yet be "numbered with the transgressors."

Chapter 15

1. What three contrasts does the writer make in this text?
2. Jesus "sits" at the right hand of God. What does this suggest?
3. Give three reasons why the ministry of our High Priest, Jesus, is better.
4. How can we speak of the old covenant as "faulty" since God made it?
5. Tell why you agree or disagree with Karl Barth's statement.

Chapter 16

1. Name the three essential elements in the Mosaic Covenant.
2. Are these three necessary today? Why, or why not?
3. How were the tabernacle and the temple different?
4. Instead of dwelling in a tent or temple where does God dwell today?
5. Tell why you agree or disagree with John Havlik's statement.

Chapter 17

1. What is suggested by the gate, the door, and the veil in the tabernacle?
2. What is symbolized by the measurements of the Holy of Holies?

3. What attribute of God is suggested by the Holy of Holies?
4. What is suggested by the brazen altar, the brass laver, the table of showbread, the seven-branched candelabrum, the golden altar of incense, the Ark of the Covenant, and the mercy seat?

Chapter 18
1. What was the difference in a "sin offering" and a "sins offering"?
2. What does it mean to have a "good conscience"?
3. Give an example of "dead works" in the physical, mental, and spiritual life.
4. How can we cleanse our conscience from dead works?

Chapter 19
1. Why does Christ's first coming demand a Second Coming?
2. How does our lifestyle witness to our belief about the Second Coming?
3. Jesus' Second Coming will be "apart from sin." What does that mean?
4. How is Hebrews 9:27 fulfilled in Christ?

Chapter 20
1. Give the definition given for man in our text.
2. Name the five sacrifices of the old Mosaic economy and tell what they symbolized.
3. What does Christ, by offering His own body, teach us about how we ought to view our own bodies?
4. What does the measure of pain we experience in the presence of sin tell about us?
5. Explain the statement "God looks upon us as perfect, but not yet perfected."

Chapter 21
1. Discuss the benefits of the three-fold covenant quoted from Jeremiah in Hebrews 8:8-12.
2. "None of them shall teach his neighbor and none his brother, saying, 'know the Lord!'" (8:11) What does this mean?

3. Which is more important – knowing God or knowing God's will?
4. What is interesting about the sequence "...from the least to the greatest"?

Chapter 22
1. "Let us draw near..." (v. 22) has to do with _____; "Let us hold fast the confession of our faith" (v. 23) has to do with _____, and "Let us consider one another" (v. 24) has to do with _____.
2. "Access to God's presence is based on the value God attaches to _____ _____.
3. Why is this way called "new and living"?
4. Is our religion a private matter? Why?
5. What is the basis of our faithfulness?
6. Why is it important that we "forsake not the assembling of ourselves together"?

Chapter 23
1. What writers in Scripture use the statement "the just shall live by faith"?
2. What is the reason mentioned in our textbook concerning why the church in Korea has grown so much?
3. We quote Rom.8:28 from our hearts or from our intellects? Why?
4. Was Habakkuk satisfied because God explained the situation to him?

Chapter 24
1. Memorize the definition of faith in Hebrews 11:1.
2. Is "seeing believing"?
3. What is the difference in our faith and the devil's?
4. Study Halverson's statement about faith and write some comments on it.

Chapter 25

1. This text demands that we believe two truths about God. What are they?
2. Does the Scripture argue for the existence of God?
3. What does the word "diligently" suggest?

Chapter 26

1. What two things was Abraham's life especially associated with?
2. Is the city of God an attempt to salvage what was lost in Eden? Explain.
3. Does the city of God come because of some spiritual evolution or because of man's righteousness? Explain.
4. Do the redeemed in the city retain their ethnicity?
5. Why will there be no reason for tears in heaven? *No Death*
6. How does knowledge of the coming city effect our lives presently? *No Death*
7. What does this text have to do with racial prejudice?

Chapter 27

1. Why would we suspect that Noah may have been a lonely man?
2. How would you describe the "fear" of God that Noah had? *wisdom*
3. How is our present generation like Noah's? *They are living in sin and for*
4. Why would others judge Noah to be an eccentric person? *himself.*
5. The fact that the ark had only one door suggests what to us?
    One way to God (Jesus)

Chapter 28

1. Why is it important that we realize that God's appearance to Abraham demanding the death of his son followed six earlier appearances?
2. Having a tent and an altar Abraham centered his life on which? Why?
3. What was the truth Abraham learned in the seventh revelation of God?

4. If Abraham sacrificed Isaac did he believe that God would raise him up?
5. What is meant by "faith never dulls feelings"?

Chapter 29
1. The writer of Hebrews tells us how three men faced death. Name them.
2. Why was Abraham fearful that his son would marry a Canaanite?
3. Comment on the conflict in Isaac and Rebekah's home.
4. What could this couple have done to resolve their domestic problems?
5. What do you find interesting about Isaac's well digging?
6. What sin did Isaac commit that his father had committed?

Chapter 30
1. How did God's visits to Abraham and His appearances to Jacob differ.
2. How would you define Jacob's motives and his methods?
3. How is the beautiful Mizpah Benediction (Genesis 31:49) contradicted by the character of Jacob and Laban?
4. How did Jacob become a "prince with God"?
5. Who initiated the struggle between Jacob and God?

Chapter 31
1. Abel represented _____ through faith. Enoch exemplified the _____ of faith. Noah demonstrated the _____ of faith. Abraham manifested the _____ of faith. Isaac showed the _____ of faith. Jacob exemplified the _____ of faith. Joseph illustrated the _____ of faith.
2. Name three Hebrew men who went into foreign countries and rose to great prominence.
3. What strange request did Joseph make when he was dying?
4. Why does this request seem ridiculous?

5. Would some today claim that the dying Joseph had no faith because he was so negative about Israel's future?
6. Name Joseph's two fold motive for refusing to sin with Potiphar's wife?
7. How does Romans 8:28 apply to Joseph's life?
8. Can you relate any experience that proves Genesis 50:20 in your own life?

Chapter 32
1. How did Moses' parents manifest faith when he was a baby?
2. Tell how Jochebed's faith was rational.
3. What did Oliver Cromwell mean by "Trust in Providence, and keep your powder dry"?
4. Tell how Moses' life is divided into three 40's.
5. Write down the six actions that grew out of Moses' faith.
6. Why would Moses' choice to renounce Egypt be difficult?
7. Explain how Moses "endured as seeing Him Who is invisible."

Chapter 33
1. What two events of the 40 years of wanderings does the writer mention?
2. Tell how God delivered you from an "impossible" situation.
3. Does the strategy for taking Jericho seem logical?
4. Can cities be "taken" by God today?

Chapter 34
1. Explain how Rahab could be a harlot, a foreigner, a member of an accursed race and also be a woman of faith.
2. Is it likely that Rahab was a respected person? Why?
3. Are we wise to try to balance her good points with her bad points? Why?
4. What was her faith based upon?
5. How was her faith manifested?
6. What is amazing about Rahab's name appearing in Matthew 1?
7. Why was Jericho destroyed?

Chapter 35

1. Write one sentence about each of the five judges mentioned in this text– Gideon, Barak, Samson, Jephthah, and Samuel
2. List some of the surprising contrasts in David's life.
3. Give your opinion as to why God restored David but did not restore Judas?
4. From this chapter list nine positive experiences accomplished by faith.
5. Now list ten negative experiences they endured by faith.
6. What was the two-fold result of the faith of these heroes?

Chapter 36

1. Who makes up the "great cloud of witnesses"?
2. What five steps promise victory in our race?
3. What is "the sin which so easily ensnares us"?
4. Is the Christian race more like the 100 yard dash or more like a marathon?
5. Are the other runners our opponents in the race? Explain.
6. What does the writer mean by saying that Christ "despised the shame"?

Chapter 37

1. Why are we not to "despise the chastening of the Lord"?
2. What is the two-fold danger in chastening?
3. What is the difference between chastening and punishment?
4. How should we respond to chastening?
5. What is "an Esau spirit"?

Chapter 38

1. What significance is attached to the two mountains mentioned in the text?
2. What is the one characteristic we share with the angels?
3. What does the writer mean by "the church of the first born"?
4. What is the difference in being "innocent" and being "just"?
5. If Jesus' sprinkled blood "speaks" what does it say?

Chapter 39

1. Explain "For He must reign till He has put all enemies under His feet."
2. What are some things that are being shaken today?
3. Why is this shaking taking place?

Chapter 40

1. Why was it significant that these first century believers be reminded that they "not forget to entertain strangers"?
2. How does "remember mistreated prisoners" apply to us today?
3. Give one reason why there is such a strong attack upon marriages today?
4. Name one weakness of getting our teaching through the electronic media?

Chapter 41

1. Give your opinion on why it is theologically incorrect to say, "Jesus (rather than Jesus Christ) the same yesterday, today and forever"?
2. We often fellowship with other believers and fail to recognize the presence of Christ in them. How can we correct this?
3. What does the word "forever" mean?

Chapter 42

1. Name four Old Testament men who built altars in times of crisis.
2. What three things are suggested by Old Testament altars?
3. Explain why the Old Testament altars were to be built of dirt. Why were they not to use hewn stone and why were they not to use steps to the altar?
4. What three offerings are we to offer today?
5. How can churches help their pastors minister in an atmosphere of joy?

Chapter 43
1. How does the writer define God in this text?
2. What is the two-fold prayer in this text?
3. What is the two-fold basis upon which these requests are made?
4. What happens to our worship if it is based on the good things which happen to us?

Notes

Chapter 1
1. Dynamic Preaching, Vol. II, No. 5, May 1987, pg. 21
2. Ibid., No. 7, July 1987, pg. 24

Chapter 2
1. Family Circus
2. Dynamic Preaching, Vol. II, No. 12, December 1987, pg. 21
3. Ibid., No. 7, July 1987, pg. 8
4. Ibid., Vol. II, No. 8, August 1987, pg. 8
5. Dr Joe Harding
6. Lion and Lamb, Old Tappan, NJ, Fleming H. Revell, 1986
7. Dynamic Preaching, Vol. II, No. 4, April 1987, pg. 28
8. Ibid., No. 3, March 1987, pg. 13
9. Ibid., No. 5, May 1987, pg. 3
10. Ibid., No. 3, March 1987, pg. 16

Chapter 3
1. Christian Century, November 5, 1989, pg. 967
2. "Jesus Christ the Liberator," Ron Lavin, CSS Publishing Company, pg. 77

Chapter 4
1. Dynamic preaching, Vol. III, No. 1, January 1988, pg. 5
2. The Best of C.S. Lewis, The Great Divorce, *Christianity Today*, New York, NY, 1969
3. Don Emmitte

Chapter 5
1. Dynamic Preaching, Vol. II, No. 7, July 1987, pg. 4
2. Ibid., No. 12, December 1987, pg. 11
3. "The Insanity Plea on Trial," NEWSWEEK, 1987, pg. 57

4. Dynamic Preaching, Vol. II, No 2, November 1987, pg. 12
5. Ibid., No. 7, July 1987, pg. 20

Chapter 6
1. Dynamic Preaching, Vol. II, No. 11, October 1987, pg. 27
2. Leadership, Winter 1988, pg. 36
3. Dynamic Preaching, Vol. II, No. 8, August 1987, pg. 5
4. Ibid., No. 10, October 1987, pg. 21
5. Ibid., No. 7, July 1987, pg. 5
6. Leadership, Winter 1988, pg. 36

Chapter 7
1. Dynamic Preaching, Vol. II, No. 8, August 1987, pg. 20

Chapter 8
1. Dynamic Preaching, Vol. III, No. 3, March 1988, pg. 27
2. Ibid., pg. 29
3. Ibid., pg. 30

Chapter 9
1. Ted Koppel, Catalina (AZ) UMC Newsletter, December 13, 1987
2. Dynamic Preaching, Vol. II, No. 6, June 1987, pg. 11
3. Tony Bland
4. Dynamic Preaching, Vol. III, No. 3, March 1988, pg. 4
5. Stan McCready

Chapter 10
1. Dynamic Preaching, Vol. III, No. 2, February 1988, pg. 4
2. One Knee Equals Two Feet (New York: Jove Books, 1986)
3. Leadership Journal, Winter 1988, Vol. IX, No. 1, pg. 37

Chapter 11
1. Dynamic Preaching, Vol. III, No. 3, March 1988, pg. 12

Chapter 13
1. Dynamic Preaching, Vol. III, No. 3, March 1988, pg. 12

Chapter 14
1. Dynamic Preaching, Vol. II, No. 7, July 1987, pg. 3
2. Ibid., Vol. III, No. 2, February 1988, pg. 11
3. Ibid., pg. 18
4. Ibid., Vol. II, No. 10, October 1987, pg. 5
5. Ibid., pg. 3
6. Kiss Yourself and Hug the World, George F. Regas, (Waco: World Books, 1987)

Chapter 15
1. Dynamic Preaching, Vol. III, No. 1, January 1988, pg. 7
2. Newsweek, August 1987
3. Dynamic Preaching, Vol. III, No. 1, January 1988, pg. 4

4. Ibid.
5. Ibid., No. 4, April 1988, pg. 16

Chapter 16
1. Dynamic Preaching, Vol. II, No. 8, August 1987, pg. 26
2. Ibid., Vol. III, No. 2, February 1988, pg. 2
3. Ibid., No. 4, April 1988, pg. 20
4. Unlimited Power, Anthony Robbins (New York: Simon and Schuster, 1986)

Chapter 17
1. Told by Joe Harding
2. Dynamic Preaching, Vol. III, No. 5, May 1988, pg. 5

Chapter 19
1. Dynamic Preaching, Vol. III, No. 2, February 1988, pg. 11
2. Ibid., No. 7/8, July/August 1988, pg. 17
3. Ibid., No. 6, June 1988, pg. 24

Chapter 20
1. THE WORLD IS NOT ENOUGH. Tom Finley (Regal Books, Ventura, CA 1986)
2. Dynamic preaching, Vol. III, No. 9, September 1988, pg. 22
3. Ibid., pg. 31
4. Wade Y. Burton, Coronaca, SC

Chapter 21
1. Why Settle for More and Miss the Boat, Tom Sine (Waco: Word Books, 1987) pg. 29
2. Dynamic Preaching, Vol. III, nos. 7/8, August 1988, pg. 18

Chapter 22
1. Love and Will, Rollo May
2. The Oxford Dictionary of Saints (Oxford Press, 1987)
3. Dynamic Preaching, Vol. III. No. 9, September 1988, pg. 19
4. The Christian Ministry, September/October 1987
5. Dynamic Preaching, Vol. III, No. 3, March 1988, pg. 9

Chapter 23
1. Dynamic Preaching, Vol. III, No. 10, October 1988, pg. 9
2. Dr. Eugene Brice
3. Rising Above the Clouds, B.L. Harbour (Nashville: Broadman Press, 1988)
4. Building Your Mate's Self-Esteem (San Bernardino: Here's Life) pgs. 64,65

Chapter 24
1. Perspective, R. Halverson, Concern Ministries, Vol. XXXIX, No. 3, February 4, 1987

Chapter 25
1. Brian K. Bauknight
2. Hide and Seek, James Dobson, Old Tappan, NJ: F. Revell, 1974

Chapter 26
1. Dynamic Preaching, Vol. III, No. 2, February 1988, pg. 17
2. Ibid., No. 6, June 1988, pg. 27
3. Ibid., Nos. 11/12, November/December 1988, pg. 22
4. Ibid., pg. 23
5. Ibid., No. 9, September 1988, pg. 16
6. The Emmanuel Factor (Nashville: Broadman Press, 1987)
7. Dynamic Preaching, Vol. III, No. 9, September 1988, pg. 29

Chapter 27
1. Incredible Insurance Claims, Brian Herbert (Los Angeles: Price, Stern, Sloan Publishers, 1982)
2. "Be Careful Out There," Michael M. Masser, The Christian Ministry, July 1987
3. Dynamic Preaching, Vol. II, No. 7, July 1987, pg. 16
4. Ibid., Vol. III, No. 11/12, November/December 1988, pg. 11
5. Ibid., Vol. II, No. 12, December 1987, pg. 12
6. Ibid., Vol. III, No. 11/12, November/December 1988, pg. 13

Chapter 28
1. Kiss Yourself and Hug the World, George F. Regas (Waco: Word Books, 1987)

Chapter 29
1. Hebrews, Everitt M. Fjordbak, Wisdom House Publishers, Dallas, Texas, 1983, pg. 470

Chapter 30
1. Dynamic Preaching, Vol. III, Nos. 11/12, November/December 1988, pg. 38
2. English and Hebrew Bible Students's Concordance, Aaron Pick, pg. 581

Chapter 31
1. Hebrews, Everitt M. Fjordbak, Wisdom House, Dallas, Texas, 1983, pg. 493
2. Great Men of the Bible, John R. Rice: Sword of the Lord Publishers, Murfreesboro, TN; 1976, pg. 38

Chapter 34
1. Tarbell's Teacher's Guide, Vol. 82 (Old Tappan, NJ; Fleming H. Revell, 1980)

Chapter 36
1. Dynamic Preaching, Vol. III, Nos. 11/12, November/December 1988, pg. 41
2. Sermons Illustrated

Chapter 37
1. Proclaiming the New Testament, Vol. III; Earle, Ralph; Baker Book House, Grand Rapids, Michigan, 1968

Chapter 38
1. Holy, Holy, Is What the Angels Sing, Johnson Oatman, Jr.; Al's Smith Collection of Gospel Songs; Zondervan Publishing House, Grand Rapids, Michigan; 1945; pg. 24
2. An Expository Dictionary of New Testament Words; Vine, W.E.; Fleming M. Revell Co., Westword, NJ, pg. 84
3. Foursquare Hymnal, Frank M. Davis, A.S.M. Publishing Co., Los Angeles, CA, 1935, pg. 90
4. Hebrews, Everitt M. Fjordbak, Wisdom House Publishers, Dallas, Texas; 1983, pg. 634
5. Foursquare Hymnal, Oliver Holden, A.S.M. Publishing Co., Los Angeles, CA, 1935, pg. 112

Chapter 40
1. From a sermon by Rev. R. Frank Porter, Middlebrook Pike UMC, Knoxville, TN
2. Dynamic Preaching, Vol. IV, No. 3, March 1989, pg. 1
3. God's Seven Wonders For You, Charles L. Allan, (Old Tappan, NJ; Fleming H. Revell, 1987)
4. Monday Morning, Catalina (AZ) UMC News, Dr. Stan Brown

Chapter 41
1. Leadership, Vol. VIII, No. 4, Fall 1987, pg. 3
2. "Abide With Me," H.F. Lyte, Foursquare Hymnal, pg. 15
3. Dynamic Preaching, Vol. II, No. 11, November 1987, pg 22
4. Dr. Peter Rhea Jones
5. Leadership, John Ross, Vol. VIII< no. 4, Fall 1987, pg 3
6. Dynamic Preaching, Vol. II, No. 11, November 1987, pg. 3
7. Ibid., No. 9, September 1987, pg. 24
8. Ibid., No. 4, April 1987, pg. 13
9. Ibid., No. 10, October 1987, pg. 22

Chapter 43
1. Dynamic Preaching, Vol. III, No. 11/12, November/December 1988, pg. 5
2. Ernest J. Lewis
3. Dynamic Preaching, Vol. III, No. 11/12, November/December 1988, pg. 9
4. Come and Worship, Stan Cosby (Nashville: Graded Press, 1987)
5. Dynamic Preaching, Vol. III, No. 11/12, November/December 1988, pg. 3
6. The Speaker's Sourcebook, Glenn Van Ekeren, Englewood Cliffs, Prentice-Hall, 1988

Is God shakeing the Christian People in Hebrew 12:25-29

CPSIA information can be obtained at www.ICGtesting.com
Printed in the USA
LVOW060526280412

279464LV00001B/57/A